DESIGNED
FOR THE
KILL

DESIGNED
FOR THE
KILL

The Jet Fighter — Development & Experience
Mike Spick

Airlife

England

First published in the UK in 1995
by Airlife Publishing Ltd
Reprinted 1995

British Library Cataloguing in Publication Data
  A catalogue record for this book
  is available from the British Library.

ISBN 1 85310 121 4

Printed in Singapore by Kyodo Printing Co (S'pore) Pte Ltd.

Airlife Publishing Ltd

101 Longden Road, Shrewsbury SY3 9EB, England

Contents

Prologue

Four fighters swept across friendly airspace at medium altitude. Flying in wide battle formation, they had been scrambled to intercept an enemy strike force heading deep into their territory. In just one minute they should be within radar range of the low flying intruders, and then look out! The leader smiled grimly to himself at the thought before checking for the nth time that his missiles were armed and ready, and that his radar was in dummy load, with no telltale emissions to alert the enemy.

The voice of the ground controller had long since been obliterated by jamming, but information via the secure data link was still getting through. He was bringing them in for a front quarter attack. The situation display, fed by the IRST, was confused; the enemy formation was down there somewhere, but effectively masked by ground returns. When the range had closed enough, all they needed was a radar contact followed by a lock and then . . . ! The enemy formation would be disrupted by the surprise attack, and the four interceptors would close to visual range to engage the survivors with all-aspect heat seeking missiles. Once again the leader scanned the sky around and behind. As yet there had been no warning of enemy fighters, and they were not really expected this far inland, but you never knew. He was a cautious man, and his training had been thorough.

All his concentration was now on the task at hand, and the familiar noises from his radar warning receiver, sounding like a dozen Disney mice in fast forward, gave no cause for alarm. The seconds and the miles ticked away. In range at last. He thumbed the switch which activated his radar from the quiescent standby mode, and waited for the contacts to appear on his Hud. Even as he did so, his RWR gave out a more insistent tone. Adrenalin stung the back of his hands and dried his mouth. A split second of indecision as he desperately searched the vast and seemingly empty sky, then a flicker of light caught his peripheral vision. Even as his mind registered the torn and flame-wracked aircraft of his No 3 half a mile away, he wrenched the controls into the corner and broke hard downwards. His mouth opened to call a warning, but too late. A slim grey blur, moving at mind-numbing speed, came at him from above . . . !

Nine miles higher up, and travelling at better than a quarter of a mile per second, his unseen opponent grunted with satisfaction. His tactical information display now showed two contacts where only seconds earlier there had been four. The surviving bad guys were taking frantic evasive action close to the ground, and for the moment posed little threat to the strike force that he was protecting. "Alpha Romeo Fiver ready, Alpha Romeo Sixer ready! " Robotlike behind his dark visor, the pilot selected two more missiles by voice command, then hesitated. His first salvo of four had gained two kills; there would almost certainly be other enemy formations about, and his remaining weapons should be kept for them. His wingman, flying about fifteen miles astern and on a slightly offset course, could take care of the surviving pair if they got their act together in time. He reefed into a steady turn, looking for more targets.

At this speed and altitude, tight turns were impossible. By the time that the large fighter had got around to head in the opposite direction, it was laterally displaced by

OPPOSITE: *The Lockheed YF-22A, winner of the USAF Advanced Tactical Fighter competition, has been carefully shaped for minimal radar cross-section while still being able to supercruise in military power. Extra manoeuvrability is conferred by thrust-vectoring engine nozzles. (Lockheed).*

nearly six miles, and almost a minute had passed. Standard formations were not very useful for these new high speed birds, as they almost invariably operated beyond the limits of visibility. Mutual protection and support was achieved simply by being in the same area, kept in contact by the tactical information display. An offset trail was favoured, the distance determined by the time taken to get through a complete circle of 360 degrees in a sustained turn.

Sustained supersonic cruising in military power, supercruise as it was widely known, at about Mach 1.5, made the new fighter almost invulnerable to attack from astern. Sheer speed made it difficult for an enemy to get into position, and even if one succeeded in doing so, its effective missile range was reduced to the point where it had to get very close to achieve a valid firing solution. In any case, the defensive systems computer, fed by a combination of passive sensors and data from an AWACS aircraft many miles away, would give the pilot adequate warning of an impending threat, and even suggest a course of action. Supercruise combined with very high altitude also reduced the effective launch envelope of ground based missiles, rendering them much less dangerous.

The enemy's problems were compounded by the fact that the big fighter incorporated state of the art low observables. It was a tiny radar target in relation to its physical size, and a very poor heat target. This made it difficult to detect, while supercruise ensured that it could only be caught by a previous generation fighter if it was fortunate enough to be exceptionally well placed at the moment of detection. Of course, the enemy fighter pilots were aware of this. Once F-22s were known to be in the area, they became very defensive minded, and thus less effective. Their only chance was to get in close and swamp the new fighter with numbers. But this was easier said than done!

The road to the stealthy supercruise fighter has been long and beset by confusion. Until the 1950s, what a fighter did and how was clearly understood. In basic terms it intercepted enemy bombers, and escorted and protected friendly ones. It contested for control of the skies in manoeuvre combat against enemy fighters. If no longer needed in its primary role, for whatever reason, air to surface ordnance was hung on it, and it was sent off to have at the unfortunate pongoes.

These essential issues then became blurred. Galloping technology was the cause. In just a few short years in the 1950s, maximum speeds more than doubled. Climb rates nearly tripled. Detection from far beyond normal visual limits became possible. Finally, there was the promise, unfortunately never fulfilled, of homing weapons which would unerringly destroy their targets once launched.

Another factor was the changed nature of the threat. Defence procurement was based on a "worst case" scenario; an all-out world war, the primary battlefield of which would be in Central Europe. This was to be a classic case of equipping and training for a hypothetical war, and then becoming embroiled in wars of far more limited extent and differing nature. Theoretically, the hardware suitable for the "worst case" scenario would outclass the opposition encountered in lesser conflicts. But at this point political considerations invariably intervened.

The war in Vietnam was a typical example. Had the USA used its full air power and complete arsenal of weapons from the outset, Hanoi could have been reduced to cinders on day one. But this sledgehammer approach to a rather small nut was both morally and politically unacceptable. The result was that the USAF and USN were forced to fight what was basically a holding action, for which they were not equipped, and which ceded the advantages of superior air power.

The rampant technological advances had unfortunate effects on Western fighter doctrine. The perceived threat to the major nations of the West was the fast high flying jet bomber. To intercept it, high speed and rate of climb were essential. The inevitable result was that performance had been sought at the expense of all else. For a pure interceptor, designed to hack down unescorted bombers and never intended to encounter fighters, this was perfectly sensible; manoeuvre is low on the list of priorities. Even if hostile fighters were encountered, the new homing missiles would cut them down at long range, well before close combat entailing hard manoeuvre could be joined. As for the tactical fighters, they needed high speed at low level while hauling a large load of external ordnance. They also needed low gust response in order to give a smooth ride. For high speed they needed minimal drag, and for low gust response they needed a high wing loading. They could achieve both by using small wing surfaces with high wing loadings. The price paid for speed and a smooth ride was poor turning ability. For both interceptors and tactical fighters, the possibility of manoeuvre combat against other fighters was largely discounted, to the extent that many of the former carried no gun. The latter normally carried a gun, primarily for strafing targets of opportunity, but their air to air armament was minimal or non-existent. It should of course be mentioned that air to air missiles could only be carried at the expense of air to surface ordnance.

The theory was unarguable. What the theorists got wrong was the type of wars that air forces would be called upon to fight. They can hardly be blamed for this. They simply reacted to the obvious threat to the exclusion of all others, apparently discounting as over optimistic the possibility that the nuclear balance of terror would serve to keep the peace between the superpowers. It is also arguable that had they not bent all their efforts to counter the major threat, this could have been construed as a national lack of will, which might greatly have increased the possibility of world conflict.

The other error was rooted in the past. From the time that aeroplanes first contested the sky with each other, maximum speed had been of primary importance. From 1915 until Korea, nearly forty years later, most air fighting had been carried out at or near the maximum speeds attainable. Like the primary tactical advantage of height, this had become holy writ in the fighter community of all nations. Even in Korea, the cry from those at the sharp end had been for ever more speed and rate of climb; performance before all else.

By 1960, Mach 2 capability was almost obligatory, even though this could only be achieved in the thin air on the edge of the stratosphere. And at Mach 2, manoeuvre combat was generally considered to be impossible. Turn radii increased from a few hundred yards to several miles, while the time taken to turn through a complete circle more than doubled. Within these constraints, it was doubtful whether a pilot would physically be able to judge a turn in behind an opponent accurately enough to achieve a satisfactory firing solution.

These doctrines remained current for many years until experience showed that manoeuvre combat was not only possible, but necessary. The breakthrough came in the late 1960s. Air superiority gained via air combat, once thought to be outmoded, was back in vogue. The next generation of fighters was designed to be as good in close combat as they were in other missions. The following chapters trace that generation from beginning to end, right through the present and into the future.

The MiG-17 has seen service with more nations than any other jet fighter. While it has for many years been outclassed in theory, in practice the need for close combat, where its manoeuvrability at moderate speeds shows to advantage, has allowed it to oppose far more modern designs.

CHAPTER ONE

The Resurgence of Air Combat

The five years prior to 1970 saw the combat debut of the new breed of supersonic fighter in several skirmishes and four quite substantial wars. These were the Indo/Pakistan conflict of 1965; the Six Day War between Israel and its Arab neighbours in 1967, followed by the War of Attrition which commenced in June 1969; and the Rolling Thunder era over North Vietnam, which commenced in 1965 and continued until 1968. Many valuable lessons were learned in these conflicts, which were to influence fighter design and doctrine over the next two decades.

The Indo/Pakistan War completely reversed the "ever higher, ever faster" trend which had reached its peak in Korea some twelve years earlier. Almost all engagements took place at medium or low level. The reasons for this were not hard to find. In Korea, the large numbers of fighters available to the UN forces enabled them to put a defensive umbrella of F-86 Sabres over the contested area. This gave the North Korean and Chinese MiG-15s a choice; stay high and tangle with the top cover, allowing the UN fighter-bombers to operate relatively undisturbed; or to go after the fighter-bombers and risk being bounced from above by the Sabres. Almost inevitably they chose the former. Neither India nor Pakistan had a force size sufficient to use the high cover option, a factor that was aggravated by relatively long borders, and their ground radar coverage was far from comprehensive. Most combats occurred when defending fighters, often on standing patrols, encountered small raiding forces penetrating at low level. The majority of aircraft on both sides were firmly subsonic, although both forces had a small supersonic component; Pakistan the Lockheed F-104A Starfighter, and India the MiG-21. While there were no conclusive encounters between the two, their presence served to demonstrate one vital point; that previous generation subsonic fighters could survive in the same sky as the Mach 2 wonders.

The Six Day War of 1967 was notable on two counts. The main one was the famous "pre-emptive strike" against Egyptian airfields, which clearly demonstrated the vulnerability of unprotected aircraft on the ground, and also the ease with which runways could be made unusable. Following this, European military airfields sprouted a rash of hardened shelters able to protect aircraft against all but a direct hit by a heavy bomb. In those days, when precision guided munitions were still in their infancy, this was a reasonable step to take.

The equally important lesson, that aircraft dependent on long stretches of hard surfacing could be grounded by a single well-placed strike, was much slower in being accepted. There were three possible solutions.

The most obvious one was dispersed off-site basing, but this involved horrendous logistical problems. The Soviet Union made a practice of designing for rough field operations, which probably was intended more to allow operation from damaged airfields than full scale dispersal. Only Sweden, with its permanent dispersed basing, can be said to satisfactorily have solved the problem, and Sweden's tactical situation applied to few other countries.

STOVL (Short Take Off, Vertical Landing) was the next possibility, but this imposed very stringent constraints on both aircraft design and performance. Air forces were simply not prepared to accept a significant reduction to their effectiveness for the sake of STOVL, even though it would completely free them from runways. Also, if this doctrine had been accepted in toto, much of their existing hardware would have become obsolete overnight, which was both unacceptable and unaffordable.

The third solution was a compromise. It assumed that a damaged runway would always have significant stretches remaining intact. The new buzzword in fighter design became short field performance. Optimism took precedence over calculation, to judge by the rather elastic field lengths postulated at different times, which seemed to be dictated by the takeoff and landing performances of the latest jets rather than by operational analysis of airfield attack effectiveness. Takeoff was only a problem with a heavily laden strike fighter; most could get airborne within quite short distances at light weights. The fact that this made the payload/range capability of STOVL fighters, which could operate even from heavily damaged airfields, look quite advantageous, seemed to escape most commentators.

Landing a conventional aircraft on a damaged runway posed three problems for the fighter pilot. Firstly he needed to know how much room he had to get down in, and how slippery or otherwise the surface was. Next he needed to know exactly where on the runway the undamaged stretch was located. Finally he needed to touch down accurately on a given point. While reverse thrust (if fitted) could pull an aircraft up fairly quickly, the "scatter" of touchdown points inevitably showed a wide variation. The production of an avionics system making this possible for the average pilot was still being developed 24 years later, when the breakup of the Soviet Union rendered it largely academic.

The other lesson of the Six Day War was that guns were still a valid weapon in air combat. Israeli fighters claimed over fifty victories in this conflict, every single one of them with guns. This was surprising, because missiles were both available and used. Then after the conflict, the Mirage IIIC was hailed as a world-beating fighter and the gun as the basic fighter weapon. While neither was entirely true, it was nevertheless a convincing demonstration that close combat could still be fought in the air.

Meanwhile the United States was deeply embroiled in South East Asia. Addled political considerations dictated that military action must take the form of a carefully graduated response to aggression from North Vietnam, with the result that the USAF and USN went to war with one hand tied behind their backs.

For most of the Rolling Thunder period, the North Vietnamese airfields were inviolate, and the potentially overwhelming American air power was not brought to bear against them. Bombing restrictions were later eased, but the elimination of the NVAF on the ground never seems to have been given any form of priority. This was an error of the first magnitude.

The NVAF made no attempt to wrest air superiority from the Americans. Had they tried, there can be little doubt that they would have failed, with heavy losses. Instead they pursued a policy of what has been termed air deniability, putting up just enough strength to make the USAF and USN divert a considerable amount of effort from their main offensive strength to countering them. Not every American incursion was opposed by the North Vietnamese fighters. At times they responded in strength, while at others they stayed on the ground and left the defensive battle to the SAMs and AA artillery.

In theory, the NVAF opposing the might of the USAF and USN appeared a David and Goliath struggle. The numerically most important North Vietnamese fighter in the early years was the MiG-17. Firmly subsonic in level flight even though fitted with afterburning, its main armament consisted of large calibre cannon. Generally considered pleasant to fly, at speeds above 450kt the controls began to stiffen, giving very high stick forces. At high subsonic speeds this made it very slow in the rolling plane, and thus slow to commence a turn, although being lightly wing loaded it was very agile at more moderate speeds.

The MiG-17s were supplemented by a handful of early MiG-21Cs. This model MiG-21 was claimed to be capable of Mach 2, but in fact the only way in which it could get there was by running itself out of fuel. It was certainly supersonic, but had a low dynamic pressure limit, which restricted its speed below about 5,000ft to Mach 1.05. The American fighters could reach Mach 1.20 with a full head of steam, giving them nearly 100kt advantage.

Like the MiG-17, the MiG-21 was armed with large calibre cannon. It also carried a pair of AA-2 Atoll air to air missiles, as very occasionally did the MiG-17. The radar on both fighters was range-only, and they were thus dependent on close ground control to get them into position and warn them of impending attacks. Both were short legged and fuel-critical. Like the MiG-17, the MiG-21C was lightly wing loaded, and agile throughout the subsonic regime.

The USAF fielded two genuinely Mach 2 capable fighters in the theatre. The Republic F-105D Thunderchief was designed to penetrate modern defensive systems at high speed and medium altitude to deliver tactical nuclear ordnance accurately on target. It carried a 20mm M61 cannon, and a single AIM-9B Sidewinder for self defence. The heaviest single seat, single engined fighter ever to enter service, the Thud, as it was unattractively called, had a very small wing area with a consequently high wing loading, aggravated by the heavy load of conventional ordnance typically carried in Vietnam. While fast in the rolling plane, it turned like a tram. In air combat it had one great advantage; at lower altitudes it was the fastest thing in the sky.

The MiG-21 has been built in greater numbers than any other Mach-2 capable fighter. What it lacks as a weapons system, it makes up for agility in close combat.

The McDonnell Douglas F-4 Phantom II had been designed as a fleet air defence interceptor, able to patrol far out from the carrier for extended periods, detect intruders at long range on radar, and destroy them from way beyond visual distance. Twin engines improved its survivability; a two man crew coupled with a state of the art radar and avionics fit gave it the ability to detect opponents over forty miles distant under the right conditions, while a full load of eight missiles; four AIM-7D Sparrows and four AIM-9B Sidewinders, gave outstanding combat persistence. The Phantom had good acceleration and a high rate of climb; wing loading was considerably lower than that of the Thud. Neither Phantom nor Thud could match the two Russian designs in a straight co-speed turning engagement in the subsonic regime, but initially there seemed no reason why they should do so. The Thud would not seek aerial encounters; this was not its function. It would attack at high speed; hit the target, then turn around and bug out even faster. Only under exceptional circumstances could it be caught from astern, which was the only real danger area against the weaponry carried by the North Vietnamese fighters, and if anything got in its way it had the firepower to defend itself. The Phantom? Why, that could detect enemy aircraft and kill them with "shoot 'em in the face" missiles before they were even aware that they were under attack. It was too fast for its opponents, and its avionics and weapons were too clever. It was a different generation fighter; combat between Phantom and a MiG-17 looked rather like matching a Spitfire against a Sopwith Camel.

Once the shooting started, reality proved rather different from the elaborate theories. Many factors intruded which tended to level out the odds against the NVAF fighters. Supersonic speeds were only attainable with the help of afterburning, but this was so prodigal of fuel that its use had to be sparing. Full 'burner has been likened to pouring fuel through the necks of eight milk bottles at once. The American fighters operated far from home, and were often hard pressed to get back to a tanker, let alone base. Their pilots were forced to fly with one eye constantly on the fuel gauge. Consequently afterburning could only be used when the need was great; for acceleration, on the attack run, gaining height rapidly, and keeping kinetic energy levels high during hard manoeuvring. The result was that for perhaps 95 percent of the mission, the Mach 2 monsters dawdled along at speeds of between 400 and 450kt, which placed them well within the performance envelope of even the elderly MiG-17, and ensured that contrary to theory, they could be caught from astern.

Speeds in excess of Mach 1 were the exception rather than the rule, and were generally achieved only briefly during combat, or during the egress from the target area. The NVAF MiGs, short legged though they were, operated mainly within about forty miles of their bases, which made fuel shortage much less of a problem for them. Security of base, which for much of the war was ceded to them without opposition, also helped, as did "Tom Tiddler's Ground"; a no-go area along the Chinese border, in which the NVAF was safe from American pursuit.

The next levelling factor was in the field of avionics. In a pure fighter versus fighter scenario, the Westinghouse radar of the Phantoms gave tremendous theoretical advantages, allowing their crews to detect oncoming MiGs at ranges far beyond where the NVAF MiG pilots, dependent on visual acquisition, could possibly detect them. Early detection gives the initiative, which in air combat is vital. The difficulty was that a pure fighter versus fighter scenario is a peacetime training exercise, and has little to do with war.

In practice, the North Vietnamese pilots operated under tight Russian style ground control. The respected Soviet commentator, Colonel V. Dubrov, was later to comment that at this stage the controller was of equal importance to the pilot. Suffice it to say that the NVAF fighter controllers, backed by a comprehensive ground radar network, had a broader picture of the air situation than did the Phantom backseater crouched in his cockpit. Operating without the psychological pressure that comes of knowing that at any moment a missile may burst through the windshield, they calmly directed their fighters into favourable attack positions, or warned them of impending danger. As the war progressed they got very good at their work. After all, they had plenty of practice! The austere NVAF fighters were thereby enabled to operate efficiently, even without an effective on-board search radar. Only when close combat was joined were they on their own.

The Phantom crews were almost totally reliant for situation information on their on-board search radar, operated by a rated pilot in the early days, and by a specialist operator later on. This had several drawbacks. Firstly its field of look was limited to a pie shaped scanning area extending about 60 degrees to each side of the nose, and a few degrees in azimuth. While it could be trained up and down, anything outside its volume of scan would not be detected. Its "look-down" capability was limited, and targets could easily be missed in the ground clutter. Its display was of the analogue type, which needed skilled interpretation to get good results. Neither was it infallible.

It is widely known that air combat victories tend to fall to the same handful of pilots; but it is less often appreciated that in South East Asia victories often went to the same machines, regardless of who was flying them. While in a few cases this was because the successful Phantoms were fitted with special gadgets such as Combat Tree, which was a MiG IFF interrogator, the main reason was that the radar and weapons systems of some machines were far more reliable and better performing than the average. Finally, the MiG-17 and 21 were rather small radar reflectors, especially from the frontal aspect, and could only be detected when they were well within the maximum theoretical range of the Phantom radar.

Not only aircraft but weapons systems were another source of levelling the odds. The American AIM-7 Sparrow missile was a semi-active radar homer, guiding on reflected radar emissions from its parent fighter. Before launch, the radar had to be switched into attack mode, or locked on, which meant that it could look only at one target, and did not continue to scan. This gave an effect akin to target fixation in a guns attack where the pilot is aware of nothing but his opponent, and ceases to watch the sky around for further threats. Only when the attack had either succeeded or failed could the radar be used to resume a watch on the surrounding sky. But even as the radar was unable to detect the MiG-21 until it was fairly close, it could not be locked on to such a small target until it was even closer, while for the Sparrow seeker to guide successfully, the range could not exceed more than seven or eight nautical miles. If the Sparrow attack failed, the combined closing speed of the two fighters ensured that the gunless Phantom would be committed to a head-on pass against a gun armed adversary within seconds.

While the radar of the Phantom could detect MiGs at a reasonable distance, it was often unable to identify them, and a couple of "own goals" were scored in the early days of the conflict. This proved a great handicap, as in most situations it made visual identification of targets obligatory. This was further aggravated by having two services raiding the North; the USAF based mainly in Thailand, and the USN operating from carriers on Yankee Station in the Gulf of Tonkin. While attempts were made to keep the friendly forces clear of each other, the occasional overlap was inevitable and the potential for disaster always present. At a stroke the Phantom lost its greatest advantage; the ability to kill from beyond visual range, and this was responsible for forcing it into the close combat arena against lighter and better turning opponents. The gunless Phantom was therefore forced to break a cardinal rule of warfare, and fight on the enemy's terms.

Close combat quickly highlighted the weak points of the Phantom. It could not turn tightly without bleeding off energy at a very high rate. In its design stage, the accent on performance had caused the cockpit canopy to be faired closely into the fuselage to minimise drag; this also minimised rearward view, thus increasing its vulnerability to attack from behind. Its missiles were not instantly available; they needed a settling period before launch. Nor could they be launched at loadings of more than 2 to 2.5g. Finally they had a minimum range of about half a mile before they armed themselves and began to guide. An opponent inside this distance was safe from attack until Phantoms began to carry guns. Sparrow and Sidewinder had been designed to kill non-manoeuvring targets; the agile NVAF MiGs were not so co-operative, with the result that kill probabilities fell from a theoretical 80 percent to between eight and 15 percent. The Phantom did however have some good solid virtues, and these were put to work in an attempt to redress its failings. Sometimes described as a triumph of thrust over aerodynamics, it was a very powerful machine. When its radar and missiles worked well, it was deadly. It had plenty of scope for improvement; the later slatted wing F-4E with an internal gun and a better radar introduced later in the war enhanced its close combat abilities considerably. Its two man crew could be used to advantage in a visual range fight; the backseater took his head out of the office and became a spare pair of eyes checking the vulnerable six oclock area, in fact two in every five visual sightings were made by the guy in the back. In so far as tactical circumstances permitted, it became a matter of handling it to its strengths, keeping energy levels high, and avoiding energy depleting hard turns where possible.

Nor was it enough just to defeat the NVAF fighters. The defences were multi-layered, with surface to air missiles and radar directed anti-aircraft artillery. While concentrating on one, it was all too easy to fall victim to another. Watching a SAM curve through the air, even at a distance, was compulsive viewing, but with attention distracted in this way, a MiG could sneak into the vulnerable rear quadrant, launch a couple of Atolls, and depart unnoticed. A tremendous overall effort had to be made to protect the American fighters over enemy territory. These were the force multipliers. Typically, there were tankers to give fuel on both the inbound and outbound legs; Wild Weasel or Iron Hand defence suppression aircraft attacking gun and missile batteries en route; ECM birds jamming search, gunlaying and missile guidance radars; chaff bombers in the later stages of the war, laying a corridor of chaff through which the strike force could advance undetected; the airborne early warning aircraft orbiting way back and keeping a wary eye open for enemy fighter activity; and a SIGINT (signals intelligence) bird monitoring enemy electronic traffic. As a general rule, the force multipliers outnumbered the bomb carriers, often by as many as two to one, without taking escort fighters and pre-and post-strike reconnaissance aircraft into account. Often more than fifty aircraft were needed although only sixteen of them actually attacked the target. The force multipliers made no direct contribution to the weight of ordnance delivered. This was prodigal of resources, but given the state of the art at that time, and the strength of the defences, it was necessary.

The F-105D Thunderchief was designed to deliver ordnance on target at high speed and low level. For this it was given a small wing area, which made it a turkey in a turning fight. Its greatest advantage against the agile NVAF MiGs was sheer speed.

(Fairchild Republic).

The lessons of the Vietnam air war underlined the Middle Eastern experience that close range manoeuvre combat was not only possible, but certain. Future fighters must be designed for both manoeuvre and stand-off combat. They must also carry a gun, if only as a last ditch weapon. Advances in radar detection, tracking, and its presentation were urgently needed. Also AAMs should have no launch manoeuvre loading limitations, much shorter minimum range, and greater reliability. It also clearly showed that semi-active radar homing for missiles was a potential liability; it forced the launching fighter to keep flying towards its target, which made it predictable for far too long, and in extreme cases, vulnerable to a counter-strike by a front-aspect heat homer. The radar warning receiver of the target could tell the difference between search and attack mode; too long in attack mode and it might take evasive action. In addition, the "target fixation" of the illuminating radar was unsatisfactory, the radar needed to keep searching even as it tracked multiple targets. None of these goals were beyond the contemporary state of the art, although some were pushing it a bit.

Finally, although this was not so apparent at that time, and the requirements were far beyond the state of the art, the effort expended on force multiplication was badly in need of reduction. The future need was for a fighter that could operate autonomously. This will be considered later.

* * * *

While combat experience shows precisely what is needed at the present day, the perceived future threat exerts equal, if not greater influence. But threat perceptions need to be accurate, and this is not always the case. During the late 1960s the Soviet Union introduced what, due to misinterpretation by Western intelligence, became for many years the equivalent of an aerial bogeyman. This was the Mikoyan MiG-25, given the NATO reporting name of Foxbat.

Foxbat first flew in 1964, and came to the attention of the West on March 16, 1965, when it set a new world speed record of Mach 2.185 over a 1,000km closed circuit. Just over two years later four pre-production Foxbats were displayed at Domodedovo, when it was announced that they were capable of Mach 3. Three more records were taken in October 1967; the 500km closed circuit at Mach 2.808; the 1,000km closed circuit at Mach 2.75; and the absolute altitude record with a 2,000kg payload, at 98,355ft. This was impressive; all three had previously been held by the Lockheed YF-12A; the experimental fighter version of the SR-71 Blackbird. The Western intelligence world was agog, and the confusion was compounded when Western ground radars tracked what appeared to be Soviet aircraft assumed to be Foxbats at very high speeds and very high altitudes far out over the Baltic. From this it was deduced that Foxbat had quite a respectable operational radius. In fact the radar tracks came from missiles, but there was no means of knowing this at the time. Totally confounded, Western analysts assumed that Foxbat was a fully fledged multi-mission fighter able to manoeuvre at least as well as the Phantom, while totally outperforming it. Despite its shortcomings, the Phantom was widely recognised at that time as the world's most advanced multi-role aircraft, and the thought that the Soviet Union had been able to produce a fighter so superior caused something akin to panic. To make matters worse, Western intelligence had given the NATO reporting name of Fearless to a new Soviet variable geometry fighter, believed to be capable of Mach 2.5, and which also outclassed the Phantom. Fearless, which was a twin engined variant of the MiG-23 Flogger, never entered service, although at one point it was believed to be about to do so in large numbers.

Foxbat and Fearless appeared to pose a significant threat to the West; it was only when the latter faded away, and the truth about the former was revealed after Lt. Viktor Belenko defected to Japan in 1976, that the threat assumed its correct perspective. Foxbat was a very fast high altitude interceptor. As an air superiority or multi-role fighter, it was not even a contender. Neither had it a reasonable operational radius; in the full bore interception mission, it could reach out only to about 160 miles. A record it could have taken with ease was that for fuel consumption per minute. It did however serve one useful purpose; it accelerated Western fighter development beyond all recognition!

* *. * *

Fighters are called upon to perform many different missions. Briefly these are: interception; air superiority; and escort. While there tends to be a degree of overlap between these roles, each mission has its own unique requirements. Fighter design is therefore a matter of deciding the order of mission priorities, and the importance to be allotted allocated to each. A series of tradeoffs is then made to arrive at a design compromise. In most cases it is desirable to have some mud moving capability built in, but not at the expense of the main perceived mission. A true multi-role fighter which is equally capable in all missions, is not likely to be outstanding in any of them, and is therefore to be avoided.

The final consideration is affordability; in any given scenario there is a numerical value below which the size of the force will be inadequate for the task, no matter how capable the individual fighter may be. Politicians and cost cutters often seek to reduce force sizes by moving the goalposts. It hardly needs saying that theoretical modifications do not actually change the threat by one iota, and the main peacetime function of air force commanders is to resist such specious savings. But even then, air force commanders cannot have what their countries cannot afford, and the final compromise in fighter design is to ensure firstly that sufficient fighters can be procured, including attrition replacements, and that they can then be maintained at an acceptable rate of serviceability and readiness.

Interception implies air defence; whether of the homeland, an air base, vital strategic targets, or an aircraft carrier, is basically immaterial. It is modified by two factors, the first is geographical, the second is the threat hardware.

Geography determines the optimum method of defence. If the potential aggressor is situated several hundred miles away, perhaps with open sea intervening, ample early warning should be available. If this is the case, air attacks are best countered well forward, before the raiders can reach the coast or the border. Defending against a cross-border incursion by an adjoining state is far more difficult; reaction time available to the defenders is short, and interception is inevitably made at close range. These two extremes demand different qualities from their interceptors. In the first case, the interceptor has to take off; climb to altitude, make a high speed, preferably supersonic dash to intercept well forward, detect and track incoming aircraft autonomously at long range, and kill them with medium or long range missiles. The two really critical factors are how far forward the interceptor can get in the time available, and how quickly it can close to within missile range.

The F-4 Phantom II was designed initially as a carrier-based interceptor, patrolling far out from the fleet and destroying intruders from far beyond visual range with missiles. Heavy and powerful, it was never intended for manoeuvre combat at close range.
(McDonnell Douglas).

This puts a premium on endurance at high power settings. To be effective in this scenario, an interceptor needs long legs. By contrast, the short warning available in the event of a cross-border incursion means that seconds count. This demands speed of reaction above all else.

The second factor is the type of hardware to be countered. Raids coming over a long distance are likely to be one of two types. The first consists of tactical fighters backed by escorts, inflight refuelling, airborne early warning, and electronic countermeasures machines. The second consists of long ranged multi-engined aircraft carrying stand-off air to surface missiles. In the first case, air combat is unavoidable, and the missile mix should consist of both visual and BVR weapons. In the second case, the priority is to hit the strike force as far back as possible, in order to kill the bombers before they can launch air to surface missiles. For this, a full bag of long range missiles is preferable. At the same time, the interceptor must be capable of killing small targets at low level, as after launch, the ASMs become the priority targets.

Cross-border incursions will almost invariably be made by tactical fighters equipped with air to surface weapons. They will be escorted if the enemy has sufficient aircraft to spare; alternatively they will have a self defence capability. In this scenario, close combat is almost inevitable, and interceptors should be equipped accordingly. Whereas forward defence against long range threats demands highly sophisticated aircraft with BVR weapons, short range defence is often better served by quick reacting austere point defence fighters in greater numerical strength than would be affordable with the longer ranged more capable variety.

The defence of carrier task forces poses rather different problems, as they are vulnerable to attack from both long range missile carrying aircraft, and shorter range tactical fighters, depending on whether they are operating far out at sea, or close inshore. An aircraft carrier is probably the highest value single target in the world, and is worth a great deal of effort to take out. Its load of aircraft, fuel and munitions makes it vulnerable and it cannot afford to take hits, therefore its defences must be exceptional. But its capacity is limited. If it is to pose a credible threat, it must carry a significant number of attack aircraft. It must also be defended against submarine attack. The aircraft dedicated to these roles occupy a great deal of hangar space, and this severely restricts the number of interceptors that can be accommodated.

Defending such a high value target with numerically limited resources demands a very sophisticated interceptor. In high threat areas, it is not sufficient to rely on deck launched fighters to intercept forward; at any given moment standing patrols must be in the air, usually in the form of two fighters flying a racetrack pattern. The carrier-borne interceptor must therefore have exceptional endurance as well as high performance, and a long range multiple engagement weapons system. It also needs all the assistance it can get from force multipliers; tankers, AEW and jamming aircraft.

Air superiority is the next fighter mission. It is defined as creating a situation in the air favourable to the conduct of both surface operations and the air operations which directly support them. Air superiority gained through air combat alone is ephemeral; the only realistic aim is to create favourable situations over limited areas for limited periods of time. When the last fighter leaves the scene through shortage of fuel, air superiority ceases to exist.

As a result of limited wars experience in the late 'sixties and early 'seventies, it was assumed that air superiority would always have to be fought for; air superiority

The F-104A Starfighter, seen here in Pakistan Air Force markings, was designed for rate of climb and acceleration, and not much else. Its tiny wing conferred superb roll rates but gave it poor turning performance. (PAF).

became synonymous with air combat, and the expression "air superiority fighter" became commonplace. The fact that Israel achieved air superiority in the Six Day War by taking out a large proportion of the opposition on the ground was to a degree regarded as an anomaly caused by circumstances unlikely to be repeated. Until such time as PGMs entered widespread service, this was of course a fairly reasonable proposition.

Air operations over friendly territory have the full support of ECM, surface based counter-air weapons, and ground control, but over hostile territory these advantages pass to the enemy. It is therefore far more difficult to achieve air superiority over a hostile area than it is over a friendly zone, but equally it is far more valuable. The role of the air superiority fighter is to engage and destroy enemy fighters where other means are not possible. In this scenario, clever avionics and BVR missiles are not enough; a fighter must be able to outmanoeuvre its opponents if necessary. Whereas the interceptor should be optimised for medium range combat, with dogfighting a valuable if secondary capability, the air superiority fighter has dogfighting as a priority, with medium range

21

combat as a nice to have but secondary feature. It will have a moderate to low wing loading, a moderate aspect ratio, and a high thrust to weight ratio. Most importantly, bearing in mind that the dominant factor in air combat is surprise, everything possible will be done to make sure that the air superiority fighter is not surprised. Radar, radar and IR warning gadgets, and a good all-round view from the cockpit are essentials, while in the last few years, low observables have been added to the list. But more of these later. One of the most difficult fighter missions is that of escort. Historically, fighters protected bombers by clustering around and above them; and by ranging ahead and on their flanks. The missile age changed matters. No longer could protection be afforded by close escort. While it was conceivable that a flight of escort fighters could bring up the rear of a strike force, thus preventing enemy interceptors from slipping in behind them, thus tied they themselves became vulnerable. The only way to effectively protect a strike force was by combining barrier patrols in predetermined positions, with fighter sweeps freelancing in the vicinity of the strike force route. Finally there should ideally be a fighter "reception committee" to meet the whole force on the homeward leg and brush pursuers off their backs. For the escort mission, many of the qualities of both interceptor and air superiority fighter are required; long endurance; the ability to operate autonomously in a hostile countermeasures environment; enough on-board kills to give combat persistence, and the agility to prevail in the dogfight.

* * * *

The lessons of the various limited wars around the world; the obvious needs of the fighter missions, and to a fair degree, the priorities of the "worst case" scenario, were the cause of a steady progression in fighter design over the quarter century following Rolling Thunder. While in numerical terms, performance hardly improved during this time, technological progress was spectacular. But in contrast to events in the previous two decades, those responsible for defence procurement had a fair idea of what they were likely to want, if rather less idea of what they were able to afford.

CHAPTER TWO
Needs and Means

Experience gained in limited wars prior to 1970 made it appear that air superiority was the primary fighter mission, and that the next generation should be tailored to this, with other roles relegated to second place. Progress first became obvious in the West, mainly due to a technological lead over the Eastern bloc generally reckoned to be ten years, though at the time, the assumed, and as events were later to show, largely fictitious capabilities of the Foxbat were to give Western defence analysts bad dreams. In fact, Foxbat was a technological *tour de force* but not in the manner anticipated. What the Mikoyan OKB had done was to take the state of the art and stretch it to its utmost limits. The structure exposed to extremes of kinetic heating, instead of the expected titanium, was made mainly of welded nickel steel. Trading manoeuvrability for performance and fuel capacity, Foxbat was lightly stressed, while its engines were huge, crude, and very thirsty. The radar was probably the most powerful ever to be carried by a fighter, but it used old-fashioned thermionic valves. To the Soviet Union it represented the best possible response to a specific threat; whereas to the West, it at first appeared to be an incredible technical feat. Later, when the truth became known, it seemed more like deliberate disinformation.

From the Western viewpoint, what was wanted was an agile close combat fighter which yet retained all the virtues of an interceptor. It needed performance, manoeuvrability, endurance, and a large number of on-board kills coupled with superior detection, identification, and weapons aiming systems. All the formidable resources of Western technology were mustered to achieve these aims. Under review were the fields of weight saving, propulsion, aerodynamics, and electronics. Advances in these fields often directly affected the development of the fighters on which they were used; to save digressions in the main text, a brief rundown of some of these subjects follows.

Weight Saving

Weight saving reduces wing loading, giving greater turning ability, while increasing thrust loading, which improves rate of climb, acceleration, and sustained turn rates. It reduces the amount of fuel needed for a given mission, which in turn constitutes a further saving in weight, or it allows the fighter to fly farther on the same fuel volume, increasing operational effectiveness. Finally it allows a shorter takeoff run, reducing runway dependence. Weight savings are generally achieved by using specific materials which allow structural and other components to be made lighter.

Prior to 1970, the standard material for fighters had been aluminium alloy, with steel components where either great strength or heat resistance were required. Steel was however extremely heavy, and unless its use was kept to a minimum, the fighter suffered a weight penalty, with a consequent reduction in performance. A possible alternative was titanium alloy, but this was expensive and at that time, difficult to work. With one exception, it was used only in small quantities. The exception was the Lockheed A-12, the forerunner of the SR-71 Blackbird, nine tenths of the structural weight of which was composed of this metal. But as titanium was almost as strong as steel, and had excellent heat and corrosion resisting qualities for barely half the weight, its use rapidly became obligatory.

The very high yield strength of titanium, coupled with a low modulus of elasticity, makes it difficult to shape cold. It is likely to warp or wrinkle, or simply resume its former shape, while any attempt to form small radii may cause cracking. In the early '60s the method of fabrication was to preform components with roughly shaped contours, then creep-form them to their final size and shape in a press under extremes of temperature, holding them until the elasticity had sorted itself out. This worked, but was hardly suitable for efficient mass production. Later in the decade, a process of hotforming components from sheet blanks was developed. Chemical milling is used for some applications, and hot isostatic pressing for others. The latter involves pouring titanium powder into a mould, which is sealed and presurized with an inert gas before being subjected to very high temperatures. Titanium has good welding characteristics, although electron beam welding in a vacuum chamber is far from simple. This was the state of the art in 1970; further advances were made in the use of titanium over the next two decades, including superplastic forming, which uses high temperatures and pressures to enable complex shapes to be made without welding or fastening. Diffusion bonding is another method. Temperatures of 900deg C and pressures of 150lb/sq.in cause the atomic structures of the metal to fuse together into one integral component.

Later to become critical in the hunt for weight savings were advanced composites, usually carbon or boron based. Prior to 1970, non-metallics accounted for only a tiny part of the total empty weight of the fighter; the main items being the dielectric radome and acrylics in the canopy.

Composites are lighter than their metal counterparts, with a higher strength to weight ratio and a much higher stiffness to weight ratio. They are virtually corrosion-proof, resistant to wear and fatigue, and have low thermal conductivity. Basically, they are made by placing layers of fibre on top of each other, separated by a matrix material which is then cured. By carefully designing the pattern in which the fibres are laid, components can be tailored to resist the flexing or torsional movement anticipated in flight.

The drawbacks of composites are material cost, which is much higher than that of aluminium alloy, and difficulty of handling, which is very specialised, and cannot be carried out in the same way as metal. Composites are far more difficult to cut and drill than conventional metal alloys, and demand specialised tooling. Some idea of the problem can be gained when one considers that an average fighter wing contains about 5,000 holes. Battle damage is another potential problem area. Band-aid type patches have been developed to stick over simple holes, but impact damage can cause delamination, with attendant structural weakening, without it becoming immediately obvious. One obvious difficulty is in deciding the positions and the extent to which quite small perforations, say from shrapnel, will degrade the structural strength of the component to an unacceptable degree. It thus seems that entire large panels may have to be changed, which had they been of conventional light alloy, could simply have been patched. In addition, composites have a very low linear coefficient of expansion, which in areas subjected to heat, demand great precision at the interfaces with metal components. In 1970, few components were made from advanced composites, but this has gradually increased to the point where some 40 percent of structural weight is made up of composite components.

An alternative lightweight material is aluminium lithium. Lithium is the lightest metal known; so light that it floats on water. Tiny amounts combined with aluminium and other metals give an alloy both lighter and stiffer than duralumin. It is however difficult to produce, as is the basic lithium, which not only oxidises rapidly, but like titanium, has an affinity for hydrogen. Aluminium lithium was first used on the upper wing surfaces of the Mach 2 North American A-5 Vigilante, while the Soviet Union used an aluminium lithium magnesium alloy on the Foxbat. It offers a cheaper alternative to composites on aircraft skins; it is a metal, and can be fabricated, handled, and repaired using ordinary workshop practices and skills. It may also be used for more solid forged items, where weight savings will be greater. While its qualities have been known for many years, problems with casting techniques have delayed its entry into widespread usage.

Propulsion

The quest in propulsion is always for greater power at less engine weight, coupled with greater efficiency, reliability, and fuel economy. Without getting too technical, the jet engine consists of five stages. First comes the inlet. Jet engines can only accept air at relatively low speeds, and the inlet serves to draw air in, then slow it down. It does this by increasing the size of the duct downstream of the intake; as the air expands to fill the larger volume it slows down. A simple inlet serves for flight speeds of up to about twice the local speed of sound, but to fly faster than this, a variable intake is needed. At high speeds this constricts, reducing the open frontal area, and with it the volume of air being shovelled through the intake.

Next comes the compressor, a series of fans which, as its name implies, compresses the air. This has several stages, each stage compressing the air a bit more than the one in front. The General Electric J79 which powered the Phantom had no less than seventeen compressor stages, which made it a very long engine. The J79 had a single spool, but modern engines have two, and sometimes three spools. A two spool engine has low and high pressure compressors, driven by coaxial shafts. Although more complex, it is more efficient, and reduces the total number of stages needed, giving a shorter engine.

After compression, the air enters the next stage, the combustion chamber, where it is expanded by heating, typically to temperatures of between 1,200 and 1,400 deg Celsius. To put it mildly, this is very hot, and the search is always on for new metals and methods of cooling in order to prevent the combustors and the downstream engine components from deforming or melting.

After the combustor, the air enters the turbine stage. The turbines are driven by the superheated exhaust gases, in turn driving the compressor stages via concentric shafts, and as a general rule using rather more energy than the combustor stage produces. Fortunately the compressors themselves restore the balance, producing thrust on their own account. Finally, the hot exhaust gases are expelled through a fifth and final stage, the nozzle. This is designed to reduce the pressure of the hot gas as it leaves the engine by expanding it, producing a small extra thrust increment as it does so. The nozzle area is variable to suit flight conditions.

Fighter turbojets invariably feature afterburners; termed augmentors when applied to turbofans. This is a method of obtaining extra thrust for short periods by spraying fuel into the hot exhaust, with the effect that the rear end of the engine behaves like a ramjet, giving a massive thrust increase. The amount of thrust gained varies, but afterburning is most effective at higher speeds, becoming progressively less so lower down the scale.

The late 1960s saw the introduction of military turbofan engines. Turbofans, in which the low pressure compressor stages are extended in radius to become wider than the main body of the engine, combine highly efficient dry thrust with low specific fuel consumption. Much of the air which passes the low pressure compressor passes around the core of the engine, aiding cooling and allowing hotter temperatures to be used. Turbofans also permit a greater degree of afterburning due to the larger proportion of bypass air in the exhaust, albeit at a penalty in fuel consumption. But while fuel economy is important, in a fighter performance is even more so. Generally it can be said that the turbofan cannot produce as high a specific thrust performance as an equivalent turbojet, and military turbofans are therefore a compromise, with low bypass ratios compared to those of civilian engines.

The early history of the jet engine saw greater power attained by progressively using bigger and more complex engines. This could not continue. Fighter design imposes severe size constraints, and more recently, methods of improving all-round engine performance have concentrated on increasing the thrust to weight ratio. This resulted in smaller engines, with less components, giving greater simplicity and reliability. The technology has advanced by leaps and bounds; for example greater compression is now attained from fewer stages. Operating temperatures have risen, particularly at the turbine inlet, causing problems of cooling, differential expansion, etc, which can only be solved by new state of the art materials, both metallic and ceramic.

Electronics

The greatest advances on the fighter scene have been made in the field of electronics and avionics, mainly due to micro-miniaturisation techniques which allow a tonne of capacity to be squeezed into a thimbleful of volume, and to advances in the speed of processing raw data. Detection, countermeasures, self protection, attack, navigation and communications systems have all benefited greatly. Electronics have also commenced to spill over into other areas previously not considered; cockpit displays and the man/machine interface; engine management, and flight control systems.

1958 was the year of the microchip. Working independently, a Texan engineer and a Californian physicist arrived at the conclusion that the four essential elements of an electronic circuit; resistors, capacitors, inductors and transistors, could all be integrated on a small piece of silicon. The end result was that thousands of micro-miniaturised circuits could be fabricated on a single silicon wafer, or chip, with connections "printed" in copper or gold inlay. The effect was revolutionary. Equipment that would previously have occupied a small room could now be fitted into a suitcase. Nor did it stop there. Since the early days, a new generation of microchips appeared roughly every three years, each generation giving a fourfold increase in capacity. As capacity has grown, and with it capability, ever more tasks have been found for the willing electrons, with the result that both demand and capacity have now grown so great that the limiting factor has become the speed at which the data can be processed. For example, radar signals often carry far more information than the systems could handle; the problem is to process and use it, because the speed at which electrons can be made to move through silicon is limited. Active electronic countermeasures have exploited this failing in the past by inserting misleading signals. An overload of information coming in leads to an electronic traffic jam; and faster processing is the answer. It is also the key to improved electronic counter-countermeasures. Current silicon-based systems can handle up to 300 megabits of data per second, using the new Very High Speed Integrated Circuits (VHSIC), but even this is insufficient. In addition, they are vulnerable to electro-magnetic pulse, which is the byproduct of a nuclear explosion.

Two alternatives seem possible; gallium arsenide chips in place of silicon, and optical processing. Experiments to find a faster alternative to silicon began in the early 1970s, and gallium arsenide showed many advantages. Electron speed is up to ten times faster, while demanding less power. GaAs chips can also operate over a wider temperature range.

Optical processing is further into the future, but shows greater promise. It works by the reaction of light with the raw radar signal in an optical-acoustic cell, using analogue rather than digital techniques, and shows particular promise for functions where pattern recognition is required. Optical processing promises a speed of 1,000 times greater than that presently available, but digital techniques must be introduced for greater accuracy. Current problems will probably restrict its use in fighters for many years, although it has other airborne applications, such as processing synthetic aperture radar signals; a reconnaissance or attack rather than an air superiority function.

The other data processing problem lay in computers. The early solution was to bung in a computer for each task. This took a lot of space and a lot of power, while connections were made with large and complicated wire bundles which inevitably had to be altered whenever a new capability was wanted. Early computers were of the analogue type, which work by comparing incoming data with prestored patterns. It was soon found that the complicated relationships between bits of electronic data were best untangled by digital computers, and these have largely taken over.

Duplication of effort was another problem. Often two or more computers were monitoring the same function, and even worse, coming up with slightly different answers. This basically arose because of how the computers were linked together. The answer proposed in the late 1960s was the data bus. The data bus can be visualised as a single track circular railway with stations located around it. The stations represent computers, subcomputers, or sensors, while data acts like the passengers on a train, riding from station to station in turn. In this way, all the stations receive all the passengers. These data buses are known as single source/multi-sink types, and the early fighters which incorporated them tended to have a powerful central computer to handle the main data processing function, with smaller, dedicated subcomputers for specific sensors or systems all having their twopennorth on a timeshare basis. As miniaturisation improved and capacity increased, this inevitably caused traffic jams among the eager electrons, while it lacked the flexibility to re-allocate the bus capacity available on a need or priority basis.

The very factor which had caused the problem was also to solve it; as black boxes became smaller and cheaper, it became preferable to use lots of individual computers rather than one large one. But this called for a new type of data bus to cope with what had to be a much greater demand. In the form of the MIL-STD 1553, this arrived in the early 1970s. Unlike its predecessor, it is a very high capacity multi-source, multi-sink bus. This is like a multiple track circular railway, with stations as before. But instead of checking in at every station as before, each bit of data, or passenger, is given a ticket, without which he cannot board a train, and once on allows him to leave the train at a specific point only. Also, unlike earlier data buses, bits of data can flow in either direction, while the multi-track capability means that several bits of data can be transferred at the same time. Naturally this takes a great deal of management if efficient working is to be maintained, and this, plus extra functions continually demanded from the black boxes, means that processing speeds must continually improve.

Electronics-Detection

The primary means of detection are radar, infra-red, and optical. Of these, radar is the most widely used. Modern fighter radars are invariably multimode, each mode being used for a specific function. In search mode, it typically scans a pie shaped area ahead of the aircraft between 60 and 90 deg on either side of the centreline, and up to eight bars in elevation. A bar is the beamwidth in degrees, and varies according to the size of the scanner. It is calculated as follows: 60 multiplied by the wavelength in centimetres (fighter radars operate in X-band, which is approximately 3cm) divided by the diameter of the scanner in cm. For example, the AWG-9 of the Tomcat is roughly equal to 1.97 deg per bar, so the maximum elevation of eight bars gives a vertical angle of 15.76 deg. This can of course be trained to look up and down. Other modes utilise a lesser area of scan in order to concentrate the radar on a particular sector of the sky.

A radar emits large amounts of energy, which attenuates rapidly with distance, then listens for the energy bouncing back off a target. The rate of attenuation is such that a good analogy would be throwing the town hall at a concrete wall, and having a single brick bounce back. The receiver has to be very sensitive in order to detect the tiny echo at all. Pulse repetition frequency is another factor. High prfs, between 100,000 and 300,000 pulses per second, give the greatest amount of transmitted power, and therefore the best long distance detection performance, but with a long range target, many pulses are transmitted before the echo returns. This gives rise to possible ambiguity; which pulse was the return from? Was it a large target at long range, or a smaller one closer in? A technique called frequency modulation, in which the individual pulses are coded, is used to give the answer. While high prfs give the best detection results at long distance, they are not so good at calculating the range. Faster processing capability and greater capacity will provide an eventual solution.

Medium prfs range between 10,000 and 30,000 pulses per second. They also suffer from possible range ambiguities, but nowhere near to the same extent as high prfs, and they are far better for ranging, which makes them widely used in fighter applications. Range data on any specific target is obtained by making a slight variation to the prf. At the same time, if the echo returns slightly off-frequency, the amount can be measured and the relative motion of the target deduced.

Pulse Doppler is yet another capability. In addition to sorting out relative target motion, as described above, it is particularly useful for looking down at targets. Naturally the radar picks up all the ground clutter, but utilising the Doppler effect, filters screen out all returns moving in conformity with the flight path of the fighter to within a preset limit, typically 90kt, This leaves just the faster moving returns, which are likely to be true targets. The one flaw in pulse Doppler is that any co-speed targets moving in the same direction as the fighter will also be filtered out, as will targets moving at an angle of close to 90 deg from the flight path of the fighter. As the man said, there is no free lunch!

Radar is frequently seen as a sort of infallible long range flashlight, unerringly detecting targets far beyond the limits of human vision. Unfortunately this is not the case; the two characteristics of radar search are that the probability of detection reduces as the range increases, and also with the distance away from the centre of the beam. By the same token, a target which is on the border of two range bars in elevation is also more difficult to detect. There are no total guarantees of detection at longer ranges. Further handicaps actually arise from advanced technology. One of the essentials made possible by digital computers was the ability to track one or more targets while continuing to search the surrounding sky for others. Once a target is being tracked, the computer opens a file on it, and if for any reason it is not detected during the next few search sweeps, the computer will interpolate a position and continue to display it. The trouble is that the contact is historical rather than real time, and it takes perhaps 14 seconds before it self-cancels. This can be misleading. A further problem is that switching from one mode to another will sometimes leave the pilot unaware of further developments, as the radar concentrates on what it is told to, to the exclusion of all else. Modern radar systems give the appearance of being the ultimate no-brainer, but this is not the case; the pilot needs to be very discriminating in his choice of modes in any given situation.

Radar Missile Guidance

Various forms of missile guidance had been tried, and all had been found wanting in one respect or another. By 1970, both beam riding and wire guidance with active control to line of sight were long gone. Active radar, with a small set mounted in the nose of the missile was theoretically an optimum solution, but in 1970, the range attainable was not really worth the trouble. For beyond visual range combat, semi-active radar homing was the only realistic solution. This involved the fighter detecting the target on radar, then illuminating it during the entire missile time of flight, during which period it was forced to close the enemy, while being electronically oblivious to all else. This was hardly satisfactory, but there was no suitable alternative. This dilemma was partially solved when track while scan mode was introduced, allowing missile guidance while the radar continued to search for other contacts.

Infra-Red Detection and Missile Guidance

Detecting enemy aircraft by their heat emissions dates back to 1940, but it was many years before it became a viable method. The advantage of IR is that it is passive; unlike radar it gives off no telltale emissions to betray the presence of the fighter to the enemy. It possessed better angular discrimination than radar, and is thus superior to it in picking out individual targets in a tightly packed formation that only show up on the radar screen as a single large blip. Infra-red has two faults; it degrades badly in conditions of cloud, mist or rain. It also lacks any form of ranging capability, which is another severe constraint. IR detection can be regarded as complementary to radar, rather than a detection system in its own right, although the way the Russians use it in the MiG-29 and Su-27 is interesting.

As a missile guidance system IR lacks target discrimination. Launched at one target, it can easily switch to another within its "look angle", regardless of national markings. This restricts its effective use to visual distance in clear air conditions, where the fighter pilot can establish that he is shooting at a positively identified enemy.

The baseline detection system is the human eye. Pre-1970 fighters were designed for high performance, with minimal drag as a priority, with the cockpit canopy faired into the fuselage. The pilot's view out, particularly to the rear, was abysmal as a result. Strength was a further consideration, and pre-1970 cockpits generally featured very heavy metal framing, especially those designed east of Potsdam. Experience in small wars showed the folly of this, and within a few years, coupled with advances in transparent materials, soon permitted an unrivalled view in all directions.

In close combat, the human eye has always been the most used method of instant identification, limited only by distance. It was inevitable that electro-optical attempts to expand its range would be made. These have included a device which gathers and concentrates light at low intensities, to permit visident at night, and another which allows visident at ultra-long ranges. These were moderately successful, but were far too dependent on weather conditions. They also tended to increase pilot workload, and keep his head down in the office for far too long. Current progress is concentrating more on electronic means; IFF interrogation is one obvious method, while non co-operative target recognition, using the radar signatures of the type of aircraft being illuminated, and particularly its engine compressor face, holds much promise. This last naturally demands a tremendous amount of high speed computer capacity.

Advances in electronic capabilities have allowed nav/attack and countermeasures systems to be largely automated, and have gone a great way towards producing secure voice communications. This last is a great advantage; the easiest way of finding out what an enemy fighter unit is up to is to simply listen to their radio chatter and the messages sent them by base. Flight control and engine monitoring systems were also to a great degree taken over by the black boxes after 1970. But it is in the province of the man/machine interface; the cockpit, where the greatest advances have been made. As fighters have become more capable, and their systems cleverer, so the fighter pilot has become overloaded with work. This is evident even in peacetime exercises, how much more so does it become when the stress of war, and of imminent extinction, is added.

In pre-1970 fighters, the pilot spent far too much time looking down into the cockpit at a mass of instruments, dials and gauges. In addition he had to operate a whole mass of switches in the correct sequence in order to perform certain functions, such as dropping ordnance, selecting air to air weaponry, or even carrying out essential tasks such as transferring fuel between tanks to keep his centre of gravity within limits. The ideal was to have every control needed in combat to hand; with all information presented in an easily assimilable manner without the need for prolonged periods of peering down into the office. Over the past 20 years, black boxes have revolutionised the pilot's workload; he still has a lot to do, but much of the donkey work is now automated, and the essentials, where he must use his own judgement, are presented in a clear format in a place convenient to be seen. Developments in this field are outlined in the chapters devoted to the fighters on which they occur.

CHAPTER THREE

Quality versus Quantity and the American Giants

By 1970, the Cold War had reached maturity. The armed forces of the United States and the Soviet Union had, with the achievement of mutually assured destruction, reached an uneasy stand-off. Neither side wanted to trigger an all-out nuclear exchange, as this could only result in a no-win situation. There were however, other possibilities. The Soviet Union was spending a great deal of time, effort and roubles in destabilising countries in the Third World. Sometimes this was done directly; in others it was done by Communist satellite states. Marxist dogma stated that sooner or later, the workers of the world would revolt against their rulers, and that gradually, country by country, the world would fall under communist domination. This concept was widely accepted in the West, where it became known as the Domino Effect. Naturally there were many regimes that resisted it, and these looked to the United States as their ally. Local wars involving the great powers were and would be the inevitable result. The War of Attrition, in which Soviet flyers and missileers took an active part for Egypt against an American-backed Israel; and the on-going conflict in South-East Asia, were just two of the more visible facets of this process.

There was also the projected "worst case" scenario; a conflict in Central Europe in which the Superpowers would directly confront each other. While this involved a high risk of nuclear escalation, the West thought it possible to limit it by graduating their response, rather like raising the stakes in a poker game. The huge ICBMs in their silos would be merely pawns in this scenario, posing a threat or a bluff, no-one could be sure which, that would only reluctantly be used. Conventional forces were all-important, as was the ability to project armed might rapidly at a distance. Air power, with its speed and flexibility, was the obvious way of doing this, and the tactical air assets of both sides were critical for the battles assumed to be ahead. At the same time, the air defence of the respective homelands could not be neglected, in case apparent physical weakness, or lack of resolution, should tempt exploitation.

In many ways, fighter aircraft are the status symbols of nations. They represent the peak of advanced technology, and are a visible indicator of a country's prestige, wealth, and industrial power. There is no record of any nation settling for second best in the field of fighter acquisition. Even when faced with a relatively low level threat, they will always buy the best that they can afford.

Political idiocy having emasculated the British aircraft industry during the previous fifteen years, the United States had taken over as the world leader in the field. They had always set out to design and build the world's best fighters, and now they were to succeed with a vengeance. The problem was that the world's best fighters were also the world's most expensive fighters. Less than 20 years earlier, the American Joint Chiefs of Staff had recommended an Air Force strength of no less than 155 wings; 138 of them combat wings. Needless to say, this had never been achieved, and in fact the USAF had shrunk to less than half this figure by 1970. The underlying reason for this reduction was cost. On the other side of the world, the Soviet Air Forces kept their numerical strength at a much higher level.

The USA found itself locked into a self-perpetuating upward spiral. In any wealthy and democratic state, the military are fairly low in the pecking order. The number of young men with the ability to fly hot fighters is always a very small percentage of the population. This being the case, and also as an expression of national pride, they must be given the best possible aircraft. In a democracy, defence is just one of many calls on the national budget, and only a tiny proportion of the gross national product can be allocated to fighters. At the same time, in an advanced society, technology ensures the best fighters are being produced, albeit at a cost. The spiral then becomes; better fighters = advanced technology = more expensive fighters = fewer fighters = more outnumbered than ever = better quality pilots needed = fewer suitable recruits = fewer fighters = better fighters needed etc.

The Soviet Union was differently situated. The USSR was often described as technologically backward. This is only true in relative terms; the Soviet Union was a major industrial nation which a few years earlier had pioneered spaceflight and unmanned moon landings. In 1970 it lagged the United States mainly in the field of computers and high speed processing.

Being a totalitarian state had its advantages. The Soviet career officer was accorded higher status in society than his Western counterpart, and was rewarded accordingly. Conscription brought all suitable young men into the net, while a state-funded flying scheme for the young(DOSAAF), recruited many promising young fast jet pilots. Another factor was patriotism. Mother Russia had been all but overrun by the Nazi hordes in 1941 and 1942. Defence of one's native soil was therefore very real to young Russians, founded as it was on events within living memory. By contrast, young American patriotism is more of an abstract concept based on individual freedoms and liberties. Obtaining suitable recruits was therefore less of a problem in the USSR. Nor were budgets the supreme arbiters that they were in the West. A totalitarian state could deprive its civilian population to fund the military. As for the technology gap, there is an old saying, often proved in battle, that numbers degrade technology. Taking all these factors into account, the Soviet Union made a virtue of a necessity, and built up air forces which were huge in comparison with those of the Western nations. Judged on a one for one basis, Soviet aircraft were inferior to those of the West, but *en masse* they were formidable.

This had the unwitting effect of locking the Americans even more tightly into the spiral. In the event of war they would be heavily outnumbered, and could only seek to redress the balance through superior technology. In the air, they needed ace pilots. Throughout the history of air combat, a few outstanding fighter pilots, typically less than five percent of the whole, had run up large scores at the expense of their less gifted brethren. The numerical imbalance was such that a large number of high scorers was needed. The quest was on to turn each fighter pilot into an ace, and technology seemed the easiest, and indeed the only way to achieve it. This was the idea underlying the first two American superfighters; the F-14 Tomcat, and the F-15 Eagle.

The theoretical ideal was a single fighter for both the US Navy and Air Force. This would yield enormous savings through large production runs, commonality of parts, and similar training. In the mid-sixties the aircraft selected was General Dynamics' F-111, the swing wing wonder. Heavily laden with air to air missiles, it was intended to fill the interceptor/fighter role for the USAF, the USN, and the RAF. However it soon became obvious that the F-111 would never be a fighter; it lacked manoeuvrability, and its engines were sensitive to disturbed airflow. Moreover, as the Phantom had previously shown, it is far easier to adapt a naval fighter for land-based use; the opposite course is far more difficult. The naval F-111B variant was a disaster; in addition to other flaws, it was too heavy for carrier operations and was eventually scrapped.

Grumman F-14 Tomcat

Grumman had been responsible for developing the General Dynamics F-111B into a carrier-based aircraft. When this project started to run into trouble, they sought an alternative. The result, after literally thousands of design studies and several years of work, emerged as the F-14 Tomcat.

The Tomcat, contrary to popular opinion, was designed for the air superiority mission, although it was known from the start that it would also have to be an outstanding interceptor. In the early design studies, the only real concession to the fleet air defence mission was to make it a very large aeroplane in order to carry a two man crew and a heavy load of long range missiles. Apart from scaling it down, everything possible was done to make it an outstanding performer in the close combat arena. In addition to the usual air superiority requirements of high speed, high rate of climb, and agility, it needed long range and extended endurance. The weapons system chosen was the Hughes AWG-9 with its huge radar scanner, and a load of six large and heavy long ranged AIM-54 Phoenix missiles, both originally intended for the F-111B. A smaller fighter could simply not have carried the kit. A two man crew was necessary to operate the complex weapons and avionics, and inevitably, two engines were required to give sufficient thrust.

When late in 1970, the prototype was rolled out, the F-14 looked very different to anything previously seen. It had been designed around engines that had given trouble in the F-111; Pratt & Whitney TF30 turbofans. In order to minimise the effects of disturbed airflow which was such a feature of the earlier machine, the engines were widely spaced, keeping the intakes well away from the front fuselage. For the same reason, the flow through them ran in a dead straight line from from inlet to nozzle. It was not intended that the TF30-P-412 would be the definitive engine for the Tomcat, but in the initial stages it was the only engine in sight. The TF30-powered F-14A was to be an interim machine until a new and more powerful advanced technology engine, Pratt & Whitney's F401, came on stream about two years into F-14 production. The definitive Tomcat was to be the F-14B, and all F-14As were to be retrofitted with the F401 when the original TF30s reached the end of their natural life

The wide spacing of the engines gave rise to a novel layout. A nacelle holding the huge radar and the crew was mounted centrally between the intakes, tapering into a flattish pancake aft of the cockpit. This housed a considerable amount of fuel in locations where battle damage was unlikely to cause it to spill into the engines. It also provided a great deal of lifting area, effectively reducing wing loading, which by orthodox standards was rather high, by some 40 percent. It was also responsible for twin fins being adopted, supplemented by twin ventral strakes for additional stability at high angles of attack. Originally a single large dorsal fin supplemented by a sideways-folding ventral fin had been considered, but this was deemed unsuitable for carrier work.

At the time that the Tomcat was designed, a fierce debate was raging as to whether the optimum fighter crew was one man or two. The Phantom of course had been a two holer, with the back seater looking after all the electronic magic. Statistics from the Vietnam War showed that roughly four in every ten visual sightings were made by the guy in the back, and he also played an important part in close combat by taking his head out of the office to keep a watch on the vulnerable rear quadrant. With a well-trained crew accustomed to flying together, this worked well, but when pilots and back seaters were teamed ad hoc, there could be crew coordination problems. The extremely sophisticated AWG-9 weapons system in the Tomcat demanded a specialist operator, and a single holer was never seriously considered. One basic flaw of the Phantom had been its poor rearward visibility. This was corrected in the Tomcat by the provision of a huge canopy which gave a near perfect all-round view from the cockpit, setting a trend for all future fighters.

It is easy to design a wing for supersonic flight; it is equally easy to design one for economic subsonic cruising. Combining these two conflicting requirements in the late '60s was more difficult. Add the need for hard manoeuvre and the difficulty is compounded. The Tomcat had yet another essential requirement; it had to be easy to land on an aircraft carrier. A fighter in motion contains a great deal of kinetic energy which is imparted to the carrier on landing, to the deck on touchdown and to the arrester gear. This had to be held to a minimum for obvious reasons. By far the most important factor in kinetic energy is velocity. While it is important to keep the weight of the fighter down, even a small reduction in landing speed produces a disproportionate advantage. In addition, to land on a relatively small object such as a carrier calls for very precise flying, and the pilot needs a good forward view. This can only be achieved if the nose is not cocked up at a high angle on the final approach.

Economic cruising, especially at high altitudes, high rates of turn, and a low landing speed with a low angle of attack (alpha) is best achieved by a high aspect ratio straight wing; i.e. a long narrow wing as on a glider. Supersonic speed, fast acceleration, and a fast rate of roll, which is essential for a rapid change of direction, are conferred by a low aspect ratio sharply swept wing which is short and broad, as on the French Mirage deltas. The compromise selected for the Tomcat was a variable sweep wing, which could be adjusted in flight to suit the requirements of the moment. A further factor was thickness/chord ratio; the depth of the wing in relation to its width measured front to back parallel with the aircraft centreline. High t/c ratios give more lift in the lower speed range, while low t/c ratios are less draggy at high speeds. Variable geometry has the best of both worlds; while the physical thickness of the wing remains constant, the chord increases with the sweep angle, decreasing the t/c ratio. As Grumman's Bob Kress said, "it's not what you've got but the way that you swing it!"

The variable sweep wing has many advantages, but it also has certain drawbacks. It is complex, but this must be accepted. It is relatively small in area, which leads to a high wing loading. With the Tomcat, this was to a great degree offset by the extra lifting area of the pancake. The only other swing wing fighter of that era was the Russian MiG-23, which had just three sweep angles. They were; fully forward for takeoff and landing, fully swept for acceleration and high speed flight, and intermediate sweep for combat. At minimum sweep, which gave the greatest lift, it was severely restricted as to the g loading it could sustain.

Grumman, with the advantage of high speed on-board computers, decided to take full advantage by making the sweep infinitely variable, the angle changing to give the optimum setting for every flight regime. Nor was it load restricted in any way even at minimum sweep. Computer controlled extending slats ran the entire length of the leading edge while flaps made up most of the trailing edge. Spoilers on the top surface augmented roll control at subsonic speeds only; roll and pitch control was by differentially moving tailerons. Both deck and hangar space on an aircraft carrier is very limited, and wing folding is a normal feature of carrier aircraft. Grumman found a

OPPOSITE TOP: *A Grumman F-14A Tomcat seen over Saudi Arabia during operation Desert Shield in 1990. The long canopy was a reaction against poor rearward visibility in previous US fighters. (Grumman).*

OPPOSITE BOTTOM: *For improved supersonic manoeuvrability, the Tomcat was fitted with glove vanes, seen here deployed, as a stabilising measure. (Grumman).*

simpler way of minimising the parking space needed; they provided an oversweep wing position which reduced the width required to that of the tailplane.

A feature of supersonic flight is that the centre of lift moves aft. A variable sweep wing aggravates this, because as the wings move backwards, a great deal of the lift moves with them, but not a lot of the weight. This causes significant differences between the centre of lift and the centre of gravity, which causes the aircraft to become nose heavy. To balance things out, the aircraft must be trimmed tail heavy, which causes excessive drag, and also excessive stability, with disastrous effects on supersonic manoevrability. It had been precisely this which had made the F-111B such a turkey as a fighter, unable to pull more than 3g at high altitudes and Mach numbers. The solution adopted was the glove vane; a small triangular surface which extended automatically from the leading edge of the wing glove when the speed exceeded Mach 1.4. This destabilised the forward area of the Tomcat, relieving downloads on the tailerons. At the same time, it reduced fuselage bending moments, permitting weight savings in the structure.

The wings of the F-111B pivoted around single enormous pins carried in a steel box structure, part bolted and part welded. Not only was this enormously heavy, but failures occurred on Air Force F-111s. Grumman chose a different route. They went for two spherical bearings for each wing, each strong enough to carry the load if the other failed. These were mounted in an all-welded titanium wing box. The largest all-titanium component of its time, it gave a weight saving over steel of some 900lbs. This approach was justified; not one Tomcat ever suffered a wing box or wing bearing failure. In all, titanium accounted for roughly 25 percent of the structural weight of the big fighter; 15 percent was steel, and 36 percent aluminium alloy. The first major use of composites in a fighter was boron epoxy for the upper taileron surfaces. The ventral strakes were of fibreglass epoxy, as was the radome.

The AIM-54A Phoenix is 13.15ft long; 15 inches in diameter, and weighs 985lb, which is pretty large as air to air missiles go. The Tomcat carries up to six of these monsters, and minimising drag was a problem. The solution adopted was to carry four on semi-conformal pallets beneath the fuselage, with the other two on hardpoints beneath the wing gloves. Phoenix is widely quoted as having a high altitude V_{max} of Mach 5, and a range of 110 nautical miles. In fact, the rocket all-burnt speed of the AIM-54A was Mach 3.8, and its maximum range 75-80nm. The figure of 110nm arose from a spectacular test in which a Tomcat "killed" a supersonic drone approaching from near head-on and rather higher. The big missile was launched when the drone was still 110nm away, but after a time of flight of 2.62 minutes, when the Phoenix passed within lethal distance of its target, the distance had closed down to 72.5nm. To maximise the reach, the launching fighter had accelerated to Mach 1.5, and the missile was pre-programmed to fly a high trajectory, peaking at over 100,000ft before using the downhill slope to maintain speed and manoeuvrability while maximising the range.

Phoenix uses semi-active radar midcourse homing, switching to active radar for the terminal phase, which is limited by seeker head sensitivity to about 10nm. Unlike the AIM-7 Sparrow, which can only be used singly, Phoenix can be used for multiple simultaneous attacks, the semi-active midcourse homing being used by up to six missiles at once on a time-share basis.

Other weapons routinely carried by the Tomcat are the AIM-7E/F Sparrow and the AIM-9L/P Sidewinder, with AIM-120 Amraam to replace Sparrow shortly. The maximum number of missiles possible is eight, in various combinations. Two 'winders can supplement Phoenix, or four each of the smaller missiles, with Sparrows carried semi-recessed under the fuselage once the Phoenix pallets have been removed. The harsh lessons of South East Asia ensured that an internal cannon was installed; the 20mm M61 Vulcan six barrelled cannon with 675 rounds, and a rate of fire of 100 rounds per second.

The Hughes AWG-9 weapons system represented a massive advance in technology. A travelling wave tube replaced the magnetron used in earlier radars. This gave much higher pulse repetition frequencies than were previously obtainable, while pulses were coherent, or exactly in phase. This gave two significant advantages; by allowing the Doppler shift of the returning emissions to be analysed, ground clutter could be filtered out, giving an effective look-down radar capability for the first time, while the increase in transmitted power gave longer range detection than had previously been possible by an airborne radar. It was the first coherent pulse-Doppler radar to be mass-produced. Advances in lightweight solid state computers gave a tremendous increase in capacity, which was used to give radar modes previously unobtainable.

AWG-9 can detect targets with a radar cross-section of $5m^2$ out to more than 115nm. Closer in, at 90nm it can track up to 24 targets simultaneously, but this many would be enough to swamp the Tactical Information Display(TID) in the back seat, which can only manage six at a time if its information is to remain readable. The system automatically presents the six contacts which appear to be the greatest threats, while continuing to track the remainder. If the Naval Flight Officer, as the backseater is called, wishes to have a look at any of the other target files, he can call the information up on the Detail Data Display(DDD), a small screen set above the TID. He can also overrule the computer's selection of which contacts are displayed. Subject to the maximum of 24, further contacts can be fed in via data link from other Tomcats; Hawkeye AEW aircraft, Prowler EW aircraft, or the carrier. AWG-9 has six channels dedicated to Phoenix missile guidance, which can be used for a simultaneous attack on six separate targets, and this which gives the Tomcat its unrivalled capacity for mass destruction.

The information is displayed on clutter-free screens in an alpha-numeric format; a tremendous advance over the old analogue displays which needed a lot of skilled interpretation. The TID can be oriented in two ways; either with the F-14 at the bottom of the scope pointing up, or geostabilised with north at the top, showing both the F-14 and its contacts. The former is preferred in a straightforward attack situation, but in a confused scenario, with contacts coming in via data link, possibly with some in the rear quadrants, where they are outside the scan of the radar, the latter has advantages. The pilot has access to the same information as the NFO, on displays and HUD. Either can launch Phoenix or Sparrows, but only the pilot can use Sidewinders. In combat, the NFO is more than a mere radar operator. In addition to monitoring the systems, he acts as a battle manager, advising the pilot of the all-round situation.

While the reputation of the Tomcat is of a long range killer, it is remarkably good in close combat for such a big machine. Its predecessor, the Phantom, was notoriously twitchy at low speeds and high weights. By contrast, the Tomcat is reckoned to be easy to handle. Roll rate is good, while pitch rate is exceptional. Unlike the majority of later fighters, notably the F-16, it has no angle of attack limiter; nor does it need one. It is also highly spin-resistant. These attributes allow the pilot to keep on hauling with little fear of departing controlled flight. The variable sweep wings with a battery of high lift devices make it very manoeuvrable at low speeds, while in mock dogfights, even F-15 drivers have to keep their energy levels high if they don't want to get waxed.

As we saw earlier, the TF30 should have been a stopgap pending the development of the F401-PW-400 Advanced Technology Engine. The seventh prototype, the sole F-14B, flew just 33 hours with the new engine before escalating costs caused the F401 to be cancelled, and the TF30 became the standard power plant by default. Measures to reduce compressor stalling at first seemed to succeed, and when power settings were left high, there were few problems. The previous generation of fighters bled off speed rapidly in hard manoeuvring, and needed to keep power on at all times. The Tomcat didn't, mainly due to its automatic wing sweep, which provided optimum lift throughout the speed range. The result was that in simulated combat, squadron pilots were continually banging the throttles back and forward, and the TF30 was simply not up such hard usage. Compressors shed blades, and all sorts of problems were encountered. Engine failures were responsible for roughly 25 percent of Tomcats written off in accidents, and pilots had to learn to fly the engine in order to minimise the risks. Another shortcoming was that the F-14A was a bit underpowered by comparison with its close contemporary, the F-15. The F-14B would have been a far more potent fighter.

The Tomcat was a very expensive aeroplane to start with, and in 1974, escalating costs nearly caused it to be cancelled. Only a loan from an Iranian bank enabled work to continue, for which the quid pro quo was an order for 80 Tomcats for the Imperial Iranian Air Force. When the Shah was ousted in 1979, this was renamed the Iranian Islamic Revolutionary Air Force. US assistance ceased immediately, making maintenance a problem, with the result that Tomcats played little part in the eight year war against Iraq, which broke out in 1980. In two highly publicised actions against Libya, they shot down two Su-22 Fitters in August 1981, and two MiG-23 Floggers in January 1989. In neither action was Phoenix used; three kills were with Sidewinders and the fourth with a Sparrow. During the Gulf War, an Iraqi Mi-8 helicopter was shot down by a Tomcat on 6 February 1991, the only F-14 air to air kill of the war. This reflects lack of opportunity rather than any other reason.

McDonnell Douglas designed the F-15 Eagle as a totally uncompromised air combat fighter. Seen here is the first F-15A to undergo the multi-staged improvement programme. (McDonnell Douglas).

An Eagle driver's view of beyond visual range combat, as a missile streaks towards an unseen distant target indicated only on the head-up display. (McDonnell Douglas).

The McDonnell Douglas F-15 Eagle

The Eagle, slightly later in time than Tomcat, was designed to counter much the same threat, and in particular Foxbat, which at that time was still believed to be an air superiority fighter. The nature of the threat now appeared dual; large numbers of tactical fighters, including the new swing wing MiG-23, combined with the ultra-high speed and altitude capabilities of Foxbat. Whereas the USN was confident in the F-14s ability to hold its own in a multi-bogey scenario, and content to counter the ultra-high speed and altitude Foxbat threat with the unique qualities of AWG-9/Phoenix, the USAF held different views. They wanted a sophisticated weapons system with outstanding performance and the agility to hold its own in a multi-bogey situation, outstanding rate of climb, and Mach 3 top speed, in order to outmatch the Foxbat. It should also be a single seater.

This was a tall order, and as the Mach 3 requirement directly conflicted with the need for agility, it was soon dropped. It was considered that provided the F-15 could reach Mach 2.5, and had a climb rate sufficient to reach the operating altitude of the Foxbat before it arrived, it would normally be able to reach a position for a front quarter or head-on attack in sufficient time. The air to air weapons load was specified as four Sparrows and four Sidewinders; the same as that of the Phantom, but for close combat a 25mm cannon firing caseless ammunition was to be developed. In the event this last was unsuccessful, and the Eagle was fitted with the proven 20mm M61 Vulcan cannon with 940 rounds of ammunition, located in the starboard wing root.

Inevitably the F-15 was large. In order to obtain the climb rate and acceleration specified, the thrust/weight ratio had to be far higher than anything previous. In addition, the specified load of AAMs was heavy, weighing roughly 2,750lb excluding launch rails and pylons. This was nearly 12 percent of the maximum thrust of the best engine available at that time, which meant that two engines were essential. Two engines need more volume, more structure, and double the number of systems and accessories. This amounted to a large and heavy aircraft.

In addition to high performance, the Eagle had to be superbly manoeuvrable. Endowed with a very high thrust/weight ratio, it also needed low wing loading for turning ability, and moderate aspect ratio to give a fast roll rate. On such a heavy fighter, this meant a large wing area. The layout adopted was almost a cropped delta with 45deg of leading edge sweep, and a straight inboard trailing edge with a minimally swept outer section. Aspect ratio was 3. Remarkably, the leading edge was plain, with no slats or other high lift devices, and the angle of incidence was zero, to maximise acceleration in level flight by minimising induced, or lift dependent, drag. The entire profile of the F-15 was designed to minimise wave drag to improve performance between Mach 0.9 and Mach 1.2.

Like its near contemporary the Tomcat, the Eagle had twin fins and differentially moving stabilizers. The fins were of high aspect ratio, and were necessary to counteract increasing lateral instability encountered at speeds exceeding Mach 2. Both fins and stabilizers were mounted on booms outside the line of the main fuselage, where they were less likely to be blanketed at high alpha. Following the trend set by the Tomcat, the canopy was large, with the sills cut down slightly, giving the pilot a superb all-round view from the cockpit. For conversion training, every seventh aircraft was a two seater.

The engines selected were Pratt & Whitney F100-PW-100 turbofans rated at 14,670lb static thrust in dry power, and 23,830lb with augmentation. The F100 was developed specifically for the F-15, and represented a major technological advance; producing considerably more thrust than the TF30 powering the F-14 while being much smaller and lighter. This was achieved in two main ways; a more efficient compressor to achieve a high overall pressure ratio with less stages; and running the engine much hotter. Pressure rises per compressor stage were of the order of 1.25:1 with 13 stages in the F100, compared to 1.2:1 with 16 stages in the TF30. Turbine entry temperatures reached about 1,400 deg Celsius in the F100, as compared with 1,093deg Celsius in the TF30. New technologies were developed to handle these high temperatures.

The compound inlets were two dimensional, and were sharply raked. Moving ramps controlled by the air data computer operate at supersonic speeds, creating a low pressure area to slow the air before it reaches the compressor face. A feature unique to the F-15 was the use of pivoting inlet hoods. Intended to keep the intakes pointed into the local airflow at high alpha, thus minimising compressor stalls, they were hinged at the top, and controlled by the air data computer, pivoted between four degrees above and 11deg below the horizontal. They also have a secondary function. At supersonic speeds, they can be used to create a download in front of the centre of gravity, thus unloading the tail surfaces, reducing drag and increasing manoeuvre ability.

The heart of the F-15 weapons system was the Hughes APG-63 radar. Like Tomcat's AWG-9, it was a multi-mode, pulse Doppler type, with a detection range against fighter sized targets in excess of 86nm(160km). While lacking the range of AWG-9, APG-63 had one great advantage. AWG-9 used high prfs for long range But as high prfs are not particularly accurate in measuring range, and had limitations in detection of low closure

FAST packs, later known as CFTs, are seen here on this two seater F-15B. Also clearly indicated are the 'nodding' intakes; compare with the picture on page 38.
(McDonnell Douglas).

rate targets, medium prfs were needed. Medium prfs, interleaved with high prfs, provided high quality tracking data.

All this radar magic, coupled with the need to monitor and use other electronic systems such as communications, navigation, and electronic warfare kit, made heavy demands on the pilot, who also had to fly, and if necessary fight the F-15. Experience in South East Asia showed that fleeting opportunities could easily be missed simply because a sequence of switch settings could not be completed in time, or even, in the heat of combat, at all. It was to overcome this deficiency that McDonnell Douglas came up with the Hands On Throttle And Stick(HOTAS) concept.

HOTAS was an attempt to put all the controls and switches that the pilot would need in combat, ready under his hands. In combat, a pilot flies with his right hand on the control column and his left hand on the throttle(s). The simplest example of HOTAS dates from 1916, when gun triggers were mounted on the control column. McDonnell Douglas took this to the ultimate. Like all twin engined aircraft, the F-15 has two throttle levers mounted close together so that they can be operated with one hand as a single unit. On the throttle levers were mounted a microphone switch, IFF interrogation button; target designation control; gunsight reticle stiffen button, also used to reject a heat missile; radar elevation control; chaff and flare dispenser switch; weapon selection switch; and the speed brake. On the control column were housed the gun trigger, which also operates the Hud camera; the weapons release(pickle) button; the radar auto-acquisition switch; the heat missile/electro-optical weapon head cage/uncage lever; and trim button. Given that everything needed was to hand, the pilot no longer needed to take his attention from a distant fleeting target in order to fumble for the correct switch. On the other hand, he needed the manual dexterity of a piccolo player in order to get the best out of the system.

In contrast to the advanced HOTAS concept, the rest of the Eagle cockpit was strictly conventional by the standards of the time. Old fashioned analogue dials and switches filled the dash and the side consoles, while the small radar display was located high on the left. The Hud had a narrow field of view by later standards, and the splendid view astern was optimised by three mirrors on the canopy bow.

The first F-15 prototype took to the air at Edwards AFB on July 27, 1972, nineteen months later than the first Tomcat. A few problem areas were identified and fixes found. The chord to the outboard section of the stabilizers was increased to cure a flutter problem, resulting in a notched leading edge. Buffet in certain flight regimes was corrected, after a brief flirtation with wing fences, by cropping back the wingtips at an angle. The speedbrake was increased in size, and various systems modified.

It was soon clear that the USAF had a winner, and the chance of depriving Foxbat of some of its hatful of world records was too good to be missed. Streak Eagle, the seventh full scale development aircraft, was stripped down for the attempt, and in a dazzling series of flights between 16 January and 1 February 1975 it set eight new time to height records. Three of these, to 20,000m; 25,000m; and 30,000m, had previously been held by Foxbat, and these were bettered by 28, 16, and 15 percent respectively.

The F-15A first entered service at Luke AFB in November 1974 with a training wing, and the first operational unit to be so equipped, 1st Tactical Fighter Wing at Langley, had two of its three squadrons mission ready by the end of 1976. The next wing to convert onto type was 36 TFW at Bitburg in Germany, which received its first Eagles in January 1977, and re-equipment of Phantom units proceeded apace.

The Eagle was generally regarded as easy to fly, if a little sensitive in pitch. In terms of sheer performance, it was everything a fighter pilot could want, although perhaps a little lacking in rate of roll. It was however quite a while before the early Eagle drivers mastered HOTAS well enough to get the best out of it. HOTAS demands practice in order to achieve a high level of proficiency, and this took time to achieve. There were however technical problems. As with the Tomcat, it was found that constant throttle cycling was needed in simulated combat, and the engine was simply not durable enough. Stagnation stalls were common, as were turbine failures, which could be quite spectacular. In addition, problems were experienced with the augmentation system, which did not always light up on cue. Mistrusting the 'burner, many pilots left it on minimum rather than have it fail to light. The result of this was that fuel was used at a higher than predicted rate, making the F-15 far shorter legged in practice than it should have been. Various fixes were found to cure the problem, and an acceptable level of reliability was finally attained.

The good can always be made better, and while the USN stayed with the baseline F-14A Tomcat for nearly two decades, the F-15C and its two-seater D variant, with improved radar and more fuel, replaced the F-15A and B on the production lines in 1978.

Improvements to the APG-63 radar were made possible by a further technical advance, a digital programmable signal processor able to control radar modes through software rather than circuits. This, plus greater computer capacity, allowed new modes to be added; raid assessment, which could resolve the returns from a close formation into individual contacts at up to 40nm, and track while scan. Later, synthetic aperture imagery was used to improve the quality of the ground mapping modes.

The simplest way of giving a fighter greater range or endurance is to hang external fuel tanks on it. These have two disadvantages. Firstly they occupy hardpoints which could otherwise be used for ordnance. Secondly, they cause so much extra drag that only about half the contents can be used to actually extend either range or endurance.

Two methods were used to overcome the problem. Extra tanks were located in the forward fuselage, and in front of and behind the existing wing tanks, increasing internal capacity by 1,820lb. An innovatory approach at this point was the FAST (Fuel And Sensor Tactical) pack. The FAST pack was a particularly neat solution, consisting of conformal tanks fitted to the fuselage sides beneath the wings, which allowed a further 9,750lb of fuel to be carried for a minimal drag penalty. With FAST and three 600 US gallon drop tanks, the F-15C can be ferried across the Atlantic without refuelling. FAST packs can also be fitted with laser designators, infra-red seekers, electronic jammers, or reconnaissance cameras.

The undercarriage of the F-15C/D was beefed up to handle the extra weight, but the engines and wing areas remained the same, with the result that t/w ratios shrank and wing loadings increased. This naturally had a detrimental effect on performance, although the Eagle still outclassed all adversary fighters in service.

Many nations would like the Eagle, but few can afford it. So far, only Israel, Saudi Arabia, and Japan operate the type. It first saw action in Israeli service, in which it has so far accounted for 56.5 air to air kills, including three Foxbats, for no loss. It provided escort on the raid against the Iraqi nuclear reactor in 1981, and carried out the attack on the PLO Headquarters in Tunis in October 1985. Saudi Eagles next saw combat, knocking down two Iranian Phantoms over the Persian Gulf in June 1984. The type played a distinguished part in the Gulf War of 1991, in both USAF and Saudi service, accounting for the majority of air to air kills in that conflict, including several Soviet-built MiG-29 Fulcrums. Not one F-15 was so much as damaged in air combat during the conflict.

An F-15C is readied during Operation Desert Storm in 1991. This will be a lengthy mission, judging by the three external fuel tanks carried. A Sparrow can be seen, carried conformally on the angle of the starboard intake. (McDonnell Douglas).

The CL-1200 Lancer was Lockheed's contender for the USAF Lightweight Fighter competition. With a larger wing and a low-set horizontal tail, this is how the Starfighter should have looked. It is however just a mock-up. (Lockheed).

CHAPTER FOUR
The Lightweights, Falcon and Cobra

The argument for quality to defeat quantity has its limitations. Attrition works on the side of the big battalions. No matter how capable a fighter may be, and how well it performs in a few versus many scenario, it can always be ground down by superior numbers. Leonidas and his 300 Spartans may have held the pass at Thermopylae against Xerxes and his Persian hordes, but in the end they were annihilated. The Alamo is yet another example. In the air, the classic example is the Messerschmitt Me 262 jet fighter in 1944-5, which in spite of its overwhelming performance advantage, was gradually shot from the skies. The lesson of history is that even though many battles may be won, the war can still be lost. If qualitative advantages are held, numerical inferiority can be accepted, but this must be kept within reasonable limits.

As we saw in the preceding chapter, quality is a very costly commodity, which inevitably leads to reductions in force sizes. The F-14 came very near to being completely unaffordable, while the F-15 could not be bought in the numbers that the USAF thought necessary. The answer to this was the hi-lo mix; very advanced fighters capable of dealing with the best the enemy had in a few versus many scenario, preferably from beyond visual distance, backed by a larger number of austere, and therefore more affordable fighters agile enough to hold their own in visual distance manoeuvre combat against greater numbers.

Down in the Pentagon, something stirred. The inadequacies of the Phantom in South East Asia became apparent early in that conflict, and a small group of like-minded individuals, later to become known as the "Fighter Mafia", started some original research. Among them were Major (later Colonel) John Boyd, and defence analyst Pierre Sprey. Previous fighters had been designed to meet certain performance requirements; maximum speed, endurance, and rate of climb being considered the most important. The Mafia evaluated the needs of a fighter pilot in combat, and came up with some startling (for the time) conclusions.

The first priority was the ability to achieve surprise while avoiding being surprised. Statistics showed that from WW1 to Vietnam, between 65 and 85 percent of victims in fighter versus fighter combat never saw the one that got them. What was needed to achieve this was small size and smokeless engines to delay visual acquisition; sparing use of radar, which could betray presence, relative position, and even possibly intent; a cruising speed significantly higher than that of the enemy to reduce the time between sighting and attack, while increasing the chance of spotting an attacker; and excellent all-round view from the cockpit.

The second priority was to outnumber the enemy in the air. This required a large force size, with many well trained pilots, and a high sortie rate. The force size, both aircraft and pilots, would be limited by budgetary constraints but could be optimised by purchasing light fighters designed for close combat rather than large expensive interceptors. A high sortie rate was to be achieved by a combination of numerical strength and maintainability, attainable in part by simplicity, the austere fighter being both affordable, and having far less to go wrong and keep it on the ground. The point of outnumbering the enemy in the air was to maintain a high threat level over a wide area, not necessarily to outnumber him in the dogfight. The rationale behind this was that in an outnumbered scenario, the exchange rate is always better. The author's own research tends to conflict with this finding, and shows that while kill ratios per 100 sorties tend to be high in an outnumbered scenario, mainly due to a greater number of opportunities, loss ratios often go through the roof. Also, to be continually outnumbered is not good for morale. Be that as it may, in an air campaign as opposed to a single engagement, the figures show that numbers are very important, which justifies outnumbering the enemy in the air as the second priority.

The third priority was the ability to outmanoeuvre the enemy in close combat. The requirements for this were rapid acceleration, a high rate of climb; a fast rate of turn with the ability to sustain high g loads, and snappy pitch and roll rates. Another essential sneaked in here; the ability to outlast the enemy in the fight.

Acceleration, climb, and sustained turn all call for a high thrust/weight ratio, which is achieved by wrapping the smallest possible airframe around the most powerful available engine. The remainder of the requirements are conflicting; a wing design is needed which gives a compromise between wing loading, which should be low; aspect ratio which should be high for sustained turn but low for roll rate; lift co-efficient, and lift/drag ratio, both of which should be high. The ability to outlast the enemy in the fight requires adequate fuel. Prior to 1970, it was widely thought that only large size gave endurance; the Mafia established that this was not so; the critical parameter was fuel fraction, the weight of the internal fuel expressed as a proportion of clean takeoff weight, and which ideally should be about 0.30. Much less than this, say about 0.26, makes a fighter short on endurance, while much more, say 0.35, needs extra volume, tank and structure weight, which penalises performance.

The fourth and final priority was the ability to use split second firing opportunities at ranges between 100ft and maximum visual identification distances, an area where the Phantom had proved to be sadly lacking. The requirements for this were a high kill probability against close-in manoeuvring targets; enough munitions for multiple engagements; minimum time between recognizing an opportunity and completing an attack; and minimum vulnerability to ECM or tactical countermeasures. Given the state of the art around 1970, this presupposed the gun to be the primary fighter weapon, backed by Sidewinder heat missiles for longer range work. Once again the keynote was simplicity.

The lightweight fighter programme would probably have emerged sooner than it did had not Foxbat phobia swept the Pentagon in the late 'sixties, concentrating their attention almost exclusively on the Grumman and McDonnell Douglas giants. It was not until January 1972 that a Request For Proposals(RFP) for a lightweight fighter (LWF) was issued by the USAF, and this was viewed as a technology demonstrator, to see what could be done with the resources to hand. There were five competitors; Lockheed with the CL-1200 Lancer, which was basically how their F-104 Starfighter should have been in the first place; LTV with the V-1100 based on the Crusader/Corsair; two entries from Northrop with similar configurations, the single engined P.610 and the twin engined P.600 Cobra; and General Dynamics Model 401. Of these, the P.600 and Model 401 were selected for development, and contracts for two prototypes of each were placed. For the first time in many years, aircraft types were to be evaluated against each other in flight. Specifications and performance targets were kept to a minimum on the LWF project. Where rigid specs and performance targets are laid down, penalties in cost, weight, and complexity are often incurred in getting that last five percent, which are out of all proportion to the gains. This would not happen on LWF, which gave the designers a free hand to trade off one aspect against another.

Neither of the two winners was starting from scratch. GD had initiated work on the Model 401 back in 1968, while Northrop's P.600 dated back to 1966 as a low cost export fighter to replace the earlier F-5, with Holland confidently expected to be the launch customer. Now, with their projects designated YF-16 and YF-17 respectively, and the possibility of an order from the USAF, their prospects looked rosy. The first flight of YF-16 No 1 took place by accident on 20 January 1974 when speed on a taxying trial got too high. It was followed by YF-17 No 1 on 9 June of that year. The second prototypes of each followed, and the competitive flyoff was completed by the end of the year. But long before this, the LWF technology demonstration had become the Air Combat Fighter(ACF) programme for the USAF.

General Dynamics YF-16

The YF-16 was a small single seat fighter powered by the same F100 engine used in the F-15, which gave it a thrust/weight ratio exceeding unity. The wing was of moderate sweep and aspect ratio, and at first sight it looked very ordinary. Closer examination revealed that it was nothing of the sort. A thickness/chord ratio of just four percent had been adopted to give high speed and acceleration, while for manoeuvre and other flight regimes, variable camber was used, with leading and trailing edge flaps automatically operated by the flight control system to give optimum performance in all flight conditions. The wing was blended smoothly into the fuselage, giving three main advantages. It minimised wave drag at transonic and supersonic speeds; it gave extra stiffness, and it provided extra volume for fuel. While not designed to do so, it also reduced the radar cross-section by a fair amount. In front of the wings were long root extensions(LERX). These generated vortices across the wing upper surface which inhibited spanwise drift of the airflow, scrubbing off the turgid boundary layer air and providing good handling at high alpha.

The small nose was intended to hold a basic search radar, and the engine intake, plain because Mach 2 capability was not required, was mounted ventrally, the underside of the nose acting as a wedge at high alpha to angle the airflow into it. A single tall fin and rudder was augmented by small ventral strakes for longitudinal stability at high alpha. Basic fighter armament was a 20mm M61A Vulcan cannon mounted in the left wing root, with the ammunition drum holding 511 rounds behind the cockpit. In all, the YF-16 was a *tour de force* in packaging.

Exotic materials were kept to a minimum in the structure, but it was under the skin that the most advanced features lay. Previous fighters had been designed to have the centre of lift and the centre of gravity very close to one another, to give flight stability. At supersonic speeds, the centre of lift moves aft, and the tailplane has to impart downward thrust to compensate. When turning, the aircraft is banked over and the stick hauled back. Firstly inherent stability must be overcome; secondly a very high level of downward force has to be exerted by the tailplane. In the YF-16, the centre of gravity was set aft of the centre of lift, to give a degree of instability; relaxed stability as it has become known. The benefits of this were threefold. There was no inherent stability to be overcome. At subsonic speeds the horizontal tail was required to give positive rather than negative lift, which supplemented wing lift. At supersonic speeds, with the centre of lift aft, the downloads on the tail were only a fraction of what they would have been had relaxed stability not been adopted. All this added up to improved manoeuvrability across the entire speed range. Furthermore the tail surfaces could be made smaller, giving an appreciable weight saving.

There remained however the problem of controlling an unstable aircraft. This was overcome by using a quadruplex fly-by-wire(FBW) system with computerized stability augmentation. This four channel analogue system worked on a concensus basis, in which agreement by any two channels would overrule failures in the others. The fail-safe reliability of this allowed mechanical backup to be omitted, giving a considerable saving in both weight and complexity. This was a bold step at the time.

The cockpit of the YF-16 also showed the effects of radical thinking. To give near-perfect all-round vision, even the traditional canopy bow was omitted, the canopy consisting of a single piece bubble transparency, its only disadvantage being that there was nowhere to hang rear view mirrors. The sides of the cockpit were cut low to give a 40deg downward angle of vision. The seat was raked back at a 30deg angle, and the pilot's heel line was raised. This increased his g tolerance, although it also decreased the usable instrument panel area. Finally, the central control column was replaced by a sidestick controller mounted under the pilot's right hand.

Northrop YF-17

The YF-17 looked rather more futuristic than its GD rival. It was small, it was a single seater, and it had a moderately swept wing, but there the similarities ended. It was powered by two General Electric YJ101-100 turbofans with a bypass ratio so low (0.2) that they were unkindly dubbed "leaky turbojets". A simple, modular engine, the YJ101 was rated at 14,800lb maximum and 9,000lb military power. While two YJ101s theoretically provided more thrust than the single F100 of the YF-16, they were early development engines not yet giving their full rated output. Any remaining advantage was dissipated by the extra structure and systems weight, volume and drag of a twin-engined installation, to say nothing of the greater area needed to keep wing loading down. The empty weight of the YF-17 was 25 percent greater than that of the YF-16.

Like GD, Northrop used computerized variable cambered wings combined with leading edge root extensions for optimum manoeuvre and good high alpha capability. Northrop had in fact used LERX previously on their F-5E fighter, and were well aware of the benefits. But the size and shape of the LERX was something else. They were huge and very subtly contoured, and from the frontal aspect gave a hooded appearance which suggested the name Cobra. The LERX of the YF-17 provided a destabilizing effect to minimise the effects of tail download, also known as trim drag, at supersonic speeds. Located above the intakes, they also served to deflect the airflow at high alpha, while acting as compression wedges to reduce the Mach number at the compressor face. This allowed the intakes to be set well back, giving a short duct; another weight saving factor. Large slots between the LERX and the fuselage took the sluggish boundary layer air clear of the intakes, expelling it into the low pressure area above the wings.

The airframe was mainly aluminium, with steel and titanium limited to highly stressed or heated areas. Carbon composites were widely used for the skin; vertical tail surfaces, flaps, wing leading and trailing edges, fuselage panels, and access doors. Like its GD rival, the YF-17 used quadruplex FBW, but it retain a mechanical backup to the stabilizers for emergency pitch and roll control as a "get you home" facility.

The tail surfaces were quite unusual for the time. The all-moving horizontal surfaces were of high aspect ratio, and were more sharply swept than the wings. The twin fin and rudder assemblies were located forward between the wing and the horizontal tail, and canted outward at a steep angle. This position, in the vortices shed by the LERX, gave good lateral stability, while avoiding blanketing at high alpha.

The forward fuselage was relatively conventional. The nose radome housed a Rockwell air to air ranging radar, and like the YF-16, the avionics were basic in the extreme. The transparency was divided into windshield and canopy in the orthodox manner. The cockpit layout was also orthodox, and the only oddball thing was the location of the 20mm M61A Vulcan cannon. Firing the gun caused extremely high levels of vibration, and an offset position was used in the F-15 and YF-16 to keep it away from the sensitive radar and avionics. On the YF-17 this was just not feasible, as it would have spoiled the lines of the carefully contoured LERX. This reduced the options. After abortive attempts to shoehorn it in beneath the nose, Northrop located it high on the centreline, with the muzzle directly ahead of the pilot. Apart from vibration, there were two possible drawbacks to this position. Firstly, muzzle flash could interfere with the pilot's night vision, and secondly, sticky gun gases would flow straight back over the windshield. Experience was later to show that these fears were unfounded, while the vibration was successfully damped to acceptable levels.

The flight evaluation of the two contenders would normally have taken the best part of two years, but other factors were to intervene. Four European nations; Belgium, Denmark, Holland and Norway, were seeking a new fighter, and the projected low costs of ACF, coupled with economic benefits of co-production, made the winner of the ACF competition look very attractive. As a result, the evaluation was completed by the end of 1974. The result was announced on 13 January 1975. The new USAF Air Combat Fighter would be developed from the YF-16.

General Dynamics' YF-16 was the eventual winner of the USAF LWF competition, after a close contest with the YF-17. It was designed as the ultimate close combat fighter, armed with a single M61 cannon and two wingtip Sidewinders as seen here. (GD).

The contest was much closer than it is sometimes portrayed. For a start, the dice were loaded. While the Northrop contender was, as requested, a technology demonstrator, the YF-16 could actually have been produced as it stood. As noted earlier, the YJ101 was still in the process of development, running at about 92 percent of its eventual rating, whereas the F100 was, despite the teething troubles related in the previous chapter, a fairly mature engine. But the fact remains, a superb fighter was passed over in favour of a better. In terms of pure performance there had been little to choose. In some areas one would be superior, while in others the reverse would apply. For example, the YF-17 could outturn the YF-16 at Mach 0.7 at medium altitudes, but the YF-16 became progressivly superior as speeds increased. As part of the evaluation, the two fighters were matched against each other in mock combat. Differences in flying ability were ironed out by having the pilots swap aircraft and repeat the mission. In this part of the evaluation, the YF-16 emerged the winner more often than not. But while the pilots knew which aircraft they were winning in, it was awfully difficult to find out exactly why. It took three days of debriefing and analysis to discover the reason, and it might surprise anyone who believes that 9g sustained turn is the supreme arbiter in air combat. It finally emerged that while the YF-16 was generally the better turning aircraft, the primary reason for its success was that it had better transient performance. It had better acceleration and a faster roll rate, and it was these factors that gave overall superiority. Finally, the YF-16 was smaller and lighter than the YF-17, and would therefore be cheaper to acquire, and with one engine rather than two, easier to maintain.

Having won the flyoff, and with large orders for both the USAF and the four European nations in prospect, it might be thought that the YF-16 would go straight into production. But not a bit of it!

The Belgians, and to a lesser degree the other European customers wanted a multi-role aircraft, able to carry out the attack and nuclear strike missions as well as air superiority, while the USAF had traditionally hung air to ground ordnance on their fighters and also wanted greater capability. All this meant that changes were needed. In the words of Pierre Sprey, speaking in 1980, "we ripped up the plans, spent $1.5 million in redesign, added 3,000lbs extra weight, and came close to doubling the cost! And what was a great fighter, sadly enough became an almost great."

While this overstated the case a bit, the alterations were certainly wide ranging. The small search radar was replaced by a more capable multi-mode type, and the nose was extended by 0.58ft in length and 0.33ft in diameter to accommodate it. Two more hardpoints were fitted, bringing the total to nine. As heavy external loads moved the cg forward, the area of the horizontal tail was increased by 15 percent to cope. The fuselage length grew by 1.14ft, the fin was raised by 0.42ft. Total weight growth was nearly 2,000lb, and while the wing loading was held down by the addition of a further 20 square feet of area, the outstanding t/w ratio of the YF-16 was degraded in the production model. While the author does not agree with the comment that the F-16 had become an "almost great" fighter as a result, it was certainly not quite as good a pure dogfighter as the prototype, although better in many other ways.

Lockheed F-16 Fighting Falcon

Weight growth notwithstanding, the F-16 was for many years the world's most agile fighter, and even in 1994 it is widely regarded as the yardstick by which all other close combat fighters are measured. The new radar was the Westinghouse APG-66 pulse-Doppler type. In its original form it had 11 modes, four of them air to air; the rest air to

Some F-16As have been modified to carry and guide AIM-7 Sparrows in the Air Defense role. As can be seen, it is a small fighter carrying a big missile. (GD).

surface or navigation. Of the air to air modes, Uplook Search utilised low prfs to detect medium or high flying targets at the longest possible range; about 39nm against a MiG-23 Flogger or 70nm against the huge Tu-95 Bear. Downlook Search was a medium prf mode used against low flying targets. Downlook detection ranges were about 26nm against a Flogger and 54nm against a Bear. Air Combat mode covered a smaller scan area than Search; either 20deg x 20deg or 40deg x 10deg field of view. When the range reduced to 10nm, lock-on was automatic, with Sidewinders slaved to the radar contact. Against several contacts in close formation, Narrow Beam enabled one to be cut out of the pack. NB was either boresight or slewable. Other modes included air to ground ranging, ground mapping, and beacon. Sea surface search and display freeze modes were added at the request of the Europeans. Following the trend set by the F-15, the radar displays were alpha-numeric, with the modes operated by switches on the throttle and side controller.

Like the F-15 before it, the F-16 had trouble with its F100-PW-200 powerplant, and for much the same reasons. In a single engined aircraft, this was far more serious, and was aggravated by the fact that in terms of engine cycles, the F100 was worked more than a third harder than it was in the McDonnell Douglas fighter. A device called the proximate splitter had been developed for the F-15, although never fitted, and this was installed in the F-16. Basically it was an extension to the engine casing aft of the compressor which divided the airflow, sending some through the core, and the rest through the bypass. By this means, pressure surge from the afterburner was largely diverted around the engine core. Other engine modifications devised for the F-15 were also incorporated, and by 1981 reliability had improved dramatically.

The first operational F-16 unit was the 388th TFW at Hill AFB, Utah, which also acted as the conversion unit for the type, both for the USAF and for overseas customers. The first F-16 arrived in January 1979, and IOC(Initial Operational Capability) was attained by its 4th TFS in November 1980. Like the F-15, the F-16 had a two seater trainer variant, the F-16B, which was fully combat capable, although provision for the second seat reduced internal fuel by 17 percent to 5,785lb. Deliveries to the four European air arms commenced very quickly. Belgium got its first F-16 in January 1979, followed by Holland in June of that year, and Denmark and Norway in January 1980.

No matter how agile a fighter is, sooner or later it gets the kitchen sink hung on it. The F-16 was no exception. Designed as a clear weather fighter, the climate of Europe, which differs from that of Texas, quickly exposed its limitations, and those responsible for defence procurement realised that they needed more capability. Of course, this should have been foreseen much earlier. The answer was a series of upgrades, some retrofitted to the F-16A /B, while others resulted first in the F-16C/D, and then in the F-16C /D MSIP (Multi-Staged Improvement Programmes).

The improvements which went to make up the F-16C and MSIP, which was in three stages, are too numerous to list in full, and only the most important are given here. First was a new radar; the Westinghouse APG-68. The range of Uplook and Downlook Search was increased by a third, while a new mode, Velocity Search, allowed detection of head-on closing targets at up to 160nm. Other new air to air modes were Range While Search, and Track While Scan, which could track up to ten targets simultaneously. A track retention feature when looking down gave a certain amount of capability to continue tracking even when the target turned through 90deg angle off. New air to surface modes used synthetic aperture techniques to give Ground Moving Target Indication and Ground Moving Target Tracking. Continuous wave guidance was provided for the SARH Sparrow, while software changes later allowed Amraam to be carried. The cockpit was modified to suit the new radar and other avionics, with two multi-function displays and a wide angle Hud compatible with the Lantirn (Low Altitude Navigation Targeting and Infra-Red for Night) pod, while providing an enhanced envelope gun sight.

The only visible change to the F-16C/D is the tail root housing, which was enlarged to contain two units of the ALQ-165 Advanced Self Protection Jammer. Everything else is hidden, including a digital flight control system in place of the original analogue, several new avionics and navigation boxes, and wiring for smart air to surface missiles such as Harm, Maverick, Harpoon and Penguin. Neither is the structural strengthening needed to increase the takeoff gross weight to an enormous 42,300lb evident.

Upgrades may improve capabilities in some ways, but they invariably add weight. This increases wing loading and reduces the t/w ratio; with a consequent loss of performance. In 1986, Block 30 F-16C/Ds were configured to accept the F110-GE-100, rated at 17,260lb military and 28,982lb maximum thrust, which was enough to restore the t/w ratio. An enlarged intake was needed to cope with the greater mass flow of the bigger engine. Block 50 aircraft have the F110-GE-129, and Block 52 aircraft have the F100-PW-229, both in the 17,500/29,000 lb class.

Barring major redesign, nothing can be done to reduce wing loading. Also, weight growth has degraded the fuel fraction which was designed into the original LWF. On the other hand, the high military thrust of the GE engine, coupled with low specific fuel consumption, may in part offset this, as it means that use of afterburner will be less frequent and less prolonged, and operational radius and endurance will not be as badly affected as the bare figures might indicate, although heavier reliance on external fuel tanks may have to be made.

The F-16 is popular with its pilots for its agility and sparkling performance. Alpha and g limiters are fitted, which prevent the aircraft being inadvertently overstressed, giving carefree handling, leaving the pilot to concentrate on fighting the aircraft. As an old Aggressor pal once commented, "the Electric Jet does it all for you!" If it has any weaknesses at all, it is probably a bit short on high alpha capability, the limiter holding it to a 26deg angle. This has been demonstrated at Farnborough and Paris in the "Limiter Spiral".

Two further variants are currently in service. The F-16A Air Defence Fighter has replaced the aging F-106 Delta Dart in the continental air defence role. It lacks the multi-role capability of the standard version, and its APG-66 radar has been modified and given different modes to guide AIM-7 Sparrow, and AIM-120 Amraam. It has the advanced cockpit displays of the F-16C, and improved ECCM, while a quick reaction inertial navigation system allows takeoff just 60 seconds after engine start. The other variant is the F-16N, used as an adversary aircraft by the USN. This is an austere version with no cannon, and carries one tethered Sidewinder and an Air Combat Manoeuvring Instrumentation (ACMI) pod.

The F-16 has notched up a remarkable record in air combat, mainly in Israeli service. In the Beka'a Valley action against the Russian-equipped Syrian Air Force in 1982 it was credited with 44 victories for no loss. Prior to that it carried out the long range precision strike against the Iraqi nuclear reactor at Osirak. The Pakistan Air Force has also notched up a hatful of victories defending the border against incursions by Afghan fighters. USAF F-16s gave sterling service in the Gulf War, but mainly in the attack role, with just one air to air victory. Since then it has become the first fighter to score with Amraam, while enforcing the no-fly zones over Iraq.

Only two minor criticisms have emerged. The steeply raked seat has been blamed for neck and shoulder strains when the pilot has been looking backwards under high g. The Israelis have also commented that whereas a pilot with his right arm incapacitated has a good chance of getting a conventional fighter back to base, the sidestick controller of the F-16 rules out this option. While this is a valid point, it happily remains purely theoretical.

CHAPTER FIVE
From Cobra to Hornet

In 1971 the United States Navy faced a quandary. The F-14 was proving unaffordable in the numbers required, procurement being only sufficient to equip 18 of 24 Navy fighter squadrons. In addition the US Marine Corps had 18 more fighter squadrons, including reserve units, that would need re-equipment, plus 30 attack squadrons flying the A-7 Corsair. Replacement was scheduled to start at the end of the decade, with a minimum requirement of 800 aircraft.

The USN set up a group called Fighter Study IV to examine the problem. The alternatives were a low cost F-14, a navalised F-15, or an improved Phantom. None were judged suitable. What the Navy really wanted was a true dual role aircraft able to supplement the Tomcat in fleet air defence and in providing fighter escort to the strike squadrons, while equally able to fly the attack mission, a single airframe varied only in the avionics fit. A new specification was drawn up, designated VFAX; a Sparrow-armed air combat fighter with a secondary attack capability. Ideally VFAX should have been a totally new aircraft, but in their infinite wisdom the politicians decided that it should be based on one of the two ACF contenders. This was done apparently in the belief that the winner would be selected, thus gaining the greatest economic benefit from a huge production run.

The requirements of carrier operations differ considerably from those of land based aircraft, and neither GD nor Northrop had ever built a naval fighter. To overcome this, they teamed with experienced makers; GD with LTV and Northrop with McDonnell Douglas, to produce navalised variants of their contenders.

After an exhaustive evaluation, the USN concluded that while both aircraft were a bit small for the job, the YF-17 offered the greatest growth potential. Its two engines offered a greater margin of safety for operations far out over the ocean, and it had demonstrated better carrier compatibility. On 2 May 1975 the USN announced that their VFAX choice was the scaled-up YF-17, with McDonnell Douglas as the main contractor and Northrop as the primary subcontractor. Designations of F-18 for the fighter and A-18 for the attack aircraft were allotted.

Turning the YF-17 lightweight fighter into a carrier-compatible multi-mission aircraft was a major undertaking, far larger than the redesign of the F-16 for nuclear strike had been. The most demanding parts of the flight regime of a carrier fighter are catapult launches and arrested deck landings. In the former, the aircraft is attached to the catapult by a slender bar on the nosewheel leg, and with engines running flat out, it is accelerated to roughly 120kt in a matter of four seconds. A deck landing, or trap, is even worse. Standard procedure is to open the throttles fully just before touchdown so that if the aircraft misses the arrester wires it can overshoot, or bolter. When the hook takes the wire, the aircraft is brought to a halt from something over 100kt in just two seconds, even with the engines at full power. The forces exerted on the arrester hook and its attachments are enormous, and a great deal of local structural strengthening is needed to withstand them. In addition, the aircraft is almost literally falling out of the sky. As a worst case specification, a vertical speed of 24ft/sec, or more than 16mph, must be withstood, making heavy demands on both undercarriage and structure.

The weight of the new fighter increased rapidly, taking it well out of the original lightweight class. Structural strengthening and a totally redesigned, more robust gear was just part of the story. Other kit added specifically for carrier operations included the catapult towbar, arrester hook, and wing folding to minimise hangar and deck parking space. Internal fuel capacity was increased by a massive 70 percent to bring the total to 10,680lb, involving extra tankage and plumbing. The nose was widened to take a multi-mode radar, and the LERX refined and extended forward to give a flatter carrier approach angle at a lower speed. The fuselage sides were reshaped in order to carry Sparrow missiles semi-conformally on the corners. Sparrow carriage brought its own problems in that it fouled the retraction path of the main gear, which had to be redesigned to clear the big missiles. Every attempt was made to keep weight down, but there were limits. In contrast to the Fighting Falcon, which used little titanium and almost no advanced composites,the Hornet contained over 12 percent titanium and nearly 10 percent of composite material, which covered roughly 40 percent of the surface area; far more than any other aircraft at that time.

Wing loading rapidly exceeded acceptable limits, and to reduce it, the area was raised from 350 to 400ft^2. This was done by increasing the span by 2.5ft while extending the chord by adding to the leading and trailing edges. The horizontal tail surfaces were redesigned to give a lower aspect ratio, and with McDonnell Douglas drawing on F-15 experience, a dogtooth was added to the leading edges of both wings and tails to generate vortices to inhibit spanwise drift of the airflow at low speeds.

The projected gross weight of the YF-17 had been 23,000lb; before the F-18 had even left the ground this had risen to 33,580lb with every prospect of further increases. The need for greater power had been obvious from the outset, and General Electric developed the YJ101 into the F404-400 by scaling it up about 10 percent, with increased mass flow. This necessitated larger inlets, and using the greater (although still very low) bypass ratio of 0.34 which in turn improved specific fuel consumption. In common with all naval engines, corrosion-resistant materials were used throughout. Turbine entry temperatures and pressure recovery ratio were both increased, and the result was an engine rated at 10,600lb in military and 16,000lb in maximum thrust.

The radar selected for the F-18 was the Hughes APG-65 multi-mode pulse Doppler type, the first production radar to have a programmable signal processor(PSP). Its modes could be modified, or new modes added, through software, while Doppler filter and range gate configurations were defined by programme coding. This was unlike all previous radars, in which these functions had been hard wired and could only be changed by physical modification. PSP made APG-65 the most capable and flexible radar of its era, and enabled it to go a full decade in service before being upgraded.

The original APG-65 had no less than nine air to air modes, and a whole bagful of air to surface and navigational modes. Those critics of the F-18 who complained that the USN bought the loser in the ACF flyoff would do well to compare it with the early APG-66 of the F-16. In fact, the original Hughes APG-65 handily outdoes the later Westinghouse APG-68 of the GD fighter, and has since become a yardstick for multi-mode fighter radar performance. Let's have a brief look at what was available.

Velocity Search used high prfs for long range detection of front quarter closing targets. Range While Search interleaved high and medium prfs to detect targets at any aspect and relative velocity out to about 80nm. Track While Scan used medium prfs during the closing stage of an engagement out to 40nm, maintaining track files on ten targets while displaying a maximum of eight, at the same time giving target data on the greatest threat in terms of aspect, speed, and altitude. Raid Assessment is effective out to 30nm, and can resolve individual contacts in a close formation. Single Target Track uses monopulse angle tracking to follow a manoeuvring target, with computer logic to extrapolate manoeuvres designed to break radar lock, such as the Immelmann or Split-S. The three air combat manoeuvre modes are Boresight, Vertical Acquisition, and Hud Acquisition, and give an automatic radar lock out to 5nm. The final air to air mode is Gun Director, which drives the aiming dot on the Hud, using frequency agility to counter erratic changes in the apparent radar centre of the target, or glint.

An F/A-18C Hornet of VFA-15 Valions races skyward near its base at NAS Cecil Field in Florida. (McDonnell Douglas).

Air to surface modes included Real Beam Ground Mapping to give a crude small scale picture of the terrain ahead, processed to present the display from a vertical rather than a true angle for ease of recognition. For better resolution over smaller areas, Doppler Beam Sharpening Sector Mode gave a magnification of 19:1, while DBS Patch Mode increased this to 67:1. Terrain Avoidance Mode allowed low level penetration in poor visibility by showing obstacles in the projected flightpath, while Precision Velocity Update provided data for both navigation and attack. Other modes were concerned with target ranging and attack, and most essential for a naval fighter, the detection of targets at sea, with automatic suppression of sea state clutter.

The capability of APG-65 allowed a far-reaching decision to be taken at a very early stage; that one aircraft could fly both the air superiority and attack missions, using pretty much the same avionics fit. This had important implications in that it allowed the same aircraft to switch from one mission to another at will. Leaving aside force multipliers and anti-submarine aircraft, a normal carrier complement consisted of two fighter squadrons, two light attack squadrons, and one all-weather attack squadron.

The all round capability of the new fighter would, according to the scenario, give a choice between four fighter squadrons to defend the carrier, or two fighter squadrons plus two light attack squadrons able to provide their own fighter escort, or two light attack squadrons with an enviable self defence capability. This decision taken, the designation of F/A-18 Hornet was adopted.

For self-defence in the attack role, the Hornet was to carry two Sidewinders on wingtip rails, plus of course the Vulcan cannon with 570 rounds. This left the conformal Sparrow positions empty, and it was decided to capitalise on this by wiring them to take two avionics pods to improve the attack capabilities. These were a AAS-38 Forward Looking Infra-Red (FLIR), and a Laser Spot Tracker/Strike Camera (LST/SCAM) pods, both of which could be fitted in a matter of minutes. The FLIR provided a cockpit picture of the terrain below in weather or light conditions too bad for visual target identification, while the LST/SCAM provided a blind strike capability against a pre-designated target, plus a photographic record of strike accuracy.

The aircraft from which the Hornet was developed; Northrop's YF-17. Note the forward position of the outward canted fins, spanning the gap between the trailing edge of the wing and the leading edge of the stabilizer. (Northrop).

RIGHT: *This 'Heath Robinson' flange mounted on the LERX of the Hornet modified the vortices, relieving stresses in the fins.* (Author).

BELOW: *Three F/A-18Cs of VFA-81 return to USS* Saratoga *after carrying out a mission during Desert Storm in 1991. Aircraft of this unit proved the dual role in action during the Gulf War by shooting down two Iraqi aircraft during a bombing mission.* (McDonnell Douglas).

High pilot workload had been a problem in the Eagle. The dual role of the Hornet appeared to make this even worse, and McDonnell Douglas, as prime contractors, addressed this aspect with care. HOTAS, tried and proven on the larger fighter, was an obvious choice to minimise the switchology workload, leaving the main problem the vast amount of information to be presented to the pilot at different times. Finding a solution was aggravated by two factors; firstly the cockpit was smaller than that of the Eagle, while the ejection seat was raked back at an angle of 18deg, raising the pilot's knees and reducing the dash area. In all, the available dash and console area of the Hornet was less than two thirds that of the F-15, with far more information to display.

The solution was radical. In previous fighters, the only two electronic displays had been the Hud and the radar scope. In the Hornet the Hud was supplemented by no less than three 5in square television-type screens on which all flight, attack, navigation, weaponry and system status information could be displayed at need, called up by one of the 20 pushbuttons that surrounded each. High on the left of the instrument panel was the Master Monitor Display, the primary functions of which were armament, warning, electro-optical and IR sensors. It also handled cautionary and advisory information on aircraft systems. High on the right was the Multi-Function Display, concerned with radar attack and radar mapping, with flight information such as aircraft speed, attitude and altitude. The functions of the MMD and MFD were made interchangeable in flight, and the failure of one does not lead to the mission being scrubbed. Centrally below these two is the Horizontal Situation Display, a coloured moving map as pioneered by the Harrier, on which attack and navigation data could be superimposed. It was also linked to the radar warning system and electronic warfare suite, and could display threats complete with identification. So capable were these displays that conventional dials and instruments were almost totally lacking. The layout of the Hornet cockpit set standards that the rest of the world has since tried to emulate.

The workings of the Hornet were highly computerized, and the total memory requirement, at 741K, was nearly half as great again as that of the Eagle. It was the first production aircraft to use a digital rather than an analogue FBW control system. Virtually everything was controlled by smart electrons, including pre-flight checks and fault-finding.

The initial order was for 11 Full Scale Development(FSD) aircraft; nine single and two twin seaters. Space for the rear seat was provided by a 600lb reduction in internal fuel capacity, which was nowhere near as drastic as that of the two seater F-16. The first flight of an FSD Hornet took place on 18 November 1978 at St. Louis International Airport, where McDonnell Douglas share the facilities, and an intensive flight test programme began.

Flight testing, much of which was carried out at NAS Patuxent River, was generally successful, although it did uncover a few blemishes. Nosewheel lift-off speed was too high, due to a rearward shift of the main gear location which moved the rotation axis aft, which had been done to reduce the risk of the Hornet tipping on its tail on a heaving carrier deck. This was reduced by a full 25kt by eliminating the dogtooth in the leading edge of the horizontal tail surfaces, while programming the rudders to "toe in" while the weight was on the wheels, thus imparting a downward force to the rear end. More serious was a significant range and acceleration shortfall caused mainly by excess drag. The fixes for this were to fill in the LERX slots; fair over the environmental control system exhaust; and increase the radius of the wing leading edges. Rate of roll was also well down, caused by wing flexing, and roll damping by the tipmounted Sidewinders. Again, multiple fixes were needed; some structural "tweaks" were made to the wing, the ailerons were extended, giving an extra 36 percent of area, the leading edge dogtooth was eliminated, and tailplane control authority was increased.

The F404-GE-400 turbofan was one of the success stories of the programme. An untried engine, it was put through accelerated flight testing in the early stages, and was found to be almost completely free of compressor stalling regardless of alpha; easy to relight, with very rapid throttle response. In fact it was found to be quite insensitive to throttle slams from flight idle to maximum power and back again, unlike the F100 of the F-15 and F-16. A few problems were encountered, notably fatigue failures of the compressor, but on the whole the F404 proved remarkably trouble-free.

A Full Scale Development Hornet, resplendent in white, gold and blue. It differs from the production aircraft in having a pitot nose probe, dogtooth leading edges, and long slots on the inside of the LERXes.
(McDonnell Douglas).

The first Hornet squadron was VFA-125 Rough Raiders, based at NAS Lemoore in California, who received their first Hornets in February 1981. The Raiders were a Replacement Air Group(RAG) for converting pilots onto type, and the first operational Hornet squadron was VMFA-314 Black Knights, based at MCAS El Toro, who were inaugurated in January 1983. The Hornet proved remarkably easy to fly, with no alpha limits, and was virtually spin-proof. Early reports suggested that the pilots had successfully mastered the extremely complex weapons and avionics systems, but it was later revealed that there was a definite tendency for pilots to stick with that part of the system that was best known and leave the rest, which meant that full operational capability was not always attained. There was also the problem that some pilots are naturals in air combat, while others enjoy moving mud, and rarely is one man very good at both. This was resolved by assigning squadrons different primary tasks; some to air superiority and others to ground attack, where the best use could be made of natural abilities.

In the air, the Hornet was worked hard, and this caused problems. At medium speeds and high alpha, vortices from the LERX impinged on the canted fins, setting up stresses which caused fatigue fractures in the tail and rear engine mounts. Structural strengthening was tried but proved insufficient, and finally McDonnell Douglas developed a flange which, mounted on the LERX, modifies the vortices and reduces the stress to acceptable levels.

The original designations for single and two seater Hornets were F-18A and TF-18A respectively. These were later amended to F/A-18A and F/A-18B. In September 1987 the first production F/A-18C rolled out, followed closely by the two seater F/A-18D. Apart from a few excrescences housing aerials, these were identical in appearance to the earlier models, all upgrades being beneath the skin. The main changes were improved mission computers, provision for up to six AIM-120 Amraam missiles, the APG-165 Advanced Self Protection Jammer, reconnaissance equipment, ACES ejection seats, and compatibility with the Imaging Infra-Red AGM-65 Maverick. Since then, the Night Attack Hornet has made its appearance. The USMC intends to operate the two seater as a primary all-weather attack machine, with a Naval Flight Officer in the back looking after the magic. Night Attack Hornets have the AAR-50 FLIR, which projects an image directly onto the Hud, coupled with night vision goggles, and a helmet mounted sight is scheduled. All this has increased weight, and from 1992 the F404-GE-402 engine, giving about ten percent more thrust, was introduced.

Before leaving the subject, we should touch upon the Hornet that never was. The F/A-18 was built by McDonnell Douglas with Northrop as the main subcontractor, with the work share split 60/40. It had however been agreed that while the former company had been brought in to ensure carrier compatibility, Northrop was free to develop and market a land based version on which the work share would be reversed. Northrop, their European market for the Cobra having largely gone to the F-16, responded with the F-18L, and the two YF-17s were redesignated as F-18L demonstrators.

While retaining commonality in most respects, the F-18L did not need the arrester hook, nose gear strut, wing folding, or heavyweight gear of the carrier fighter. Extra fuel tanks in the wings were an optional extra, as was the flight refuelling probe. The overall result was that empty weight of the basic bird was 2,230lb less, while fighter takeoff weight, with full internal fuel, guns loaded and four missiles, was 3,000lb less than the F/A-18A. This was reflected in the performance, which was considerably better. V_{max} was given as Mach 2, compared to the brochure figure of Mach 1.8 for the F/A-18A, which has since fallen to Mach 1.7 for the F/A-18C. Combat ceiling was 10 percent higher, and initial climb rate 12 percent better. Wing loading in fighter configuration was 10lb/ft^2 lower, while t/w ratio was up by 0.11 at unity, giving better sustained turn and acceleration performance.

Proposed air to air armament for the F-18L was either six AIM-7 Sparrows, six AIM-9 Sidewinders, or a mix of the two. It was proposed to strengthen the wingtip rails to carry Sparrow, although whether this would have proved feasible considering the probable roll damping effects is open to question. With the six missiles, two 610 US gallon and one 450 US gallon drop tanks could be carried. Two extra hard points were fitted under the wings, to give a total of 11, and it was proposed to give the radar a terrain following mode.

There can be little doubt that as a fighter, the F-18L would have been a rather hotter ship than the F/A-18A, while lacking nothing in the air to surface role. However, even though it was offered under a USN-endorsed joint foreign sales plan, there were no takers. The reasons were twofold. Firstly, the much more affordable F-16 had cornered most of the market, and secondly where customers requirements were more stringent, the Northrop Hornet found itself in direct competition with the McDonnell Douglas Hornet. While McDD could show flying hardware in USN and USMC service, all Northrop had to offer was a brace of thinly disguised YF-17s and some impressive brochures. Where the Hornet beat the Fighting Falcon for export sales, it was always the naval variant that won.

The Hornet has done well in the export market, and is currently in service with Canada, Australia, Spain and Kuwait, and has been ordered by Switzerland and Finland.

The Hornet that never was. A mock-up of the Northrop F-18L in two-seater form, showing the extra hardpoints, and rather ambitiously, Sparrows on the wingtip rails. (Northrop).

A trio of Saab JA-37 Viggens of the Swedish Air Force. While the canard delta configuration appears to predate the current European trend for this layout, it can be seen that it is a fixed plane with a moving control surface on the trailing edge, adopted for short field performance rather than manoeuvrability. (Foto A. Anderson).

TOP: *An F-14A Tomcat launches an AIM-54A Phoenix missile. While this gave an unsurpassed long range kill capability, it has never been used in action, even in the Gulf War of 1991.* (Hughes).

BOTTOM: *Four F-15A Eagles of the 21st Fighter Wing, armed with Sparrows and Sidewinders, patrol the frozen wastes of Alaska.* (McDonnell Douglas).

TOP: *Symbols of resistance. An Israeli F-16A overflies the ancient Zealot stronghold of Masada.* (Lockheed Fort Worth).
BOTTOM: *The fourth Full Scale Development F/A-18 Hornet flies in an unpainted state, clearly showing the amount of advanced composites in its skin.* (McDonnell Douglas).

TOP: *Squadron Leader Sami Toor of the Pakistan Air Force formates on his Wing Commander over the Himalayas. The F-16 has done well in the export field. (Lockheed Fort Worth).*

BOTTOM: *Huge flaps deployed for take-off, this F/A-18A Hornet launches from USS Constellation using military power only. (McDonnell Douglas).*

OVERLEAF *Planform view of the Northrop YF-17, showing the long slots on the inside of the LERX. On the Hornet these were found to cause excess drag and covered over. (Northrop).*

TOP: *The advanced cockpit of the Mirage 2000, showing a "look-level" display beneath the Hud, and three colour multi-function displays.* (AMD-BA/Aviaplans).

BOTTOM: *The Mirage 2000-5 is the export version. It is seen here armed with four Super 530D and two Magic 2 AAMs.* (AMD-BA/Aviaplans).

TOP: *In an attempt to gain the advantages of VSTOL with Mach 2 performance, Dassault used a combination of lift engines and an unvectored conventional engine in the Mirage IIIV. (Dassault).*

BOTTOM: *The most capable STOVL aircraft in service is the AV-8B of the USMC, which doubles as the Harrier GR.7 with the RAF. (McDonnell Douglas).*

CHAPTER SIX

European Problems and Solutions

By the turn of the century, younger readers may find it hard to imagine conditions in Western Europe some 30 years earlier. The Cold War was at its height, and a situation of armed neutrality, rather than a genuine peace prevailed. Sooner or later a surprise attack from the Warsaw Pact countries, spearheaded by the Soviet Union, was expected, and some pundits dourly forecast that they could reach the North Sea coast in three days flat. Only a massive and timely reinforcement from the USA might just redress the situation in the event of war.

This should have provided the climate for a thriving aerospace industry to match that of America. In fact, only four indigenous European fighters, as opposed to attack aircraft, entered service between 1970 and 1990. These were the Saab JA.37 Viggen; the Dassault Mirage 2000, the Panavia Tornado Air Defence Variant, and the Sea Harrier. Of these the Sea Harrier will be dealt with in a later chapter, while the Viggen was the fighter version of an attack aircraft first flown in February 1967. The JA.37 had all the faults of an earlier era; poor cockpit visibility, high fuel burn, short legs, poor turn capability, and a radar that could only be described as adequate. Its saving grace was its ability to operate from short stretches of road, using dispersed basing. The JA.37 was essentially a previous generation aircraft and therefore does not merit further mention.

The remaining two were primarily interceptors, but there the resemblance ends. For reasons which will become clear later, Dassault optimised the Mirage 2000 for the top right hand corner of the flight performance envelope, on the assumption that it would also prove more than adequate at slower speeds and lower altitudes. It also became the basis for a series of multi-role aircraft.

By contrast, the air defence variant of Tornado was very much a single mission aircraft. Its basic function was the defence of the United Kingdom Air Defence Region, a vast area encompassing most of the North Sea, north across the Denmark Strait nearly to Iceland, and the Western and South Western Approaches. The threat that it was designed to counter were fast long range Soviet aircraft armed with stand-off missiles, notably the Tu-22M Backfire, which would in times of war attempt to interdict the strategic sea lanes from North America. Nor was it totally beyond the bounds of possibility that the East Coast of the British Isles could come under low level attack from Soviet bases in what was then East Germany.

Originally the British defences were oriented in an easterly and north-easterly direction, but it was later realised that some threat aircraft had sufficient range to sneak in by the back door. The first supersonic defenders had been BAe Lightnings, high on performance but low on range. These were later supplemented by American-built Phantoms, but RAF Air Staff Target 395, issued in 1971, called for something to replace both types, able to patrol for at least two hours 400nm out over the sea, operating autonomously in all weather conditions and in the face of intense countermeasures, and with a superior weapons system. Several existing aircraft were evaluated for the role. The Tomcat seemed ideal in many ways, but its TF30 engines did not inspire confidence, and the AWG-9 fire control system was considered to be old technology, bearing in mind that the new fighter would not be required for some years to come, which would give time for a state of the art radar to be developed. Also it was unaffordable. The F-15 lacked range, and its radar and one man crew were deemed inadequate for the task. The F-16 was too deficient in avionics and weaponry to be seriously considered. It was finally decided to take the Panavia Tornado interdictor and modify it for the interceptor mission. Full scale development was initiated in March 1976.

Panavia Tornado Air Defence Variant

Like all Western fighters of the period, Tornado had a bad press. Its original acronym of MRCA (Multi-Role Combat Aircraft) was variously interpreted as Must Refurbish Canberras Again and Mother Riley's Cardboard Aeroplane. It must have come as a terrible shock to the knockers when the interdiction/strike Tornado proved outstandingly capable in service. This was underlined in 1984 by No 617 Squadron Royal Air Force, which picked up two first and two second places in the USAF Strategic Air Command Bombing Competition at the first time of entering. Just to prove it was no fluke, No 27 Squadron did even better the following year. In 1986, there was no RAF entry, as a third set of wins could only have been embarrassing.

Tornado IDS was uniquely qualified to form the basis of a long range interceptor. It had a two-man crew, the engines were expressly designed for economy, and its variable sweep wings, equipped with a battery of high lift devices, could give an optimum for both high speed flight and economical cruise. An international project undertaken by Britain, Germany and Italy, there had originally been other participants. Two of these, Canada, which later bought the Hornet, and Holland, an F-16 customer, had expressed requirements for acceleration and climb rates which called for a level of specific excess power above that normally needed by a low level penetrator. When these two countries pulled out of the programme, this was their legacy. Of the remaining participants, neither Germany or Italy wanted a long range interceptor, and so development of the Tornado Air Defence Variant was entirely a British project, although the manufacturing split remained the same.

Tornado IDS was quite a small aeroplane. It had variable sweep wings for much the same reasons as the Tomcat; economical cruise for long range, Mach 2 dash speed at high altitude, and low takeoff and landing speeds, plus good ride qualities at low altitude and high speed. The wings were liberally festooned with high lift devices; plain slats and double slotted Fowler flaps ran the entire length of the leading and trailing edges respectively. Like the Tomcat, roll control was provided by differentially moving stabilizers augmented by spoilers on the upper surfaces of the wings. A triplex FBW control system with mechanical backup was used. Unlike the Tomcat, wing sweep was not automatic; the three angles available had to be selected manually. Tornado had a single vertical tail surface; sized for stability at speeds beyond Mach 2. It was huge, giving rise to the soubriquet "The Mighty Fin", and in RAF machines this was used to house 750lb of extra fuel. The IDS variant was slightly too early in time for advanced composites, with the result that traditional materials were used throughout, which was also the case with the later ADV.

The engines, which were also a tri-national project, were tailored to the interdiction mission; high maximum thrust for takeoff and Mach 2 dash, the ability to use afterburner for extended periods, low fuel consumption, particularly at low altitude, and unusually for the time, rapid spool-up. The RB.199 was quite remarkable. With a bypass ratio of 1:1 for economy, which was too high for a dedicated fighter engine, it was very comparable in both static thrust and weight to GE's low bypass ratio F404 as used in the Hornet, while being a good 20 percent shorter in length. This was achieved by using a three spool layout that in 1994 remains unique in afterburning turbofans. Two-dimensional variable geometry inlets were needed to meet the Mach 2 plus requirement. The nose of Tornado IDS held a large terrain-following radar, and this determined the size of the forward fuselage, which in turn permitted the cockpits to be spacious; an advantage for lengthy missions. Aft of the cockpit the fuselage was of square cross-section with a flat underside. Variable sweep wings pose problems for underwing stores carriage; the pylons have to pivot as the wing moves in order to keep the stores pointing in the right direction. Provisions were made for two pivoting pylons per wing, while the rest of the hardpoints (for the really heavy munitions) were on the flat ventral surface of the fuselage.

Converting IDS Tornado into an interceptor involved rather more than simply shoehorning a new radar into the nose and hanging a few air to air missiles on the outside. Many of the changes made were quite radical.

Tornado IDS routinely carried a pair of Sidewinders for self defence, and the ADV would do the same, so the next step was to adapt the airframe to carry four Skyflash missiles. Skyflash was a British adaptation of the AIM-7E2 Sparrow, with identical flight performance. Where it differed was in having a completely new monopulse homing head, which gave it greater resistance to jamming, improved shoot-down capability, and more accurate tracking. Fuzing reliability had been a problem with Sparrow; a British active radar fuze was fitted to Skyflash to overcome this. Finally, missile warm-up time was reduced from 15 to just two seconds, eliminating the obligatory "four potatoes" prelaunch count needed for the American weapon, coming closer to the ideal of an instantly available missile. BAe Dynamics began development in 1969; the trials programme, carried out at Point Mugu in California, was the best ever, with a success rate of 91 percent. Further development would have seen an active radar homing Skyflash, which would have eliminated the need for the launching fighter to keep illuminating the target, but this was later abandoned in favour of AIM-120 Amraam.

Tornado IDS was designed for short field performance. This German example is seen with thrust reversing buckets fully deployed, together with spoilers on the upper wing surfaces. (Panavia).

The simple way to stick four Skyflash missiles on a Tornado IDS airframe would have been to hang them on pylons, but this solution would have caused a lot of drag, with a consequently unacceptable reduction in performance. Like its Sparrow ancestor, the drag of Skyflash could be minimised by carrying it semi-submerged in wells on the underside of the aircraft. But Skyflash is a big missile; over 12ft long and 3.33ft span across the fins, and there was simply not enough room to house four of them beneath Tornado IDS, even in tandem pairs. Only one answer was possible; the fuselage was stretched by inserting a new section just behind the cockpit. Even then, the tandem pairs had to be staggered longitudinally to prevent the fins of the missiles from overlapping.

In fighter design, nothing is ever allowed to go to waste, and the Tornado ADV fuselage stretch was no exception. The space was used for avionics, and a bag tank holding an extra 1,250lb of fuel. In this connection it should perhaps be noted that Tornado, despite its long range capability, had rather a low fuel fraction, and extra internal juice was welcome.

Further changes had to be made to accommodate the new air interception radar. The nose ahead of the cockpit was lengthened a few inches, while a longer and more sharply pointed radome more compatible with the operating frequency replaced that of the IDS. The combined stretches improved the fineness ratio of the fuselage, giving lower wave

To turn Tornado into an interceptor, it had to be lengthened to carry four Skyflash AAMs semi-submerged on the underside. Even then the big missiles had to be staggered, as can be seen here. (Panavia).

drag which led to better supersonic acceleration, but had also shifted the centre of gravity. To compensate for this, the centre of lift had to be moved forward. This was done by changing the wing glove sweep angle from 60deg to 68deg, which gave a little more area, deleting the Kruger flaps on the glove leading edge.

Amendments were made to the flight control system. The IDS had three wing sweep settings; 25deg to Mach 0.73; 45deg to Mach 0.88, and 67deg for higher speeds. The ADV was given an extra setting of 58deg. Also fitted was SPILS (Spin and Incidence Limiting System), which prevented marginal flight parameters being exceeded, thus guarding against inadvertent departure, and giving carefree handling. Also, the ADV controls were some 30 percent lighter than those of the IDS.

Of the four primary user air arms, only the RAF had a requirement for in-flight refuelling, and a probe had been incorporated as an "add-on" extra for the IDS. The ADV was given a permanent retractable refuelling probe from the outset. Another difference between the two was that where the IDS carried two 27mm Mauser cannon, the ADV had only one, set low on the starboard side of the fuselage. The Mauser was a revolver-type gun, with a rate of fire considerably less than that of the American M61, but this was compensated to a degree in that it went to full rate instantly, unlike the Vulcan, which takes half a second to wind up. Furthermore, both the ballistic qualities and hitting power of the 27mm projectile were far superior.

The prototype ADV first took to the skies in October 1979 from Warton, crewed by Dave Eagles and Roy Kenward. Four dummy Skyflash missiles were fitted, and these were carried through most of the trials. Handling proved excellent, even though the engines were not of final production standard, and it was quickly established that an indicated air speed of 800kt at low level could be attained, whereas most other combat aircraft were "q" limited to between 700 and 750kt for structural reasons. In fact Tornado could go even faster, as when the air speed indicator needle was hard against the stop at 800kt, telemetry showed the aircraft to be still accelerating.

The ADV entered service with 229 OCU at Coningsby towards the end of 1985. The aircraft was an interim type, the Tornado F.2, of which only 18 were built and later updated into the F.2A. The definitive version was Tornado F.3, which quickly followed the F.2 into service. This differed in having fully variable, fully automated wing sweep, operating as a function of Mach number, while fully automated slats and flaps, variable with Mach number and alpha, replaced the previous manually operated controls. Extra avionics, doubled computer capacity, four Sidewinders instead of two, and more powerful engines were the other basic differences.

The RB 199 was not really suitable as an interceptor engine. While the fairly high bypass ratio is great for low sfc at cruising speeds, at high speeds military thrust diminishes alarmingly, and must be supplemented with afterburner. The TF30 used in the F-111 had had the same bypass ratio, but was reduced to 0.9 for the Tomcat. The answer, although still not ideal, was the Mk 104, with the same bypass ratio but with a 14in extension just aft of the flameholders in the afterburner, which provides additional burning volume, and an afterburning thrust increment of between seven and 15 percent, for slightly lower afterburning sfc. The engine extension needed a fairing; oddly this reduced drag slightly without affecting handling. To enable the engine to run closer to its ideal parameters, a Digital Engine Control Unit was installed on the Mk 104, replacing the earlier analogue type used on the Mk 103 of the IDS Tornado.

In the eyes of many people, Tornado F.3 was fatally flawed by its AI24 Foxhunter radar. Certainly it failed to perform as advertised, and efforts to improve it were at first less than 100 percent successful. It had been developed under two wrong premises. Firstly that its development time would not exceed that of the development of the stretched airframe. Secondly that close combat was not a likely scenario. These were the conditions which sowed the seeds of a near disaster.

Foxhunter was required to detect low level fighter-sized targets at ranges of up to 100nm. Closer in, it was required to track up to 40 targets while displaying the 10 greatest threats. Other information could be accepted via data link. Continuous wave semi-active homing was needed for Skyflash. In addition it was to be very resistant to hostile jamming. Close combat modes were not included originally, nor was any means of maintaining contact with a co-speed low level target in a tail chase. These deficiencies showed lamentable short-sightedness, and later led to a tremendous amount of justified criticism.

Long range detection of fighter-sized targets at low level at 100nm range was a very onerous requirement. To obtain a 100nm horizon, the interceptor would need to be at medium altitudes at least, so look-down was required, which in turn demanded pulse Doppler. Pulse mode could only be used against crossing targets in situations when the pD filters would have thrown the baby out with the bathwater; the contact out with the clutter. High prfs were the only way of achieving such a range, by emitting very high power. A Cassegrain antenna was selected in preference to the more modern planar array type, as it was thought to be more resistant to jamming. To resolve range ambiguities, Frequency Modulated Interrupted Continuous Wave(FMICW) techniques were used to identify specific radar returns from distant targets.

Continuous updating added close combat modes by using medium prfs, while non-cooperative target recognition based on the identification of the engine compressor harmonics of the target, were made available by means of a software change. Not until 1991 was it announced that Foxhunter had finally met its original specifications.

The operational philosophy for Tornado F.3 was similar to that of the Tomcat, with the navigator acting as battle manager. Automatic target sequencing was one facility, in which the crew nominated up to four targets to be engaged, the type of weapon to be used and whether afterburner should be engaged. The smart electrons then sorted out an attack pattern which met all the requirements in minimum time.

While Tornado F.3 was never intended as a close combat fighter, as is evidenced by its high wing loading and low t/w ratio, opponents regarding it as a turkey often got a nasty shock. The high lift devices combined with a high aspect ratio gave it excellent turn performance in the lower speed ranges, backed by a superb rate of roll, even at minimum sweep, which often surprised a theoretically better turning adversary. Neither was it a slouch in the supersonic regime, where its roll ability was phenomenal. Acceleration was surprisingly good, in part due to the exceptionally clean lines. To put things into perspective, a comparison is needed. Tornado totally outperformed the Phantom in all departments, and in addition could act as a mini-AWACS, controlling a whole bunch of light fighters. Nobody pretended that Tornado F.3 could hold its own in close combat against a well-flown F-16 in a one versus one encounter, but it should be remembered that one versus one is a peacetime exercise which is little to do with war. The F-16 has first to close the range without getting a Skyflash in the face, while secondly, unless it is well-flown, it may still lose.

To summarize, Tornado F.3 became a first class interceptor, which was its primary function, and it was also better than expected in the close combat arena, to the surprise of many who thought otherwise.

Dassault Mirage 2000

The immediate forerunner of Tornado had been the ill-fated AFVG, or Anglo-French Variable Geometry aircraft. This was cancelled amid a welter of political infighting, and shortly after, Avions Marcel Dassault unveiled their variable sweep Mirage G, followed in 1971 by the two seater Mirage G.8. Neither entered production, but the series formed the basis of the proposed *avion de combat futur*(ACF), a large twin engined single seat multi-role fighter with a fixed swept wing with "complex lift augmentation devices". The Super Mirage, as it was known, was to have carried a large multimode radar. Very agile, its performance requirements included a V_{max} of Mach 3, then later, as the real world intruded, Mach 2.7 and finally Mach 2.5; and a combat ceiling of over 59,000ft. In the event it proved unaffordable and was cancelled in December 1975.

Dassault saw this coming, and secure in the knowledge that France was most unlikely to buy a foreign aircraft, commenced studies for a cheaper alternative in 1972. For this they reverted to the tail-less delta planform. This had many advantages over a more orthodox tailed layout. The very broad chord inboard allowed both a deep wing and a low t/c ratio. The depth gave plenty of fuel tankage space, and eased structural and manufacturing problems. The delta wing had low drag in supersonic flight, and no clearly defined point of stall, which gave controllability at very low airspeeds. The large area gave low wing loading, with consequent benefits to instantaneous turn rates. It was easily blended to the fuselage to minimise radar cross-section. Finally, it made for simplicity and light weight, as it needed fewer control surfaces.

There were however drawbacks. The delta configuration reached its maximum lift at very high alpha, but with this came very high lift-induced drag. While the low wing loading gave excellent instantaneous turn rates, the extra drag caused a very high rate of speed loss, and sustained turn suffered. Alpha for maximum lift at low speeds was too high for takeoff and landing, as the tailpipe would ground long before the wheels, and so takeoff and landing speeds were high, and ground runs long. The centre of gravity was ahead of the centre of lift, and a wide margin of static stability was needed to counter it, especially when carrying external stores. To achieve a balance, the elevons, which were control surfaces acting differentially in roll but in unison for pitch, were deflected upwards, creating drag and reducing lift. At supersonic speeds, when the centre of lift moved aft, this adversely affected manoeuvrability.

Dassault's most successful previous fighter had been the Mirage III delta, but the handicaps inherent in this planform had convinced them to move to a conventional layout for its successor, the Mirage F.1. Returning to a delta layout seemed a retrograde step to many people, not least the writer, who in 1984 questioned Dassault's Henri Suisse on the subject.

As he said, the answer was (of course) relaxed stability, already adopted by the F-16 to give enhanced manoeuvrability. By moving the cg aft and using artificial stability, the control surfaces could be configured to give extra lift in most conditions of normal and manoeuvring flight rather than killing it by imposing downloads, while there was little or no inherent static stability to be overcome in the manoeuvre regime. This, coupled with variable camber; full span leading edge slats and full span two piece elevons to the trailing edge, overcame all the worst handicaps of the tail-less delta configuration, while conferring all the benefits. Small strakes mounted on the engine intakes just above the wings generated vortices, improving high alpha capability still more.

With typical Gallic pragmatism, the Armee de l'Air adopted the new Dassault proposal simultaneously with the cancellation of the Super Mirage, and by March 1976 had written their new fighter requirements around it rather than, as is more usual, designing a fighter to the requirement! Trimming their coat to match their cloth, they wanted the highest possible performance figures permitted by the technological level of French industry; affordable in numbers sufficient to maintain an appropriate force size; and delivery to commence in 1982 to replace elderly Mirage IIICs in A de l'A service. It was to meet France's air defence and air superiority needs over a period of 20 years; i.e. past the year 2000 from which the new fighter took its appellation, while other variants, such as reconnaissance and attack, plus a two seater trainer, would be developed. It was also required to pay for itself, at least in part, via the export market.

Progress was swift, and the first prototype flew in March 1978, a mere 27 months after its official adoption. A very pleasing looking aircraft, dimensionally it was slightly smaller than the F-16A, although volumetrically larger, and rather heavier at combat weight.

The overall aerodynamic configuration was aimed at minimal drag for high acceleration, and maximum lift at high alpha. Leading edge sweep was 58deg; two degrees less than the Mirage III, while the trailing edge was swept forward at slightly more than three degrees. Careful wing/body blending, in addition to the advantages mentioned earlier, increased body lift at high alpha while reducing wave drag. Unlike contemporary American fighters, the canopy was faired into the fuselage, restricting the rear view a bit. This was due to the accent on reduced drag, which was particularly important as the French had not got an engine in the same thrust class as the F100. Composite materials were widely used to save weight; carbon fibre composites were used in some wing panels, the fin, elevons, front undercarriage doors, and certain access panels, notably to the avionics compartment situated just behind the cockpit, while both carbon and boron composites were used for the rudder.

The flight control system to the wing moving surfaces was quadruplex FBW, with no mechanical backup, although the rudder, with its lesser importance, had only a three channel system. FBW was vulnerable to electro-magnetic pulses emitted by nuclear explosions, and to cover against this eventuality, a completely separate channel, well protected against this eventuality, was fitted. A simple "get you home" device, this provided just enough control for a return to base with main systems disabled.

Like the majority of modern fighters, the Mirage 2000 was stressed for +9 and -3g, and FBW gave carefree handling, but the pilot could over-ride the system to reach +13.5g at need. This would only be used in extremis to force a flythrough or to defeat a missile, as the speed loss would be horrendous, leaving the Mirage 2000 vulnerable to a further attack.

The Mirage 2000 carried marginally more internal fuel than the F-16A, but its normal missile load was heavier, which gave it a lower fuel fraction, calculated at combat takeoff weight. Its aspect ratio was much lower, as was its wing loading, due to the large wing area, but while thrust loading was comparable in military power, at full 'burner it was not in the same league.

Power for the Mirage 2000 was provided by the SNECMA M53. The M53-5, rated at 19,840lb, was fitted to early production batches, but from 1985, the standard engine became the M53-P2, rated at 21,360lb maximum and 14,360lb military thrust. The M53 was unusual in being a single spool turbofan, or more correctly a continuous bleed turbojet. The bypass ratio was low at 0.35 in the -5, increased to 0.4 in the -P2 , and the pressure ratio moderate, resulting in high sfc at subsonic speeds, although when supersonic it was as good as anything else of its era. The M53 was cleared for flight at speeds up to Mach 2.5, and had no operating restrictions, although the Mirage 2000 was restricted to Mach 2.2 by kinetic heating considerations. The variable side inlets were typical Dassault, with translating halfcones known as "souris", or mice. It would be fair to say that the M53 was well suited to the primary Mirage 2000 mission of high altitude supersonic interception, but less good at lower heights and speeds.

The interceptor/air superiority fighter variant was the Mirage 2000C, early versions of which carried the Thomson-CSF RDM radar. A multi-mode type with a conventional Cassegrain antenna, this used medium PRFs, and had a detection range of about 50nm against fighter targets, with target tracking in TWS mode at between 30 and 37nm. Pulse compression techniques were used to obtain range information when looking up, while pulse Doppler provided a look-down capability at ranges of between 18 and 25nm. RDM also featured air to ground modes, including terrain avoidance, and both stationary and moving target ranging and attack information.

A Mirage 2000C launches a Super 530D AAM. Unusually, this missile has very long chord wings to improve its powers of manoeuvre at extreme range. (CEV Cazaux).

The definitive air to air radar for the Mirage 2000C was the RDI, also by Thomson-CSF. An X-band radar with a planar array antenna, this used very high PRFs (the actual value has not been released, but exceeds 100kHz) to provide unambiguous range and velocity data on distant targets while in search mode, not just when tracking, as with previous types. The maximum range is stated as 65nm against head-on fighter-sized targets, and up to 30nm from astern or against low flyers in the look-down mode. It can also guide missiles against very high targets where there is a large altitude disparity by using a snap-up facility, thus giving a credible interception capability against the MiG-25 Foxbat. While the ranges did not match those of comparable American radars, performance of RDI was considered to be better than that of any adversary radar likely to be encountered. In this connection, Dassault pointed out that the RCS of the Mirage 2000 is so small that enemy aircraft are likely to be well within RDI detection range before the Mirage can be detected by them. Close combat modes included boresight, vertical scan, and spiral scan, all with automatic lockon for heat missiles, and guns mode for ranges of less than 1,000m. Air to ground modes included terrain avoidance, ranging, and ground mapping for navigation, although this did not have Doppler beam sharpening.

73

The cockpit of the Mirage 2000 was designed on much the same principles as that of the Hornet. HOTAS ensured that every control and switch needed in combat was under hand, while three TV type displays dominated the instrument panel. Two of these, one head-down, the other head-level, presented flight and radar information, systems and weapons status, on demand as called up by the pilot. The third was dedicated to external threat indications after they had been located and identified by the internal electronic warfare suite. Information from either of the first two displays could be switched to the Thomson-CSF VEM 130 Hud.

Standard air to air armament of the Mirage 2000 consisted of two internal 30mm DEFA 554 cannon with 125 rounds each, giving a firing time of just over four seconds, and typically two Super 530D and two Magic 2 missiles.

The Super 530D entered production in 1986, and despite its suffix (standing for Doppler), was a later model than the Super 530F. A SARH homer, it was altogether larger and heavier than Sparrow. Unusually it had four very long chord wings to provide extra lift when the speed fell away after burnout, which improved its powers of manoeuvre near the end of its run, aerodynamic control being by cruciform tail surfaces. All-burnt speed exceeded Mach 4.6, and range was more than 22nm. High speed digital processing made it very effective in the shoot-down mode against low flying targets, against which it could be launched from level flight, after which it snapped down; while trials confirmed its ability to hit a Mach 2.5 target at 80,000ft after being launched from more than 30,000ft lower.

Magic 2 was a heat homer capable of more than Mach 2 and a range of roughly 7nm. An all-aspect weapon like the later Sidewinders, it could be slaved to the radar, or used for autonomous search. It had few launch limitations, and could be released at airspeeds down to zero, high alpha, and up to 8g.

Both types of missile will be replaced in the mid-1990s by MICA (*Missile Intermediat de Combat Aerien*). Super 530D is heavy and draggy; the short ranged Magic lacks versatility. The ideal was a small lightweight missile to handle both long and medium range interception, plus close combat. This resulted in MICA, a tour de force in packaging, with interchangeable active radar and infra-red seeker heads, range potentially exceeding 27nm, and an inertial guidance system, while being only slightly larger and heavier than Magic 2. Thrust vectoring augments the aerodynamic controls and increases powers of manoeuvre in short range engagements. Like the larger Amraam, it will be launched at the projected position of a medium distance target, and can accept midcourse updating in flight before switching to AR or IR terminal homing for the last few seconds. The Mirage 2000 will carry a total of six MICA missiles when they become available, with a mix of AR and IR seeker heads.

Like its contemporaries, the Mirage 2000 was built in a two seater conversion trainer variant, with the second hole in tandem. This displaced the gun bay, some of the avionics, and reduced internal fuel by 140lb, which at two percent of the total, was hardly enough to worry about. The second seat was raised slightly, and this plus the enlarged canopy caused a distinct dorsal spine to be formed, which housed some of the displaced avionics. The 2000B, as the two seat trainer was designated, could also be fitted with a pod holding two 30mm DEFA cannon to replace the missing internal guns.

A few non-fighter variants of the Mirage 2000 are worthy of mention. Based on the two seater was a nuclear strike variant, the Mirage 2000N, beefed up to carry a medium range stand-off missile at high speed and low level, and fitted with Antilope 5 terrain-following and attack radar. This will be followed by the 2000N', a two seat attack aircraft

Dassault built two variable geometry Mirage G.8s, one single seater and one two seater. They were not however adopted by the Armee de l'Air. (Dassault).

having no nuclear capability. The 2000E is a single seat multi-role type, while the 2000S is based on the 2000N' and optimised for low level penetration.

In 1991 the APSI cockpit layout was introduced. This consisted of no less than five electronic displays. The Thomson-CSF VEH 3020 wide angle Hud gave a field of view 30deg x 20deg, on which visual and Flir pictures could be superimposed, in addition to normal flight and attack data. Just beneath this was a Head Level Display for optronic sensor information with a field of view of 10deg x 14deg. A collimated multi-mode display, it provides the pilot with Flir, radar, or laser designator imagery without him having to glance down into the cockpit. Below the HLD and on either side of the panel are two multi-mode displays. As a general rule that on the left handles weapon delivery and management, navigation etc, while on the right is the horizontal situation display, ECM etc. Functions are interchangeable at need between these two displays. Finally the Head Down Display, low in the centre of the panel, is the one already existing in the Mirage 2000, and shows radar imagery plus alpha-numeric information in colour. This variant will be known as the Mirage 2000-3. Finally, the Thomson-CSF RDY multi-mode radar has been fitted to the Mirage 2000-5 export aircraft.

The Mirage 2000 is highly rated as a pilot's aircraft. It is snappy in both roll and pitch, roll rates reaching about 270deg/sec. Instantaneous turn rates are high, as one would expect from such a lightly wing loaded aircraft, stated as being between 20 and 30deg. Sustained turn is not quite so good, the delta wing acting as a giant speedbrake at high alpha, but again this gives the Mirage 2000 good transient performance, as in close combat it can dump speed very fast to force an overshoot while leaving the throttle wide open for rapid energy recovery the instant it unloads. Sustained turn rates max out at 17deg/sec at 5,000ft and Mach 0.9 with two heat missiles and half internal fuel. As at late 1994, there is no fighter in service which outclasses the Mirage 2000 across the board in close combat, although there are several with superior weapons systems. At low altitudes and subsonic speeds, the MiG-29 Fulcrum has greater powers of manoeuvre, but as altitude and speed increase, the Mirage 2000 becomes progressively superior.

CHAPTER SEVEN

Short Takeoff, Vertical Landing

The quest for ever more capability brought increases in cost, weight, and complexity. Taking these in turn, cost increases meant a reduction in force size. This made each aircraft more valuable to its operator and more difficult to replace; i.e. each fighter in a 100 strong force would be ten times more valuable operationally than each fighter in a 1,000 strong force, and equally hard to replace. Then as the number of fighters diminished, so would the number of fighter units also shrink, and fewer airfields would be required. A reduction in the number of airfields automatically gave an aggressor fewer targets to hit. This was counterproductive, as it automatically reduced the effort needed to take them out, thus increasing enemy force effectiveness, which to say the least, was not a good idea.

The simple answer to this was to deploy aircraft away from fixed bases so that they formed diffuse rather than concentrated targets. This was all very well, but increased weight became a major factor at this stage. Whereas in the Second World War fighters could easily be deployed to temporary grass fields, the much heavier jets of the sixties and seventies needed far longer takeoff and landing runs, and concrete surfaces on which to do them. Few Western fighters of the period could even risk taxying across grass as the chances of bogging down were too great, while soil erosion was likely to throw up stones and other matter to FOD their engines. Concrete runways up to 10,000ft long, plus hard taxiways, became essential for fighter operations.

Complexity was also a player here. The sheer amount of equipment and effort needed to keep a modern fighter serviceable virtually ensured that the squadrons were tied to huge fixed bases which had all the necessary support facilities. Fighter squadrons have always been regarded as high value targets, and large fixed bases made them relatively easy to find, bearing in mind that even the most efficient and maintainable fighter spends most of its time on the ground where it is at its most vulnerable. Even if it was in the air at the time of the attack it would still be vulnerable. If the home base was too badly damaged for the fighter to land back, it would be lost unless it could divert to an alternative, less damaged airfield. Nor were attacks with conventional weapons the only threat. Nuclear warheads, carried by long range ballistic missiles, were capable of destroying an airfield and all its assets with a single hit. In an all-out war, airfields seemed to have little future. This was underlined by the highly successful Israeli pre-emptive strike against Egyptian airfields in 1967.

Assuming that a war was to be fought, what was needed was to reduce the dependence of the fighter squadrons on large fixed bases. Complete independence was of course impracticable. The vehicle in largest scale use in the world is the motor car, yet even this has to return to the garage occasionally. What could conceivably be done was to make a fighter that could be deployed offbase for extended periods.

Vertical takeoff and landing (VTOL) was perceived as a possible solution. It would remove the fighters from the vicinity of the two mile long runway which was a magnet for air or missile attack. It would allow operations to be carried out from the most unlikely places, making an enemy's reconnaissance task far harder and his counter-air operations infinitely more difficult. Nor was it totally beyond the bounds of possibility that a new sort of air base could be devised; one without runways or taxiways, or even orthodox hangars; from the air looking like a perfectly normal cluster of farm buildings. These were heady thoughts in the days when not a few prophets had forecast the demise of the manned fighter.

Many early attempts to produce a VSTOL fighter involved tail-sitters, which on takeoff rose vertically before nosing over into horizontal flight. This was fairly easy, but landing was far more difficult. The pilot had to halt his machine in the vertical position before reversing it downwards, balanced on its own thrust. Quite apart from the stability problems involved, this was generally judged to be beyond the capability of the average squadron driver. Only one feasible alternative remained; the flat riser, which took off and landed in a horizontal attitude, translating from vertical to forward flight as required. The obvious way of achieving this was to build a more or less orthodox fighter which also had separate engines for lift. Technically this was perfectly feasible, and in fact the only Mach 2 capable VTOL fighter ever to fly used this system. The Dassault Mirage IIIV used no less than eight lift engines to get it off the ground, plus a single large cruise engine for conventional forward flight. The drawback was that eight lift engines added an awful lot of weight and complexity which reduced conventional flight performance. They also took up a lot of volume which would have been better used for other things. The Mirage IIIV was extremely fuel limited; its performance was rather lower than that of the standard IIIC, and it was quietly laid back in the closet when still in the prototype stage.

The less obvious way of producing a flat riser was to use a more or less standard engine and alter the direction of its thrust as required. The Soviet Union compromised with its Yak-36 Freehand VTOL demonstrator, combining a vectored thrust cruise engine with two lift engines placed amidships. This aircraft was later developed into the Yak-38 Forger carrier aircraft. Great Britain went the whole hog with what was eventually to become the Harrier, using a large turbofan with two ducts taking fan air to two cold nozzles (although I don't advise you to put your fingers in them) in front, and a bifurcated duct blasting the hot efflux downstream of the turbine out through two rear hot nozzles. In what looked a real Heath Robinson arrangement, all four nozzles were chain driven to swivel in unison.

The real British VTOL fighter should have been the Hawker P1154. This, in the words of Hawker test pilot Duncan Simpson, would have been a VTOL fighter with Phantom capability. Two versions were planned; a single seater for the Royal Air Force and a two seater for the Royal Navy, which at that time still operated conventional aircraft carriers. Either a single BS100 turbofan, or two Rolls Royce Spey turbofans would provide power, using plenum chamber burning(PCB), which is afterburning set in the duct upstream of the "cold" nozzles to balance orthodox afterburning at the rear end.

When designing a conventional fighter, a twin engined layout is used for two main reasons. Firstly it may be the only way to provide sufficient power when high performance or payload are major factors. Secondly it provides an extra measure of flight safety and combat survivability, albeit at a penalty in structural weight and systems complexity. Twin engined layouts are widely favoured by naval air arms, where engine failure over water may easily lead to the loss of the pilot as well as his aircraft. But in VTOL designs, two engines can be something of an embarrassment. Firstly the thrust from each engine has to be exactly matched with the other for stability in hovering flight, which is not the easiest thing to achieve. Secondly, failure in one engine eliminates VTOL capability entirely, as there is insufficient power remaining, added to

RIGHT: *Cutaway of the Pegasus Mk 105 (F402-RR-406 in McDonnell Douglas-built aircraft), showing the layout of the vectoring nozzles and over-sized compressor.* (Rolls-Royce).

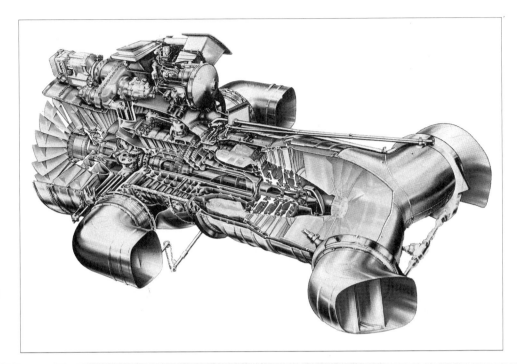

BELOW: *The Hawker P.1154 was the original design aim, a VTOL aircraft with Phantom capability. Failure of the RAF and RN to agree led to its cancellation, and left the way clear for the development of the Harrier.* (BAe).

which, asymetric thrust, while not too much of a problem in conventional flight, is a real no-no in jet-borne flight. While flying near land, a non-catastrophic failure in one engine would normally allow the fighter to recover to a conventional airfield, but at sea, all the pilot could do was to return to the vicinity of the carrier before taking a Martin Baker departure and an early bath. Rather cynically, it can be argued in the latter case that safety is greater with a single engine than with two, as there is only half as much to go wrong.

Another difficulty with vectored thrust VTOL aircraft was that the rotating nozzles had to be located about the centre of gravity with the engine(s) in the middle. The engine(s) and ducting took up a great deal of prime volume in just about the position where much of the fuel and many of the black boxes were normally kept, meaning that these necessities had to be squeezed in elsewhere. The fuel situation would not only be exacerbated by PCB and afterburning, which let it be said, are not very efficient ways of obtaining extra thrust at speeds below 200kt, but because fuel weight constantly changes in flight, the bulk of it should ideally be housed close to the centre of gravity if this is to stay within reasonable limits. Furthermore, the engine intakes have to be matched to the hover condition, which is rather at variance with a Mach 2 capability. In retrospect it seems questionable whether Hawker Siddeley could really have made the P.1154 work given the state of the art at that time. Problems such as hot gas recirculation and ingestion, and ground erosion, would have been far more severe with PCB and afterburning than they are with a straightforward vectored thrust turbofan.

When the P.1154 was cancelled, a new and much less complex aeroplane was initiated, based on the vectored thrust principle. This was the Harrier, a dedicated close air support machine which proved the concepts of both VTOL and offbase operations.

One of the main limitations of vertical takeoff was the amount of power available, which had to exceed weight by something like 25 percent. A single vectored thrust engine limited gross takeoff weight severely, and in consequence the Harrier was small. However, gross takeoff weight could be increased by using a short roll to gain a modicum of wing lift priot to takeoff, permitting a greater warload to be carried. By contrast, vertical landing with stores expended and most of the fuel used posed few problems. The accent thus moved from VTOL to STOVL (Short TakeOff, Vertical Landing).

The Harrier was a simple aircraft well suited to operating away from fixed base facilities for extended periods. The operational concept was to deploy it close to the battle area to reduce reaction time, on the principle that when the troops asked for help, they usually needed it in a hurry. The problem then became keeping the Harriers supplied with munitions and fuel. In the early days of Harrier deployments, they were often pictured peeping shyly out of deep woodland, dropping gently down into clearings, or emerging stealthily from a leafy glade to go a'hunting. For a variety of reasons, it was soon found that such arboreal deployments were less than perfect. Firstly they could be difficult for friendly forces to find, which complicated resupply. Secondly, as infra-red and other reconnaissance gismos became available, concealment in a leafy bower was inadequate. Thirdly, basic facilities such as water and sanitation were absent, increasing the logistics demands. Fourthly soil erosion would rapidly become a major problem. Finally, while the ideal means of resupply was by helicopter, availability was lacking, and surface transport often had to be used, and like helicopters, cross country vehicles were at a premium.

The answers were simple. Turn a farm into a temporary base; use barns as hangars to screen against inquisitive IR sensors, use the farm facilities, including made-up roads. Urban basing was in many ways even better, using a factory or a supermarket with a wall

pulled out, with a whole network of hard roads, all facilities hopefully in working order, and a large car park as a flight pad.

Except in a dive the Harrier was firmly subsonic; its wing loading was a bit on the high side for good turning performance although it gave plenty of lift at subsonic speeds; it carried no radar suitable for air to air, and apart from 30mm Aden cannon pods under the belly, its only offensive weaponry (in USMC service only, RAF machines were cleared but not wired) was two Sidewinders.

In the air superiority role the Harrier looked distinctly unpromising material, with only one thing to commend it. This was VIFF (Vectoring In Forward Flight). At the design stage the nozzles were only intended to be moved during transition from vertical to forward flight and vice versa, but it was only a question of time before someone tried it in normal flight, if only from curiosity. While it seems that that honour went to a company test pilot, it was the US Marines who first used it as a combat aid. By varying the nozzle angle in manoeuvring flight, some most unexpected effects resulted. Full reverse nozzle could force a pursuer to overshoot in double quick time. In a hard turn, nozzle could be used to decelerate, tightening the turn too much for a conventional fighter to follow. In a turning fight, a little nozzle could be used to nibble away a few degrees of angle in order to bring the guns to bear. In the hover, pitch and roll control was effected by small puffer jets on the wingtips, nose and tail. These had sufficient authority to keep the Harrier under control at speeds well below the stall; the post-stall manoeuvring regime which the MBB-Rockwell X-31 commenced exploring in 1991, which at that time was still far in the future. Finally, VIFF allowed the Harrier to swap ends very quickly in order to offer a pursuer some head-on discouragement. VIFF lacked precision during hard manoeuvres, and its effects could be rather unpredictable, but it was definitely a combat asset. On the other hand, as thrust fell away at high altitudes, so did the effects of VIFF, which was only a significant advantage at low and medium altitudes.

Oddly, it was none of these things which led to a fighter variant of the Harrier. The fixed wing element of the Royal Navy was lost when HMS *Ark Royal*, their last conventional carrier, was stood down, and its replacement cancelled. The main function of the Royal Navy was perceived to be the protection of convoys across the North Atlantic in time of war. Air cover was to be provided by the RAF.

This slightly potty concept rapidly broke down in practice because of the long reaction time of a force based perhaps 1,000 miles away. The RN had however retained rotary wing air, and had a few Invincible class helicopter ASW ships on order. As the word "carrier" was anathema to the politicians, these were referred to as "through deck cruisers", a cover so transparent as to make the name "see-through cruisers" almost obligatory. It was screamingly obvious that these ships could carry a complement of STOVL aircraft if necessary, and the RN, needing organic air cover against the possibility of attack by long range Soviet maritime aircraft, decided to use this option. They ordered a variant optimised for their needs, the Sea Harrier FRS.1. This decision had far reaching consequences for the future.

Meanwhile a young naval officer, Lt Cdr Doug Taylor, had propounded a theory that if a Harrier could be launched uphill, it could carry a greater payload at takeoff than if it performed a short rolling takeoff on the flat. In simple terms, the upward trajectory would more than offset the force of gravity for the few seconds while the Harrier accelerated to wingborne flying speed. This was confirmed by Hawker engineers, and a variable angle ramp was built. Trials commenced in August 1977 proved its viability, and the Invincible class ships were all built with what became known as "ski-jumps" in the bows. One existing helicopter carrier, HMS *Hermes*, was also modified in this way. One tremendous advantage of a ramp takeoff was that regardless of how badly the ship was pitching, the aircraft would always be launched upwards, away from the water, which was not always the case with conventional carriers making catapult launches.

The Sea Harrier FRS 2 is fitted with the far more capable Blue Vixen radar, a pulse-Doppler multi-mode set, which can provide guidance for Amraam missiles. (BAe).

The first Sea Harrier flight took place at Dunsfold on 20 August 1978, piloted by John Farley. It was a production model, being sufficiently similar to previous variants as not to warrant a prototype, though in appearance it differed considerably. The main requirement of a fighter variant was a capable radar. This called for a revised radome nose to house it, which gave a slight increase in length; and more panel space in the cockpit than the original Harrier layout could provide. To make room, the cockpit was raised by eleven inches, with the useful spinoff that rear visibility was greatly improved, while the canopy was bulged to give better vision sideways and downwards.

Raising the cockpit was expected to reduce longitudinal stability and to compensate for this, the fin was increased in height by four inches, and RWR aerials were installed in it. When under way, the superstructure of the ship caused turbulence over the deck. Greater roll authority was needed to counter the worst effects of this, and the diameter of the puffer jets on the wingtips was increased. Mooring lugs were added to the forward main gear leg, and horizontal stabiliser travel was increased slightly. While wing folding might have been desirable to save space below deck, the wingtip outriggers which supplemented the bicycle-type main gear virtually ruled out this possibility. Fortunately the baseline Harrier was small enough to fit on the carrier lifts without modification.

A larger alternator was fitted to cope with the power demands of the radar and other avionics kit, and the aircraft was navalised by replacing most of the magnesium alloy components, which were very vulnerable to the corrosive effects of seawater, with other materials. The engine was also treated in this way to become the Pegasus 104. The weight increase of navalisation was barely 100lb, remarkably little when compared with the galloping weight growth undergone by the YF-17 in its metamorphosis into the F/A-18.

The radar selected for the Sea Harrier was Ferranti's Blue Fox. A non-coherent pulse radar, it had just four modes; search, air/air attack; air/surface attack; and boresight for close combat. While this was very elementary for the time, it was considered adequate for the needs of the missions and the air to air weapons fit; which was two 30mm Aden cannon under the belly, and two AIM-9 Sidewinders. Pilot workload was high. To reduce this a bit, an autopilot with holds for direction, turn rate and altitude was added.

The Sea Harrier FRS.1 was very much a cheap and cheerful fighter, intended as much as anything to prove the dual concepts of STOVL at sea and the small "Harrier-carrier", while providing a measure of air defence which, by comparison with that of the huge American Tomcat, was little more than nominal. By 1981, with both concepts proven, further advances were considered worth pursuing. A state of the art pulse Doppler radar with a look-down capability was needed, as was a beyond visual range "shoot 'em in the face" missile capability, plus a multiple target engagement facility. But while these things were under consideration, the FRS.1 faced the ultimate test of battle.

The South Atlantic War of 1982 saw a handful of Sea Harriers on two small carriers set out to perform a task for which they were never intended. They were heavily outnumbered by the Argentine Air Force and Armada fast jets, which included supersonic Mirage IIICs and Daggers. While these were previous generation fighters, numbers could have been used to overwhelm the small British fighter force by making slashing attacks from different directions, using sheer speed to prevent the position being reversed. Even the small and subsonic Argentine Skyhawk light bombers were agile enough to prove worthy opponents in a turning fight had their pilots been so minded.

The outcome is now history. Twenty Argentine jet aircraft and a handful of other types were destroyed by Sea Harriers, which sustained no losses in air combat. While it is arguable that the most decisive factors were pilot quality and training, and the AIM-9L Sidewinder missile, the effectiveness of the Sea Harrier cannot be denied. A much overlooked point is that the British fighters were able to operate in weather conditions which would have grounded (or should I say carriered?) conventional types, taking off and landing back in minimal visibility and high sea states, and without the carrier having to turn into wind before landing on.

Prior to the conflict, the survivability of the type had often been questioned. In action it proved very survivable indeed. Serviceability rates were also high at around 97 percent; Sea Harriers flew a total of 1,435 operational sorties, the bulk of them defensive, during the conflict. Finally, conventional aircraft need to retain a useful fuel margin against the need to hold before landing back, or against one or more bolters. The Sea Harriers demonstrated their ability to cut things very fine; a minute or two often being sufficient for an aircraft capable of landing vertically in a small space. This, the ramp takeoff, the lack of afterburning, and the economical Pegasus turbofan, provided the Sea Harrier with adequate "legs" even though the fuel fraction was low by conventional standards.

In 1984 it was decided to go ahead with an upgraded Sea Harrier, the FRS.2, and the first pre-production aircraft flew on September 19, 1989. The main change was the radar; Ferranti's Blue Vixen replacing Blue Fox. Blue Vixen was a coherent pulse Doppler radar with eleven operational modes, compatible with the AIM-120 Amraam missile. High, medium and low prfs were all used. Velocity Search mode used high prfs to detect high speed, low level closing targets at long distance, but without giving range or velocity data, while low prfs were used in the Look Up mode. Medium prfs were used to give accurate range and target data in the Look Down, Air Combat, Track While Scan and Single Target Track modes. Mode selection automatically gave correct prfs. Air to surface modes were Sea Surface Search, Ranging, Real Beam Ground Mapping, Freeze, and Beacon Interrogation.

The main problem was that Blue Vixen and its associated black boxes could not possibly be shoehorned into the available space. One of the more limiting requirements for the FRS.2 was that although a few new-build aircraft were ordered, the FRS.1 had to be modified to FRS.2 standard at minimum cost, which meant that airframe changes could not be too radical.

A new, rather blunter radome was designed, looking very much like an afterthought, while the fuselage was lengthened 13.75in by the addition of an extra bay behind the cockpit to provide extra avionics space. While this bay is generally referred to as a plug, the upgraded FRS.1s do in fact have a whole new rear section; this being more economical than a real plug would have been. A few minor airframe modifications were made; a noteworthy omission was the ram air turbine, used to provide emergency power in the event of engine failure. As all Harriers glide like tired pianos, the retention of this item could hardly be justified.

To reduce pilot workload to manageable proportions, the cockpit area was completely redesigned, with HOTAS controls and multi-function CRT displays. Improved nav/attack kit was fitted, plus Guardian radar warning receiver, used to identify threats by comparing emissions against a memory of 200 types.

The Sea Harrier had started with a missile armament of two AIM-9 Sidewinders, which was increased to four as a result of South Atlantic experience. The selected weapon for the FRS.2 was Amraam, a medium range missile with much greater capability than the short ranged Sidewinder. Not only was it a launch and leave weapon, but it would enable the Sea Harrier to make simultaneous attacks on up to four targets. It was however rather larger and heavier than Sidewinder, and the problem became how to screw four of them onto the Sea Harrier without causing undue drag. One under each wing was easy, but a pair would have had an unacceptably adverse effect on performance and handling. Semi-conformal carriage as used by the Hornet was not feasible, as not only would have extensive redesign been necessary, but the missiles would have been in the line of the efflux from the front nozzles when they were swivelled downwards. The solution adopted was to fit them in place of the two Aden cannon pods. This in itself was a potential problem, as the cannon pods also acted as strakes to contain the engine exhaust in hovering and vertical flight to give extra lift, but was overcome by using LAU-106 ejector launchers which had much the same effect. A further problem associated with Amraam was that it generated body lift at high speeds. Wind tunnel tests suggested that this might alter the aircraft centre of lift, with a consequent destabilising effect. To counter this, bolt-on wingtip extensions were developed and test-flown. All previous Harriers had removable ferry tips to increase range on long flights, and fitting a different wingtip presented few problems. But flight trials showed that the special Amraam tips were not necessary.

The Harrier II Plus, ordered by the US Marines and the Italian and Spanish Navies, is a dedicated fighter variant with a modified APG-65 radar as used by the Hornet. (McDonnell Douglas).

Various air to air weapons combinations are possible, perhaps the most effective of which would be two Amraams on the fuselage underside and a pair of 'winders beneath each wing, for a total of six on-board kills. On the other hand, it seems a pity that in either this or the four Amraam configuration, the FRS.2 will be a gunless fighter, as all past experience shows that guns are still needed in air combat.

Meanwhile the land based close air support Harrier had undergone a considerable transformation, into the GR.5/7 in RAF service and the AV-8B Harrier II with the US Marines. Joint development work by BAe, as Hawker had become, and McDonnell Douglas, had produced an version which could carry twice the load for the same distance, or the same load for twice the distance, as the Harrier GR.3/AV-8A. The only disadvantage was a slight reduction in maximum speed.

LEFT: *Afterburning is needed to provide added power for STOVL aircraft, but this poses extreme technical problems. This is a gantry-mounted plenum chamber burning test rig at Shoeburyness. (Rolls-Royce).*

The Harrier II wing was redesigned with a supercritical aerofoil section with greater span and increased area. LERX generated vortices which improved pitch response and also lift at high alpha. Large slotted flaps occupied the inboard trailing edges. The wing was deeper than the original, and held an extra 2,116lb of internal fuel. The outriggers were moved inboard, where they could be housed mainly within the wing, reducing the fairing necessary; the narrower track improved ground handling.

The cockpit was raised to improve all-round visibility, with a wrap-around windshield and wide angle Hud. The layout was revised to incorporate HOTAS and MFDs, and a whole new nav/attack system was fitted. The engine inlets were enlarged to increase the capture area, and the radius of the lip revised. Longer zero scarf front nozzles were used to increase dynamic thrust. Lift Improvement Devices (LIDs) were fitted in the form of two longitudinal strakes under the belly, plus a retractable dam between them under the front fuselage. The function of the LIDs was to trap the efflux bouncing back off the surface while in vertical flight and prevent the aircraft being "sucked down" as hot gases flowed up past the fuselage. The LIDs also lessened exhaust gas recirculation, with the spin-off effect of lowering engine operating temperatures in the hover. Combined with a high authority attitude hold system and pitch/roll stabilisation, this improved lift in jet-borne flight and made the Harrier II far more stable in the STOVL regime than its predecessor. It also cured the tendency for the nose to wander during the hover, making "hands off" hovering possible.

A FBW system using fibre optics rather than electrical impulses replaced the conventional hydraulic system, giving a considerable weight saving. This was a first for a combat aircraft. Composites, which are corrosion resistant, were used for 26 percent of materials; the wing structure, front fuselage and horizontal tail surfaces. Extra hard points were added, giving a total of nine in addition to the gun pod mountings, and 25mm cannon replaced the elderly 30mm Adens. The gun selected for the USMC was the GAU-12/U five barrel rotary cannon, with a cyclic firing rate of 3,600 rounds per minute and a muzzle velocity of 3,500ft/sec. The ballistic qualities of the 25mm projectile were considerably superior to the 30mm shell, giving greater accuracy at longer range. Only one gun was carried, in the left hand pod; the other pod contained 300 rounds of ammunition, a linkless feed connecting the two. The British Harrier GR.5/7 was fitted with two 25mm Aden cannon with 125 rpg. Whereas the AV-8A routinely carried two Sidewinders for self defence, the greater capacity of the AV-8B enabled four to be mounted without detriment to the air to ground load.

Self defence capability was one thing, but there is really no substitute for fighter cover. For this the USMC was forced to rely on conventional carrier aircraft, but what they needed was a STOVL fighter dedicated to the task. It was therefore hardly surprising when in 1987 McDonnell Douglas proposed an air superiority variant of the AV-8B, the Harrier II Plus.

The Harrier II Plus, for which orders were placed in 1990 by the USMC and the Spanish and Italian Navies, differs from the AV-8B in certain ways. Automatic manoeuvre flaps improve turning ability, the more powerful Pegasus 11-61 rated at 24,500lb static thrust replaces the current version, and the Hughes APG-65 multi-mode radar as fitted to the Hornet is installed, making it a true multi-role fighter. The cockpit layout has been modified to suit. Air to air weaponry for the Harrier II Plus consists of six Amraam and two Sidewinders, or any combination of the two, plus the 25mm cannon.

In the combat air patrol mission, carrying four Amraam and two 300 US gallon tanks, the Harrier II Plus can achieve a time on station of 2.7 hours at a radius of 100 nautical miles, or 2.1 hours 200 nautical miles out. Whether operating from a jungle clearing or a container ship platform, this is well worth having.

The Sea Harrier/Harrier II Plus is unique in the air combat fighter world, although the former Soviet Navy operated a STOVL aircraft from carriers. This was the Yakovlev Yak-38, NATO reporting name Forger, a fairly marginal attack aircraft which used two lift engines amidships coupled with a vectored thrust main engine with bifurcated nozzles. Its thrust/weight ratio was less and its wing loading higher than the Harrier, which could out-accelerate, out-climb, and out-turn it. Forger carried a range-only radar with no search or track capability; it had no internal gun, although 23mm cannon pods could be carried on underwing pylons, plus four AA-2 Atoll or AA-8 Aphid short ranged heat seekers. Fuel fraction was almost off the bottom of the scale, denoting a very short operational radius. Inferior to the Harrier family on all counts, it had just one item of interest. This was Eskem, an automatic ejection system engaged for takeoff and landing, which chucks the pilot overboard if certain flight parameters are exceeded. This highlights the old problem; three engines have three times as much to go wrong as a single engine, therefore the probability of engine failure in jet-borne flight is that much higher, making an automatic escape system more important.

Making its Western debut at Farnborough '92, Forger appeared rock-steady in the hover, indicating a very effective automatic flight stabilization system. Be that as it may, Eskem is reported to have saved the lives of over 40 pilots during its career. This is significant, as the total build is believed to be barely 100, and this horrendous attrition rate is almost certainly why the type has been withdrawn from service.

Another Russian debutante at Farnborough '92 was the Yakovlev Yak-141, NATO reporting name Freestyle. First flown in March 1989, Freestyle was arguably the first practical supersonic STOVL aircraft, and was widely expected to replace Forger on Russian aircraft carriers in the mid 1990s.

Freestyle is a big machine, with a maximum takeoff weight roughly 70 percent heavier than that of the Harrier II. As mentioned earlier, one of the problems of a flat riser is that the engine effluxes must be grouped around the centre of gravity. Yakovlev's approach to this was to say the least, innovative. The two Rybinsk RD-41 lift engines are located just behind the cockpit, and are angled aft at 15 deg. To give pitch control in jet-borne flight, they can be vectored fore and aft by 12.5 deg. The main engine is an afterburning Soyuz R-79V-300 turbofan rated at 34,170lb static thrust maximum, with an extraordinary three section lobsterback tailpipe which rotates through 95 deg. The problems of making this work must have been formidable indeed, and in fact vectoring to the full amount results in a loss of thrust of about 20 percent.

The enormous vectoring nozzle set well forward, close to the centre of gravity, posed the problem of where to put the tail surfaces. Yakovlev eschewed the obvious solution of a high-mounted boom, and instead, opted for twin booms on either side of the nozzle. These are the full depth of the fuselage with the undersides tapering gently up towards the end, each carrying a vertical fin and horizontal stabilizer. Air bleed ejectors are located at the end of these booms for yaw control in jet-borne flight. Pitch control is of course handled by the vectoring nozzles, while roll control is provided by wingtip ejectors. The flight control system is triplex FBW.

Maximum speed is a remarkable Mach 1.8, rate of climb is over 49,000ft/min, and operational radius in the air defence mission is 485nm while carrying four AAMs and a centreline tank. A Phazotron NO-193 multimode radar was to be housed in the large radome and it has been stated that the Vrympel AAM-AE "Amraamski" missile is one weapons option. Λ 30mm GS-301 cannon with 120 rounds is located on the port side.

While at combat weight thrust loading approaches unity, Freestyle looks a rather draggy design, and the wing loading, nearly 100lb/ft^2 is definitely on the high side. This being the case, Freestyle would not be the best performer in close combat. One operational shortcoming is the ground heating and erosion effect of a short or vertical takeoff, and it was significant that at Farnborough, this was not attempted.

Currently any discussion of Freestyle's capability seems purely academic. On October 5, 1991, a tiny manufacturing fault caused one of the two prototypes to lose power when landing on the carrier *Admiral Gorshkov* in the Barents Sea. Eskem got the pilot clear, probably without his prior agreement, but the aircraft fell some 43ft onto the deck and was badly damaged. But even before this, funding for the project had been withdrawn because Russian naval requirements could be satisfied by conventional and much higher performance Su-27 Flanker. Yakovlev looked for an overseas partner to produce the bird, with, so far as is known, no success. Shortly after its Farnborough appearance, the remaining Freestyle was placed in storage.

The Russian approach to vertical takeoff was to combine two lift engines in the fuselage with a vectored thrust cruise engine, as in this Yak-38 Forger, seen here aboard the carrier Kiev. *The type has now been withdrawn from service. (US Navy).*

A navalised Su-27 Flanker (note the canard foreplanes) is described as taking off from the deck of the Russian carrier Tbilisi *in June 1990, but more probably it is a touch-and-go. Russian carrier aviation is still at a very early stage, although they seem to be making remarkable progress. (Fotokhronika Tass).*

CHAPTER EIGHT
The Other Side of the Hill

Previous chapters have shown how fighter designers and air forces of the Western nations responded to a variety of perceived threats. There was no sure way of knowing how real these threats were, or to what degree any of them were based on misconceptions. Both the F-14 and F-15 had been strongly influenced by erroneous assessments of the mission, performance, and production figures for the Mikoyan MiG-25 Foxbat. It was like shadow-boxing. The only difference was that Soviet aircraft were developed under a cloak of secrecy, leaving the West to guess their potential from the few clues available, while the Soviet Union had to assume that their opponents were as good as the technical media and advertising blurbs said they were until such time as they could be proved right or wrong.

Traditionally, Soviet fighters were developed along two distinct lines; large and heavy interceptors such as Foxbat and Sukhoi's Su-15 Flagon, intended for the defence of the homeland, and lightweight tactical fighters such as the MiG-21 Fishbed, which for many years was numerically by far the most important, and which during this period would play the greater part in any future air superiority battle. Fishbed was small, affordable, simple to maintain, and short on endurance. The avionics fit was basic, making its all-weather capability marginal. The weapons fit of a single cannon and two rear aspect only heat homing missiles (four on later variants) restricted it to the close combat arena where its greatest advantage lay in its agility. When the Phantom began to enter US service in numbers, Fishbed looked distinctly outclassed.

Something better was needed to match the American fighter, while retaining the traditional Russian virtues of simplicity, affordability, and maintainability. This was the MiG-23 Flogger, the first prototype of which flew early in 1967. Flogger, which entered service in 1972, and which was later to supplant Fishbed as the numerically most important type in Soviet and many other aligned forces, was a single seat, single engined fighter, of completely conventional construction. It had variable sweep wings with a battery of high lift devices, and three manually operated fixed sweep angles. These were to enable it to operate from short semi-prepared strips rather than to confer agility; unlike Tomcat and Tornado the wings at minimum sweep were not stressed for high g manoeuvres. At maximum sweep the centre of lift moved well aft of the centre of gravity, making trim downloads on the tailplane high. This restricted manoeuvrability considerably; instantaneous turn rate at Mach 0.9 and 15,000ft was just 11.5deg/sec, reducing to 8.6deg/sec at Mach 0.5 at the same altitude. Flogger was powered by an afterburning Tumansky turbojet. Simple and rugged, this provided excellent acceleration despite the modest thrust loading, but lacked the economy of a turbofan.

The pulse Doppler Sapfir-23 radar had a search range of about 43nm, and a tracking range of roughly 30nm, roughly on a par with the Phantom's AWG-10. Pilot workload was high, and visibility from the cockpit was appalling; gunsights and other bits cluttered a forward view that was also restricted by a massive canopy bow. The pilot was set low, with high cockpit sills, restricting his line of sight sideways and downwards, while rearward visibility was almost non-existent. Armament was two Aphid short range IR and two Apex medium range SARH missiles, plus a 23mm cannon.

The outlook for a Flogger pilot in a 1v1 combat against a Phantom was not terribly hopeful; still less against any of the new Western fighters that entered service during the seventies, although its weapon system outreached that of the F-16. But the air superiority scenario of the period was not one versus one; it was a whole heap of Floggers making slashing attacks from different directions against lesser numbers of Western fighters. The name of the game was attrition, and attrition normally works on the side of the big battalions. There was little doubt in Soviet minds that hordes of Floggers with a full head of steam on, plunging through the furball taking shots at targets of opportunity as they went, could grind down a numerically smaller force of technically superior fighters.

It was ironic that the PVO-Strany, apparently influenced by the Phantom, switched to an unmanoeuvrable BVR fighter as their spearhead at a time when the United States, as a direct result of experience in Vietnam against agile MiG-21s, started heading in the opposite direction. But the lead time between initial concept and hardware in service had lengthened, and it was years before the trend could be reversed. Not until well into the 'eighties did the Soviet Union produce fighters which could even approach those of the West, and of these, one was a rehash of an existing design.

The technology gap was a great comfort to the United States for many years. This was the main reason that Foxbat came as such a shock to the West, as it appeared that the USSR had not only caught up but had established a lead virtually overnight. The truth was more prosaic. Faced first with the Lockheed A-12, then later the SR-71 penetrating Soviet air space at Mach 3 and 80,000ft, the Mikoyan OKB stretched the state of the art as far as it would go to produce a fast climbing high speed high altitude interceptor. To this was added a requirement for a weapons system capable of completing the interception. No other considerations were allowed to interfere with these priorities, which were only attainable by using extreme measures. Two huge Tumansky R-15 turbojets could wind Foxbat up to a V_{max} of Mach 3.2, but this invariably wrecked them through overspeeding. In practice Foxbat was redlined at Mach 2.8, which it could achieve while carrying four giant AA-6 Acrid missiles. The by Western standards crude R-15s were prodigal of fuel, and inefficient at lower speeds and altitudes. Over 14 tonnes of a special high density fuel were carried internally; more than 70 percent of the aircraft empty weight, which gave a dash speed interception radius of just 160nm. Titanium technology was in its infancy at that time in the USSR, so welded nickel steel was widely employed in both structure and skinning, involving a significant weight penalty. Manoeuvre combat was never seriously considered, and to save weight, structural limits were kept low; 4.5g at supersonic speed.

The Smertch A radar was large and crude, using thermionic valves, transistors not being available in the USSR at that time, and relied on sheer power to burn through jamming. Against a bomber-sized target, detection range was about 50nm. Intercepting a target hurtling along at nearly half a mile per second called for incredibly fine judgement and timing, and like the American F-106, Foxbat was literally controlled from the ground via data link via its automatic flight control system. This made the pilot primarily a systems manager, responsible for takeoff and landing; throttle and afterburner control, missile launch, break away after the attack and, most importantly, monitoring fuel status.

The result was essentially a single mission aircraft, a dedicated high altitude interceptor, although it was also used for high altitude reconnaissance. But meanwhile the threat was changing. The B-70 Valkyrie had not entered service; the Mach 2 capable

This MiG-23S Flogger G is representative of the family that was for some time the most important fighter numerically in the Soviet Union. Its trademarks were fast acceleration, poor turning ability, and abysmal view from the cockpit. (DoD).

B-58 Hustler was withdrawn from service in 1970, while the B-52 was switched to low level. A new dual pronged threat slowly emerged. President Carter rediscovered the cruise missile, then President Reagan gave the go-ahead for the Rockwell B-1, a long range, ultra-low level penetrator. A counter was needed for these, and the Soviet designers lived up to their reputation for screwing the last ounce from a proven design by developing Foxbat into the MiG-31 Foxhound.

Mikoyan MiG-31 Foxhound

Faced with an emerging low level penetration threat, the automated ground controlled interception system used for Foxbat, dependent on clear ground radar sightlines and uninterrupted tracking, was of little use. Ultra-low level targets can only effectively be acquired from above, so an interceptor with a powerful look-down radar and shoot-down missiles was needed. The ability to operate at least semi-autonomously was also required, as was far greater range and endurance.

Development began in the early '70s, using the proven MiG-25 as a basis. The uneconomic R-15s were replaced by far superior Perm D-30F6 turbofans and internal fuel capacity was increased to just over 16 tons. The fuselage was stretched to house a second crew member in tandem, under a canopy that was little more than an extension of the dorsal spine, with side transparencies only. Unlike Western two-holers, the Russian Bear (sorry about that) was obviously not expected to take his head out of the office to become a second pair of eyes when close combat was joined. It is in fact unlikely that Foxhound was ever intended for close combat, despite the existence of a 23mm GSh-6-23 six barrel cannon with 260 rounds mounted low on the starboard side, aft of the mainwheel bay.

The prototype was first flown by Alexsandr Fedotov on 16 September 1975, but series production was delayed until 1979, with service entry in 1983. A few tantalizing glimpses of this new interceptor were afforded from time to time when it was encountered by NATO aircraft, but for years little was known for certain. Then with the ending of the Cold War, it was exhibited at Le Bourget in 1991 and Farnborough in 1992.

To the observer, its Foxbat ancestry was unmistakable, with huge inlets and twin fins dominating all else. The radome was shorter and more rounded than that of Foxbat, and

93

housed the SBI-16 Zaslon radar. This came as a big surprise to the West. It was the first electronically steered phased array fighter radar to enter service anywhere in the world. The only other radar of this type was that of the B-1B, which is used for entirely different purposes. The antenna had a diameter of 3.61ft; even larger than that of Tomcat's AWG-9, and it was claimed that transmitted power exceeded anything in the West, although no figures were stated. Detection range is reported to be 165nm, and tracking range 145nm, although if a certain illustration in the brochure is to scale, which it almost certainly is not, detection range would drop to 125nm. Zaslon can track ten contacts and guide four missiles simultaneously. Mikoyan chief test pilot Valery Menitsky also told the author that stealth targets can be tracked, and that this had been proven during trials with an unspecified stealthy Russian aircraft. As the Russians are rapidly gaining a reputation for a warped sense of humour, this statement should be viewed with extreme caution, a view shared by my friend Jacques Navieux of Hughes Radar Systems.

Having said that, electronic scanning provides faster beam steering than a mechanically operated antenna, and is switchable in microseconds, allowing instant checks on possible contacts which would make it rather more effective than a mechanically steered antenna against stealth targets. According to Menitsky, Zaslon can guide missiles simultaneously at widely separated targets, unlike AWG-9, which has to have them all in the same area of sky. In this connection, the famous 1973 Tomcat/Phoenix trial had all six targets within a 15nm frontage, giving a fairly narrow arc, and with just 2,000ft of vertical separation.

The MiG-25 Foxbat is a high speed, high altitude interceptor, controlled from the ground via the autopilot during much of the mission, leaving the pilot as systems manager. (David Oliver).

How effective is Zaslon? Its enormous power output should give a high probability of detection, while making many forms of jamming difficult. The phased array antenna should also have very small sidelobes, increasing the difficulty of spoofing it. It is supplemented by a retractable IRST mounted beneath the fuselage.

Despite Foxhound's vast internal fuel tankage, even more was needed to extend range and endurance. Unlike its predecesor, it it can carry two 550 Imperial gallon drop tanks on underwing pylons, and the aircraft exhibited at Paris and Farnborough was fitted with a flight refueling probe in front of the cockpit.

The two Perm D-30F6 turbofans are each rated at 34,171lb static thrust at maximum power and 20,944lb in military, and have much better sfc than Foxbat's R-15BFs. With five LP stages and 10 HP stages to the compressor, both driven by two stage turbines, and a massive afterburner section, they are very long by Western standards. Engine limiting speed is Mach 2.83, so nothing has been lost in the top right hand corner of the envelope.

Foxbat had been limited to Mach 0.85 at low altitude, but supersonic speed was needed by the MiG-31. To allow this, the structure was strengthened, mainly by using structural tucks and gussets, and a third wing spar was added. An attempt was also made to improve powers of manoeuvre, an area in which Foxbat had been sadly lacking. LERX appeared on the wing root; the leading edges sprouted titanium flaps, while ailerons and flaps to the wing trailing edges were extended. The structural strengthening may have increased g limits a bit, but not a lot, which is why Foxhound was kept in the static display at Le Bourget. As Valery Menitsky commented to the writer, it could have done little other than make a very spectacular noise!

One very unusual feature was the offset tracking of the two-wheeled main gear. When taxying on soft ground, twin wheels get clogged with mud, while tandem wheels with the same track cause deep ruts. The offset tandem wheel configuration minimises both problems.

An extrapolation of Foxbat, the MiG-31 Foxhound carries a second crew member, has provision for in-flight refuelling, and carries an electronically steered phased array radar. This example is seen armed with four AA-9 Amos and two AA-7 Apex missiles. (Mikoyan OKB).

The main missile armament of Foxhound is AA-9 Amos, four of which can be carried beneath the fuselage, supplemented by four AA-8 Aphids on underwing pylons. Amos, which is apparently exclusive to Foxhound, is a large missile with a passing resemblance to the AIM-54 Phoenix. A semi-active radar homer, DoD had previously given its range as a mere 27nm, but Soviet sources state 60nm, which is far more likely. It has performed well in look-down, shoot-down trials, even against cruise missile sized targets.

Performance figures for Foxhound are maximum speeds of Mach 2.83 at altitude and Mach 1.22 at low level, which last beats the DoD estimate of Mach 0.95 by a considerable margin. Ceiling is 67,558ft, which is lower than Foxbat, although if the Amos missiles have a "snap-up" capability, this should not matter in the slightest. Tactically Foxhound operates in units of four or more, tied to ground control and to each other by data link. Intended as a single mission aircraft, it has since sprouted electronic warfare and defence suppression variants.

* * * *

To recap a moment, the "worst case" scenario of the cold war period was always a major conflict between East and West in Central Europe. The East had quantity, the West had quality. Concern in the mind of the Western fighter pilot was rooted in the possibility of being ground down by superior numbers. Many pilots questioned by the author during this period opted for simpler fighters and many more of them. In the East, there seems little doubt that the fear was of being cut to pieces by superior technology, sustaining a high loss to kill ratio. The war might be won, but the fighter pilots wanted a fair chance of surviving to see the victory. Without this, morale was sure to suffer. A cartoon of the period summed the situation up perfectly; two Soviet officers were watching the victory parade in Paris; one saying to the other "pity we lost the air battle!"

The thought of going up against fighters which could detect them first, shoot them first, and outperform and outmanoeuvre them when the range closed, must have given Soviet Flogger pilots many sobering moments. They would have felt threatened even before contact was made, and this was guaranteed to engender a defensive attitude hardly conducive to combat efficiency. Once battle had been joined, seeing their comrades blown away from ranges at which they could not strike back would have exacerbated the situation even more. All any fighter pilot asked was an even chance, something which would allow him to exercise his skill to affect the outcome. What he wanted was a new fighter with weapon systems good enough to engage in BVR combat with a fair chance of success, combined with enough performance and agility to match those of the enemy.

Somewhere about 1969, two Soviet design bureaux began work. The Mikoyan OKB had dominated the Soviet fighter scene for so long that the word MiG had become synonymous with fighter. Less well known was the Sukhoi OKB, which had been responsible for the Su-15 Flagon series of heavy interceptors and the Su-7/-17 series of attack aircraft. Mikoyan set to work on an agile tactical fighter in the F-16 class to replace Flogger in the air superiority role, while the Sukhoi project was for a long range interceptor in the F-15 class with at least similar agility. Similarities in layout between the two were the result of research carried out by the Moscow based Central Institute of Aero-Hydrodynamics (TsAGI) and adapted by each OKB to suit individual concepts.

Mikoyan MiG-29 Fulcrum

Early in 1977, the MiG-29 prototype made its first flight from the Ramenskoye (now called Zukhovsky) experimental airfield near Moscow, in the hands of test pilot

The MiG-29 Fulcrum is an agile middleweight, with a combined radar/IRST detection system combined with laser ranging which gives super-accurate air to air gunnery. It has achieved moderate success in the export field, but in combat, it achieved nothing in Iraqi service. (Swedish Air Force via FlygvapenNytt).

Alexsandr Fedotov. Series production commenced in 1982, and it entered service in 1984. By this time it had been given the NATO reporting name of Fulcrum.

The veil of secrecy surrounding Soviet military aircraft lifted a little in July 1986, when six MiG-29s visited Finland. Then in September 1988, not just one, but two Fulcrums, a single seater MiG-29A and a two seater MiG-29UB, came to Farnborough, the first visit of a modern Soviet fighter to a Western air show.

Fulcrum was dimensionally similar to the Hornet and of comparable weight. Two Isotov RD-33 low bypass ratio augmented turbofans, rated at 18,300lb wet and 11,110lb dry, gave a t/w ratio at combat weight well in excess of unity. One noticeable feature was that at full military power the engines were smoky, something that Western designers have tried hard (not always successfully) to eradicate, as it adds to the aircraft's visual signature considerably. Time between overhauls was 350 hours, low by Western standards.

The rectangular intakes were of variable geometry to permit the advertised speed of Mach 2.3 plus, and had one absolutely unique feature. The variable angle top hinged ramp could actually let down to close the intake completely, air being drawn through louvres on the LERX upper surfaces to feed the engines. This caused a flurry of speculation. One canard was that an excess of thrust at flight idle made taxying on icy surfaces hazardous (the F-16 had had a similar problem) which could be cured by reducing the airflow. Another was that the blanks shielded the compressor face from the prying emissions of enemy fighter radars, and was therefore a stealth measure.

97

Simple answers are always the best, and the Russians soon confirmed that the intake blanks are an anti-FOD measure intended to keep foreign matter out of the low-slung inlets when operating from semi-prepared or damaged airstrips. It was then speculated that they closed when weight was on the main gear legs. This was quickly disproved; in fact they close automatically when airspeed drops to 108kt, which means that they can open and close in flight. Remarkably it is permitted to fly at up to 432kt with them closed, although in this condition, Fulcrum is alpha limited to 22deg. What it did reveal however was an engine that was very tolerant of disturbed airflow.

The wing planform was reminiscent of that of the F-16, with a 40deg leading edge sweep. Leading edge slats and trailing edge flaps operated automatically to assist manoeuvrability, while huge LERX vaguely like those of the Hornet improved high alpha capability. Convex in both cross-section and chord, the LERX were remarkably deep, probably because they had to house the secondary intake louvres and hydraulics. They extended over the intakes to act as compression wedges, modifying the airflow entry angle at high alpha.

The fuselage took the form of a nacelle set between the underslung engines and tapering aft to a Tomcat-like "pancake". Construction used some new (to the Russians) materials. Metal honeycomb was used for the horizontal stabilizers and all control surfaces, while the fins and part of the wingtips were skinned with carbon fibre composites. Fibreglass was extensively used for fuselage skinning aft of the cockpit and the tips of the fins, while the wing and tail spars plus many of the more highly stressed fuselage frames were of titanium alloy. A combination of electron beam and argon welding allowed the fuselage fuel tanks to be integral. The finish was the usual Soviet "good enough", with plenty of access panels held by quick release fasteners.

In one way, Fulcrum was the last of the dinosaurs in having a conventional hydraulic control system. As the engines were contained in their own nacelles, the main gear was located inboard on the wing, retracting forward into the thick section just aft of the LERX. This position restricted ground clearance if excessive length was to be avoided, which probably gave rise to the anti-FOD doors. The nose gear, with a stone guard on its twin wheels, was set level with the front of the inlets and retracted backwards. A narrow tunnel divided the engine nacelles, and this could be used for a ferry fuel tank. An odd feature of this arrangement was that the tank masked the environmental control system efflux, and the tank had to be formed with a duct through it.

Cockpit visibility was far better than in any previous Soviet fighter, with a bubble canopy and wrap around windshield. Three rear view mirrors were mounted on the canopy bow. Forward vision was partially obstructed by heavy Hud framing, while to the rear, the canopy was faired into a dorsal spine, as in the Mirage 2000, which restricted the view astern. The cockpit layout was old fashioned in concept, with lots of dials and tape instruments. While a few switches were set on the control column, it could not be said to have a proper HOTAS layout. An inadvertent demonstration of the K-36D ejection seat was made at Le Bourget in 1989, when Mikoyan test pilot Anatoly Kvotchur suffered a bird strike at low level. Departing the aircraft just outside the seat parameters, he landed unceremoniously but unharmed a split second after his aircraft impacted the ground.

The tail surfaces were carried on booms outside the line of the engines in the manner of the Eagle. Differentially moving stabilizers were of high aspect ratio, and were more sharply swept than the wings, while the twin fins showed their MiG provenance, the shape being identical to that of Flogger. One odd feature of the fins was that on the single seater they had root extensions reaching almost to the wing leading edge. These are stated to have no aerodynamic function, but housed chaff and flare dispensers. These did not appear on the two seat MiG-29UB, which had no combat capability as it lacked the operational radar, the avionics bay for which had been displaced by moving the front seat forward in order to accommodate the second hole in tandem. Forward view from the rear seat was virtually non-existent, and a periscope was provided for the instructor pilot. Early Fulcrums had ventral strakes beneath the fins for high alpha stability, but these were not featured on the production model, which had extended chord rudders projecting past the fin trailing edges.

The NO-93 radar was a multi-mode pulse Doppler type, with a maximum detection range of 54nm, and tracking range up to 38nm, although the Indian Air Force has reported better than this in practice. Look-down ranges would of course be considerably less. In level flight the radar can be trained up to detect targets 36,000ft above, or down to detect targets 20,000ft below. Not all mode details were released, but it was claimed that up to 10 targets could be simultaneously tracked and priorities assigned automatically.

The radar is backed by other sensors. Ahead of the windshield and offset slightly is an IRST under a domed housing. The IRST gives extremely accurate results at ranges up to 15nm, but lacks ranging capability, which is provided by a laser ranger. Both radar and IRST are linked through the fire control computer; if a target vanishes from one, the other sensor can pick it up, as each sensor is automatically aligned with the other, so that the target is always within the field of view of both. Finally, a helmet mounted sight is integrated into the weapons system, which enables the pilot to make off-boresight target acquisitions. It has been reported that this allows missiles to be launched at targets in the rear hemisphere, but this takes a great deal of swallowing. In practice the AA-11 Archer has an effective off-boresight capability of 60 deg, which is still more than any Western AAM.

The main air to air armament of Fulcrum consists of six missiles carried on underwing pylons, there being insufficient ground clearance for them under the engine nacelles. These are the AA-10 Alamo (Soviet designation R-27) which uses SAR homing in its A variant, and IR homing in the B model. C(SARH) and D(IR) versions, featuring long burn rocket motors for extended range, are also available. Rather smaller than Sparrow, Alamo A and B have an estimated range of 16nm, rising to around 24m for C and D. The Russians claim rather better than this, with 27nm for the baseline R-27, which would probably make 40nm a realistic figure for the extended burn models. These figures are of course for high altitude; in the denser air at sea level they would reduce considerably, typically to one third of the stated values or even less. In the West, IR homers are regarded as essentially visual range weapons, but there is no guarantee that Russia agrees. Long burn IR homing Alamo D would be fine for interception, but might prove embarrassing in a furball at high level, but its extended range could prove very useful down in the weeds. All Alamos were claimed to have a snap-up capability, and to be effective up to 82,000ft, although the launch speed and altitude needed to achieve this level of performance was not stated.

At Farnborough 90, Fulcrum carried Alamos on the inboard pylons and AA-11 Archer (Soviet designation R-73) IR dogfight missiles on the outer pylons. Archer, which appeared to be roughly the size of the Israeli Python 3, was touted as an agile, all-aspect missile with a stated range of just over 4nm. Little was known of its actual capabilities, except that it could be launched at up to 8g, which compared well with the 1.5 to 2g limit of Atoll. Then at Farnborough 92, a Fulcrum appeared with six underwing Amraamskis.

LEFT: *Major General Vladimir Ilyushin, former chief test pilot of the Sukhoi OKB, who took both Flanker A and Flanker B aloft on their maiden flights, seen at Farnborough in 1990.* (Author).

The final air to air weapon carried by Fulcrum is a 30mm GS-301 cannon housed in the port wing root. Weighing only 110lb, it is short on ammunition by Western standards, having only 150 rounds, enough for perhaps five seconds firing. Gun aiming is via IRST, which gives more precise tracking than radar, while the laser provides super-accurate ranging information. According to MiG deputy general designer Mikhail Waldenberg, problems with the gun in the trial stages resulted in it stopping after only four to six rounds had been fired, but even so, the aim was so accurate that the target was invariably destroyed.

Fulcrum performance figures are impressive, with a Vmax of Mach 2.3 plus, service ceiling of 56,000ft, and an initial climb rate of 65,000ft/min. A short takeoff run of 790ft was matched by the 1,970ft landing roll. In the air, Fulcrum appeared closely comparable to Fighting Falcon and Hornet in manoeuvrability, with alpha normally limited to 30deg. Figures from Western sources in 1990 showed in terms of acceleration there is little to choose between the Soviet fighter and Western types. Nor is there much difference in sustained turn rates at low speeds and altitudes, although as speeds increased the Western fighters became progressively superior. At medium altitudes Fulcrum possesses a slight low speed edge, again falling away as speeds increase, while in the thin air at 30,000ft, Fulcrum again performed well at low speeds but dipped out badly in the supersonic regime. At this altitude and Mach 1.6, both the F-16C and the Mirage 2000 have a distinct advantage.

One thing very apparent when Fulcrum was turned hard was that it was a draggier design than its Western opponents, and that this was not quite offset by its tremendous thrust to weight ratio. Its time through a 360deg turn at low level was 17.5sec; marginally slower than the F-16 and almost identical with the F/A-18, but it looked rather more wobbly when rolling out afterwards than the other two. This apart, both pitch and roll

OPPOSITE TOP: *Contrary to Western practice, the two-seater MiG-29UB conversion trainer is not fully combat capable, as the extra place has been squeezed in ahead rather than behind the original seat, and this can only be done at the expense of the radar and IRST.* (Author).

OPPOSITE BELOW: *The mighty Foxhound shows its impressive display of weaponry at Le Bourget in 1991. Also visible from this angle are the flight refuelling probe, looking like an afterthought, and the weapons system operator's position.* (Author).

rates were superb, and demonstration pilots showed total confidence in hurling it around the sky close to the ground. In 1988 Fulcrum introduced the tail slide to Farnborough. Fulcrum was pulled up vertically and throttled back, coming to a halt then sliding backwards before a hard pull on the stick dropped the nose into a steep dive for recovery into normal flight. Stability seemed exceptional, without the slightest trace of wing rock or drop.

In Fulcrum, the Soviet Union produced a worthy opponent for Western fighters. Of course, it was many years later than the Fighting Falcon and Hornet, and it would be surprising if the Russians hadn't caught up, given the time lag between types. The surprising thing was that they did it without benefit of fly by wire and other goodies deemed essential by the West.

Fulcrum A was a mite short on internal fuel, and therefore range, and while the Soviets claimed that the sfc of the RD-33 turbofans was least as good as anything in the West in dry power, and rather better in max, this was wildly optimistic. The next variant was Fulcrum C, with a dorsal hump where greater fuel capacity had been added, and the more capable Zhuk radar. Then on 21 November 1989, a MiG-29K flown by Mikoyan test pilot Tahktar Aubakirov, landed on the deck of the aircraft carrier *Tbilisi*, as it was then called. This aircraft, extensively modified for carrier operations, featured wing folding, an arrester hook, and major structural strengthening to the airframe and landing gear. The IRST housing was different, looking more like the front end of a FLIR, and the fin root extensions housing chaff and flare dispensers were absent, as were the overwing intake louvres and FOD doors. Further modifications were uprated RD-33K turbofans, and two extra underwing hardpoints. On the same day, it made the first ever carrier takeoff by a non-STOVL Russian jet aircraft, using a ski-jump in the manner pioneered by the Sea Harrier. It appears however that as the navalised Flanker has been selected as the new Russian carrier fighter, the MiG-29K will not enter service.

The final variants, both of which appeared at Farnborough 92, were the MiG-29S, described as a high altitude fighter, and featuring advanced computer and sighting systems; and the MiG-29M, which has digital quadruplex FBW and a "glass cockpit" with MFDs. Like the -29K, uprated RD-33K turbofans were fitted, and the overwing intake louvres deleted, the space being occupied by extra fuel tanks. FOD protection is provided by metal grilles, as in Flanker. It has slightly more wing area and vortex generators than earlier models, and the ailerons extend out to the wingtips. It has been reported that the -29M will be redesignated MiG-33, for the export market

Sukhoi Su-27 Flanker

Flanker was the upmarket end of the Soviet fighter pair. Much larger and heavier than Fulcrum, it retained a similar layout. Design work started at about the same time, but its gestation period was considerably more troubled. There can be little doubt that the emergence of the Tomcat in 1970 and the Eagle in 1972 caused considerable reappraisal, and the hardware was a long time in coming. First flight of what was then known as the T-10-1 took place on 20 May 1977, piloted by Sukhoi chief test pilot Vladimir Ilyushin, the son of the founder of the Ilyushin OKB.

The prototype Flanker was dimensionally larger than the F-15. Whereas Western fighters relied heavily on external fuel tanks to increase operational radius, the Soviet aircraft followed the trend set by Foxbat by having simply enormous internal capacity. While this made a big fighter even bigger, it had the dual benefits of eliminating the drag of external tanks while leaving all hardpoints free for weaponry. Like its MiG contemporary, the Sukhoi fighter had two afterburning turbofans set in widely spaced nacelles, with the cockpit mounted centrally behind a large radar nose. Very high aspect ratio twin vertical fins were mounted above the engines and set forward like those of the Hornet. The wings, led by simple blended body LERX, were of also of rather high aspect ratio for a fighter, with rounded tips, and fences to inhibit spanwise flow. Three-channel analogue fly by wire was incorporated plus a mechanical backup, allowing relaxed stability to be used. The Sukhoi OKB had previously gained FBW experience with the Su-100 high speed research aircraft of 1972 vintage.

Problems were encountered during the flight test programme, chief among which was lack of directional stability at speeds above Mach 2, while operational studies showed Flanker A to be very much inferior to the F-15. Nor was the FBW software perfected without loss; two Sukhoi test pilots, one of whom was Evgeny Soloviev, died in accidents before they got it right.

The result was an almost total redesign. Speaking to Vladimir Ilyushin, by now a major general, at Farnborough 90, the author was told that while the centre section remained the same, virtually everything else was rehashed. Even the cockpit was enlarged! The result was the production article, Flanker B, which made its first flight, again piloted by Vladimir Ilyushin, on April 20, 1981. Service entry was in 1986, three years later than Fulcrum, despite the prototype's earlier first flight. The Soviet fighter pilots appeared to enjoy their new mount, and instances occurred of them buzzing Norwegian Air force Orion patrol aircraft, incidentally giving the West their first really good look at the type. One, obviously misjudging the size of his machine, actually came close enough to catch his fin tip in an Orion's propeller. Fortunately damage was slight, and both aircraft returned safely.

Late in 1986 it was announced that Sukhoi test pilot Viktor Pugachev, flying an aircraft identified as the P-42, which was a stripped Su-27 powered by two Tumansky R-32 engines, had set a new time to altitude record of 25.373sec to 3,000m. This was followed by times of 30.050sec to 6,000m; 44.176sec to 9,000m; 55.542sec to 12,000m; and 70.329sec to 15,000m. Nikolai Sadovnikov was the other pilot involved. The previous times had all been set by the F-15 Streak Eagle. This served notice on the world that if the Soviet Union had not already caught up with the West, in some areas it was closing fast.

The attendance of Fulcrum at Farnborough in 1988 had been remarkable, but was to a degree understandable in that Russia wanted to export the type. But Flanker was simply in a different league. When in October that year, rumour control mooted the possibility of Flanker appearing at Le Bourget in 1989, the idea was widely scouted. Confirmation was only forthcoming at the last minute, and two Flankers, one of them the previously unseen (in the West) two seat Su-27UB, duly arrived, having flown from Moscow on internal fuel only.

The definitive Flanker B was a large aircraft, powered by two Lyulka AL-31F afterburning turbofans, each rated at 27,557lb static thrust, giving a t/w ratio at normal combat weight well in excess of unity. Like the MiG-29, these were widely spaced, apparently a TsAGI recommendation. The huge inlets were rectangular in section, with variable ramps, side walls raked back at a steep angle, and optimised for speeds well in excess of Mach 2. The raked lips reverted to the vertical for the bottom few inches to minimise spillage drag. Retractable titanium mesh guards protected the inlets from FOD; the thought was inescapable that they were a useful measure against the inadvertent ingestion of mechanics on the ground as much as birds in flight.

The wings, fronted by large LERX, were of simple planform with a 42deg leading edge sweep, and blended smoothly into the fuselage. The wing fences seen on Flanker A were gone, and the rounded tips squared off with missile rails. Slats occupied most of the previously plain leading edge, while single control surfaces, combining the functions of both ailerons and flaps were located inboard on the trailing edges. Aspect ratio was considerably greater than that of the F-15 Eagle, presumably being tailored for sustained turn performance at the cost of a slight drag increment at high Mach numbers and a small penalty in rate of roll. The formerly plain LERX were now ogival, and set over the intakes, served to lessen airflow entry angle at high alpha.

The extremely tall vertical tail surfaces had been relocated from their former position above the engines onto booms running outside them, as in the F-15. This was the fix for a directional stability problem at speeds in excess of Mach 2. Ventral fins, another feature not seen on Flanker A, were mounted below them. The booms also carried the horizontal tail surfaces, which were of completely different design to Flanker A, with cropped tips possibly indicating the solution to a flutter problem.

Like its smaller compatriot, Flanker's fuselage took the form of a nacelle between and above the engines. Its diameter was fixed by the radar antenna, which was sized for long range detection. So large was the radome that the demands of area ruling showed an obvious slimming of the fuselage cross-section as it passed the cockpit and reached the LERX. Aft of the cockpit, the fuselage tapered away to a pancake with a long bullet fairing to reduce base drag; another modification to the earlier variant. Deputy Chief Designer Constantin Marbashev told the author that while Flanker B contained little in the way of composites, much of the structure was titanium alloy.

Flanker's internal fuel capacity is a massive 22,000lb, although the full amount is only carried in the overload condition where long range is at a premium. A digital fuel control system maintains the centre of gravity within limits. This vast capacity is only achieved at a cost in vulnerability, although like most Western fighters, Flanker is a "foam jet", with polystyrene foam in the fuel tanks to reduce the chance of an explosion due to battle damage. Almost certainly it is g limited when the overload tanks are full.

Like Fulcrum, Flanker's main gear is located beneath the wings and retracts forward into the thick section astern of the LERXs. The double wheel nose gear is located behind the cockpit and retracts forward, unlike that of Flanker A, which had been set forward and retracted aft. The location was changed when, like Fulcrum, it was found necessary to bring more weight onto the nosewheel to improve ground handling. Originally the speed brakes were also part of the main gear doors, but on Flanker B this idea was dropped, and it was fitted with a single dorsal surface similar to that of the F-15.

Flanker B's cockpit is large and roomy, with a wrap around windshield, and has three rear view mirrors on the canopy bow. The K-36DM zero/zero ejection seat is raked back at about 25deg and set high, which brings the cockpit sills well below shoulder level. This gives excellent vision down over the sides, while the rear view, through a large bubble transparency broken only by a slim intermediate arch, is as good as anything the West has to offer. The Hud restricts frontal vision very little, while the IRST tracker mounted in front of the windshield obstructs the view ahead not at all, as the author can testify. Instrumentation is conventional, though an obvious move towards HOTAS has been made, the control column being festooned with buttons and switches.

The radar is a pulse Doppler multi-mode type with a very large antenna, and has an estimated maximum detection range of 130nm, and a tracking range in the region of 100nm. While multiple tracking is no problem, Marbashev stated in 1990 that while

Flanker had no simultaneous target engagement capability, this was a shortcoming of the missiles rather than the radar. What is known for certain is that much of the long delay before service entry was caused by problems with the radar, parallelling events with Tornado F.3's Foxhunter.

Like Fulcrum, Flanker's weapons system contains an IRST and laser ranger integrated with the radar, coupled with a helmet mounted sight. A 30mm GS-301 cannon is mounted in the starboard LERX, with 240 rounds. Flanker has stations for no less than ten missiles, of the same types carried by and described with Fulcrum. Apart from wingtip rails, all are carried on pylons, with no conformal or semi-submerged carriage, although two are mounted in drag-reducing tandem in the tunnel between the engines.

If Fulcrum's flying display at Farnborough 88 had startled the West, Flanker at Paris 89 was simply amazing. It was not just the short takeoff run, the acceleration, the tight turns and the general agility shown; we had expected that. What we did not expect was Pugachev's Cobra manoeuvre in which, starting from level flight at moderate speed (about 240kt) it suddenly reared up on end to an alpha of approximately 100deg in the space of one second, before pitching nose down, apparently completely under control. This demonstration of extreme manoeuvrability, was taken to what appeared to be its limit at Farnborough 90, when alphas of about 120deg were regularly achieved, although recovery from this angle was slower and showed signs of yaw.

The Russians have stated that both the tail slide and the Cobra are valid combat manoeuvres; the first to break a radar lock and the second to force an opponent to overshoot. Who says they have no sense of humour? The tail slide involves a complete loss of speed, which is potentially suicidal when enemy fighters are around, while using the Cobra to force an overshoot implies an opponent astern and closing to guns range. All it does is present the planform with no apparent motion; the easiest possible target. In fact, Flanker is normally limited to an alpha of 26deg, while as at August 1991, only four Russian test pilots had been cleared to perform the Cobra at airshows only.

Unlike the MiG-29UB, the two seater Su-27UB is fully combat capable, retaining the radar and associated weapons systems, plus full agility. The second hole is set high in tandem, giving a good view forward for the instructor. This involves a moderate reduction in fuel tankage, and a deeper central fuselage. To preserve stability, the vertical tails were increased in size.

A prototype designated T-10-24 commenced flight trials in 1985. With moving canard foreplanes to improve short landing characteristics by allowing a flatter approach angle, this aircraft was fitted with thrust vectoring nozzles in 1988, apparently with unimpressive results. Then in 1989, the Su-27K, a navalised Flanker B-2, also with canard foreplanes, carried out deck landing trials on the *Tbilisi*. Fitted with wing folding which entailed split flaperons, and a hook for arrested landings, this featured a shortened tailcone to increase deck clearance on landing. It also had a flight refuelling probe. Flankers at sea are to operate the buddy refuelling system. Takeoff is from a ski-jump, or at light weights, from a level deck without catapult assistance. The undercarriage of all Flankers was stressed for a high sink rate, and no extra structural strengthening was needed.

Like many successful designs, Flanker seems to have spawned a whole range of variants. Shown for the first time at Minsk early in 1992 was the Su-271B, a side by side two seater with a flattened, chined nose, which was promptly dubbed the Platypus. Officially a fighter-bomber, if it can survive defence cuts, it is expected to replace early model Su-24 Fencers in Russian service from about 1996. Yet another attack variant is the Su-30MK, which was revealed at Le Bourget in 1993. More or less an F-15E equivalent, and like it retaining considerable air combat capability, it is externally almost indistinguishable from the Su-27UB. At Farnborough 90, Vladimir Ilyushin told the author that an airborne command post variant was under development. Fitted with suitable avionics and communications, the Su-30MK is apparently it. How well this concept will work is anybody's guess, but historically it has never yet succeeded.

The T-10-24 prototype first flown in 1985 finally broke cover at Farnborough in 1992 as the Su-35 Super Flanker. Slightly larger and heavier than its predecessors, it differs in detail, with wingtip pods and square tipped fins. It has retained the canards, which have led to the delightful brochure description of the Su-35 as "the first in the world production unstable integrated triplane..." It also has an "embedded 30mm gun."

Performance differs little from the Su-27, but it is much superior in other ways. It is powered by uprated Lyulka AL-31SM turbofans with modified intakes to suit. A new multi-mode radar has both terrain avoidance and terrain following modes, and in the air to air mission, detection range is stated to be up to 216nm. At least 15 targets can be tracked simultaneously, and six engaged, while the record number of 14 AAMs can be carried.

CHAPTER NINE

The Nearly Birds

The nature of competition ensures that there will be losers as well as winners. Of these, the YF-17 Cobra/F-18L Hornet has already been mentioned. Dozens of others never got past the paper aeroplane stage, while a mere handful actually became hardware, and although very impressive, failed to enter service.

In 1980, the Carter Administration reversed an earlier decision forbidding the private venture development of fighters specifically for export. The guidelines laid down stated that an export fighter should be less capable and less costly than the F-16A. This decision had been anticipated, and two contenders quickly emerged; Northrop with the single engined F-5G variant of their very successful F-5E Tiger II, and General Dynamics with the F-16/79 version of the Fighting Falcon.

General Dynamics F-16/79 Fighting Falcon

The major difference between the F-16A and the F-16/79 lay in the engine. General Electric developed a version of the tried and proven J79 turbojet, designated the -17X, to replace the F100 P&W turbofan, and one of the original development F-16Bs was modified as a demonstrator. The J79-GE-17X was a single spool turbojet rather longer and heavier than the turbofan it supplanted, with a smaller mass airflow. To accommodate it, the rear fuselage of the F-16B was extended by 18 inches aft of the horizontal tail pivots, and the intake redesigned. Fortunately the F-16 intake had been conceived as a single replaceable component. The revised intake, distinguished only by an extended upper lip, slotted into place with a minimum of fuss.

Turbofans are cooled by bypass air flowing around the hot core, whereas turbojets have no such amenity. To protect the rear fuselage from excessive heat buildup, a steel shield surrounded most of the J79, and this weighed almost 2,000lb. These changes took barely four months to complete, and the first flight of the F-16/79 came in October 1980; nearly two years ahead of its Northrop rival.

While the J79-GE-17X had a higher rating than the standard -17, thrust was still less than that of the F100. Nor, in most flight regimes, was its sfc anywhere near as low. This, plus the weight penalty of the heat shield and other structural changes, degraded performance and range. Only at high speed/high altitude combinations, where the turbojet was superior to the turbofan, was there any performance improvement, and this was marginal. The F-16/79 was evaluated by many nations, but none were willing to take such a blatantly second best aircraft, even though it was demonstrably superior to many of its rivals. It was finally buried when the Reagan Administration released the F-16A and B for general export.

Northrop F-5G (Later F-20) Tigershark

Way back in the dim and distant past, Northrop had developed a lightweight fighter under the auspices of the US Military Aid Program, for sale to aligned air forces which wanted supersonic capability but were unable to afford, or were not cleared to receive, the latest "full-up" models. Based on the T-38 Talon supersonic trainer, this was the

N-156F, armed with two 20mm revolver cannon and two Sidewinders on wingtip rails. It was powered by two small J85 turbojets designed by GE as simple disposable missile engines. Designated F-5A Freedom Fighter, it was unkindly dubbed the Air Inferiority Fighter.

The F-5A was duly developed into the much more potent F-5E Tiger II, with much more powerful J85-GE-21 engines, a slightly larger wing area with small LERX, a stretched fuselage, extended intakes, better avionics and the Emerson APQ-153 radar. Noted for its exceptional handling qualities, the F-5E remains in service world-wide, and is probably best remembered as the mount of the now defunct USAF Aggressor Squadrons.

As recounted in Chapters 4 and 5, the YF-17 had been defeated by the YF-16 in the LWF competition, while the original Cobra concept had been overtaken by events. While Northrop put much of their effort into the ill-fated F-18L Hornet, it was obvious that the F-5 series was capable of further development, and that there was a large potential market for it. Studies commenced in 1978, the goal being to achieve F-16 capability at a considerably lower price. The new fighter duly emerged as the F-5G Tigershark, and it was confidently predicted to have a great future.

The original Tigershark designation of F-5G was a serious marketing error. It implied a rehashed F-5E, with its melange of positive and negative connotations; affordable (cheap); upgraded (basically old-hat); compromise (second rate). F-20, as it was redesignated, implied a new and up to date fighter; which considering the predicted improvements in performance and capability, gave a much truer picture.

The Tigershark made its first flight on 30 August 1982 from Edwards AFB, piloted by Northrop test pilot Russ Scott. While in general appearance it was very similar to the Tiger II, some important changes had been made. The most obvious one was the powerplant; the two small J85s had been supplanted by a single F404-GE-100 augmented turbofan, a more powerful denavalised variant of the engine used in the Hornet, rated at 18,000lb static thrust at maximum throttle. This gave a t/w ratio in excess of unity with guns loaded, carrying two Sidewinders and full internal fuel.

Converting a twin engined fighter into a single was a major undertaking, especially as it was essential to retain the excellent handling characteristics of the earlier machine. The F404 was slightly longer than the J85, and while of greater diameter, did not occupy the same width as the two turbojets. To accommodate the extra length, a 5in plug was inserted, and the rear fuselage was redesigned with a basically circular cross-section. To reproduce the outstanding longitudinal stability of the F-5E, it was desirable to retain the wide and flat ventral surface of the rear fuselage. To do this, shelves were added outside the line of the engine. These commenced a little way behind the intakes and ran the full length of the aft fuselage to the trailing edge of the horizontal tail surfaces. The intakes were increased in size to suit the increased mass flow of the F404, and given fixed ramps compatible with speeds up to Mach 2.

At the front end, a revised nose shape, slightly more rounded in plan but flattened in elevation, the so-called "shark nose" which gave rise to the soubriquet of Tigershark, was used to improve stability at high alpha. Sluggishness in pitch had been the only real handling fault of the F-5E, primarily because the centre of gravity was just that bit too far forward. On the F-5G it was moved aft a trifle, and coupled with a closed loop digital pitch control augmentation system. This improved pitch rates by reducing trim drag.

The cockpit was designed from scratch. As one would have expected from a company so closely associated with the Hornet, HOTAS was fitted. An improved canopy gave

RIGHT ABOVE: *The F-20 Tigershark could be airborne with all systems combat capable one minute from start-up. Had it been bought by the USAF, it would probably have found many takers world-wide. (Northrop).*

RIGHT BELOW: *The ancestor of the Tigershark was the F-5E Tiger II, which apart from the avionics fit, differed mainly from the later fighter in having two J85 turbojets rather than a single F404. This lineup is the 527th Aggressor Squadron at Alconbury. (M. Prescott).*

better all-round vision than that of the F-5E, although as it was faired into the dorsal spine, rearward view did not match that of the F-16. The flight control system was conventional apart from the horizontal stabilisers, where duplex FBW with mechanical backup was used. This configuration actually gave one advantage. With FBW, alpha and g limiters are part of the system. The Tigershark had no such limits, and if a pilot really needed to exceed them, say in a life or death combat situation, he could. The F-5E had been virtually spinproof, (although don't try telling that to my old Aggressor pal Spence Roberts, who managed to spin one inverted when the cg got out of limits). The same quality in the Tigershark made the need for alpha limits less important than might otherwise have been the case.

The redesigned fin was rather smaller than that of the F-5E, this reduction having been made possible by improved airflow around the rear fuselage, and it was set on a squared off fairing, which was also stated to give extra lift, with the drag chute at the rear and a ram air intake at the front. Horizontal tail surfaces were increased in size and mounted on the shelves. Carbon fibre composites were extensively used on all tail surfaces, together with metal honeycomb.

The wings featured refined and extended LERX, but were otherwise generally similar to those of the F-5E, with a very moderate leading edge sweep angle, although they were beefed up to allow a 9g loading instead of the previous 7.33g, primarily by using thicker skinning. Manoeuvre flaps took up most of the leading edge, while on the trailing edge, flaps occupied the inboard section with ailerons in the centre. Like the F-5E, the main gear was wing mounted at about one third of the span, retracting inboard, while the nose gear was located forward.

In its early days, when Tigershark was viewed primarily as a lightweight fighter for export, the proposed avionics fit was basic. The missile armament consisted of just two Sidewinders mounted on wingtip rails which incidentally acted as anti-flutter weights, and the two 20mm M39A revolver cannon of the F-5E were retained. Then when the F-16A was cleared for export, the picture changed. Something much better was wanted in order to compete.

It was at this point that a glass cockpit was adopted, with two MFDs, together with a much more capable avionics fit. The radar selected was the pulse Doppler General Electric APG-67(V). This had a total of 17 modes, eight of them air to air and a further seven air to surface. Detection range against fighter sized targets was stated as 50nm and tracking range 30nm. Ten targets could be tracked simultaneously and target priority order assigned to eight of them. The two cannon were retained, and the missile armament increased to two AIM-7 Sparrows, with future Amraam capability when this weapon became available, plus two Sidewinders. An alternative missile load was six 'winders. The other black boxes were in keeping; the most impressive being the Honeywell Laser Inertial Navigation System. This last could be aligned for combat in just 22 seconds, which allowed very fast scramble times.

Tigershark performance figures were impressive. A Vmax of Mach 2 was combined with an initial climb rate of 53,800ft/min and a combat ceiling of 55,000ft. It could be at 32,000ft just 2.5 minutes after the order to scramble, and at 10,000ft it took only 28 seconds to accelerate from Mach 0.3 to Mach 0.9. At sea level it could reach 800kt indicated. Demonstrated at Le Bourget in 1983 and Farnborough in 1984, it showed up well against the all-FBW Mirage 2000, especially in transient performance, as it had very fast pitch and roll rates. On the ground it set new standards for reliability and maintainability, often flying six sorties a day. It looked a winner.

There was just one problem. Re-engining had given a thrust increment of nearly 75 percent, while weight growth was less than 20 percent. While the Tigershark was stressed for 9g, manoeuvrability is dependent on more than a high t/w ratio; it also demands a moderate wing loading. In what seems to have been a blunder of the first order, the wing area stayed the same as that of the F-5E, with the result that the extra weight made the wing loading too high. And it showed. The F-5E had not been the best turning aircraft around, and the F-20 was little better at subsonic speeds. Only in the high supersonic regime was there any real improvement, and with a much faster aircraft this was only to be expected. To give some idea of the problem, F-20 sustained turn at Mach 0.9 at 15,000ft was just 9.7deg/sec. This compared poorly against 12.8deg/sec for the F-16 and 11.8deg/sec for the F-15, and was little better than the 9deg/sec of the F-4E. What was needed was a larger wing to give more lifting surface in proportion to the weight. This was duly proposed, with a 30 percent increase in area, but by this time it was too late; potential client nations were increasingly turning to the F-16. It was also too late for two Northrop test pilots. Darrell Cornell crashed shortly after Farnborough 84, and David Barnes shortly before Le Bourget 85. Both accidents occurred when they were practicing display routines, g-induced loss of consciousness (G-loc) probably being the culprit. Just one prototype was left, plus another partly built.

Selection by the USAF or USN is widely regarded as a mark of quality by overseas clients, and the lack of this proved an obstacle to Tigershark sales. The only home slot available was as the USAF's new air defence fighter. When in the autumn of 1986 the F-16 was chosen for this role, the F-20, which with a bigger wing could have been a really great fighter, was terminated.

General Dynamics F-16F

One area in which a lot of interest was shown in the late 'eighties was supercruise, the ability to cruise at supersonic speeds for extended periods; a subject which is dealt with in Chapter 13. However, the benefits of supercruise were under investigation many years earlier. General Dynamics worked intensively on the subject between 1976 and 1980, in which year SCAMP (Supersonic Cruise and Manoeuvring Project), based on the F-16, was revealed. Initially a private venture, SCAMP was later backed by the USAF, and in mid-1981 two full scale development F-16s were transferred to GD's Fort Worth facility to be rebuilt to SCAMP standard, designated F-16XL.

The first F-16XL was a single seater powered by Pratt & Whitney's F100 turbofan, the standard F-16 powerplant at that time. The new aircraft was a tail-less delta with a wing of cranked arrow planform developed by NASA for the supersonic cruise condition. This had several effects. It more than doubled wing area, which greatly reduced wing loading, giving more instantaneous manoeuvre potential. At the same time it allowed a massive increase of over 80 percent in internal fuel, bringing the fuel fraction up to 38 percent.

On the new wing LERX did not really exist as such, and the leading edge commenced further back, level with the rear of the canopy, first curving outwards, then sweeping back at a very sharp angle on the inboard section. It then cranked back at about 30deg for the final third of the span. The Sidewinder rails were retained on the wingtips. To reduce spanwise flow, which on such a sharply swept wing would have been considerable, small fences were located at the break, with aerodynamic fairings; "Kuchemann carrots" astern of them and projecting past the trailing edge. The fixed cambered section of the leading edge inboard changed to large slats on the outboard section of the leading edge, and two piece flaperons occupied the trailing edge. The ledges which had previously carried the

horizontal tail surfaces were retained, albeit with a refined shape. The fuselage was stretched by 4.67ft, and fin height was increased by 11 inches.

The single seat F-16XL made its first flight from Fort Worth on 15 July 1982, flown by GD test pilot Jim McKinney. The two seater, propelled by the more powerful General Electric F101 Derivative Fighter Engine, the forerunner of the F110, followed on 29 October of the same year, with Alex Wolf in the front seat and Jim McKinney in the back. Handling qualities were good although very different from the standard F-16, compared to which it was stated to give a much more "solid" ride. Surprisingly, the alphas needed at takeoff and landing were much less than those required by conventional deltas.

The F-16F, as it was hopefully designated, could only supercruise by using afterburner even with the larger F101DFE engine, and despite its huge internal fuel capacity, its endurance in this regime was generally considered insufficient. And while the large wing area had brought wing loading down, it increased empty weight, and the addition of an extra 2⅔ tonnes of fuel aggravated the situation by reducing t/w ratio, with a consequent reduction in sustained turn performance. It did however show certain advantages over the standard F-16. Load for load its tactical radius was about half as far again, while its long wing chord permitted most of its bombload to be carried in drag reducing tandem. With 12 Mk 82 500lb bombs carried on low-drag pylons, it could wind up to Mach 1.2, which was outstanding.

After 940 flying hours spread over 798 sorties, the F-16F flight test programme ended in August 1985. One of the official reasons given was that in a large measure it duplicated the dual role mission of the McDonnell Douglas F-15E. Then in 1989, both F-16Fs were returned to flight status with NASA in investigations into boundary layer flow at supersonic speeds, but at this stage no possibility of service adoption remained.

The F-16XL, later redesignated F-16F, of cranked delta configuration, was built under Project SCAMP to investigate supersonic cruise and manoeuvrability. This aircraft is currently used by NASA in supersonic airliner research. (GD).

A clear view of the wing planform of the F-16F, which is also carrying no less than 12 Mk 82 500lb bombs. Even with this load, the F-16F could still attain Mach 1.2. (GD).

Israel Aircraft Industries Lavi

Israel has been embroiled in more wars in recent times than any other nation, with the result that Israeli flyers are very combat experienced, and most likely to know exactly what they want in a fighter, within the constraints of affordability. When in 1979 the Lavi programme was announced, a great deal of interest was aroused for these very reasons.

As originally conceived, Lavi was to have been a light attack aircraft to replace the elderly Skyhawks and Kfirs remaining in Israeli service. A single seater powered by a General Electric F404 turbofan, it was soon perceived that this solution gave no margin for growth, and an alternative engine was chosen, the much more powerful Pratt & Whitney PW1120, rated at 20,260lb static thrust wet and 13,550lb dry. This engine was based on the core of the F100, with a new LP compressor and turbine, and a redesigned afterburner. With the extra power came demands for greater capability, until Lavi began to rival the F-16, which was already in Israeli service.

Comparisons with the F-16 were inevitable, as the American fighter made a handy yardstick. Lavi was rather smaller and lighter, with a less powerful engine, and the t/w ratio was slightly lower across the board. The configuration adopted was that of a tail-less canard delta, although the wing was unusual in having shallow sweep on the trailing edge, giving a fleche planform. The straight leading edge was swept at 54deg, with manoeuvre flaps on the outboard sections. The tips were cropped and fitted with missile rails to carry Sidewinder, Shafrir, or Python AAMs. Two piece flaperons occupied most of the trailing edge, which was blended into the fuselage with long fillets. Wing area was 414 square feet, 38 percent greater than that of the F-16, giving an almost exactly

113

proportionally lower wing loading, while aspect ratio, at 2.1, was barely two thirds that of the American aircraft. Pitch control was provided by single piece, all-moving canard surfaces, located slightly astern of and below the pilot where they would cause minimal obstruction to vision.

Predictably, relaxed static stability and quadruplex FBW with no mechanical backup was used, linked to nine different control surfaces to give a true Control Configured Vehicle(CCV). These surfaces were programmed to give minimum drag in all flight regimes, while providing optimum handling and agility. It was stated, although to the best of the writer's knowledge never demonstrated, that Lavi had an inherent direct lift control capability.

The engine intake was a plain chin type scoop, similar to that of the F-16, which was known to be satisfactory at high alpha and sideslip angles. The landing gear was lightweight, the nose wheel located aft of the intake retracting rearwards, and the main gear was fuselage mounted, giving a rather narrow track. The sharply swept vertical tail, effective at high alpha due to interaction with the vortices shed by the canards, was mounted on a spine on top of the rear fuselage, and supplemented by two steeply canted ventral strakes mounted on the ends of the wing root fillets. Extensive use of composites allowed aeroelastic tailoring to the wings, so that the often conflicting demands of shape and rigidity could be resolved to minimise drag in all flight regimes. Composites were also used in the vertical tail, canards, and various doors and panels. IAI claimed a significant reduction in radar cross-section.

Internal fuel load was 6,000lb; some 16 percent less than the F-16, although this was claimed to be offset by the low drag of the Lavi airframe and the low sfc of its engine. Single point high pressure refuelling was adopted for quick turnaround, and provision made for air refuelling with a female type receptacle compatible with flying boom-equipped tankers. To aid the flight test programme, Lavi prototypes were also equipped with bolt-on refuelling probes.

Standard practice with high performance jets is to provide a second seat for conversion training by shoehorning it in, normally at the expense of fuel, avionics, or both. IAI adopted a different approach, designing the two seater first, then adapting it into a single seater, which left plenty of room for avionics growth. In fact, the first 30 production aircraft would all have been two seaters to aid service entry. Many of these aircraft were later to have been kitted out for the defence suppression role.

The cockpit contained some surprises. As was expected, a wrap around windshield and bubble canopy gave excellent all-round vision. But where a steeply raked seat and sidestick controller similar to the F-16 might have been expected, IAI selected a conventional upright seat and central control column. The reasoning was as follows. The raked seat raised the pilot's knees, causing a reduction in panel space which could ill be spared, while neck and shoulder strains were common in the F-16 when a pilot craned around in his steeply raked seat to search the sky astern while pulling high g. The sidestick controller was faulted on three counts. Firstly it virtually neutralised the starboard console space; secondly with a force transducer it was difficult for an instructor pilot to know precisely what a pupil was trying to do; while thirdly, in the event of quite a minor injury to the right arm, the pilot would not be able to recover the aircraft to base. With a central stick, Lavi could be flown left-handed with little difficulty. The cockpit layout was state of the art, with HOTAS, and a wide angle diffractive optics Hud surmounting an up-front control panel, through which most of the systems were operated. Three MFDs, two monochrome and one colour, dominated the dash. The avionics suite

was stated to be entirely of Israeli design, with an Elta multi-mode pulse Doppler radar. Flexibility and situational awareness were emphasised to reduce pilot workload. An electronic warning system capable of threat identification and automatic deception and jamming was carried internally.

Weapons carriage was mainly semi-conformal, thus reducing drag, with three hardpoints beneath each wing, plus the tip rail. The main air to air weapon was the Python 3, an Israeli-designed short range IR homing dogfight missile, while a 30mm DEFA cannon was housed in the starboard wing root.

The first Lavi flew on 30 December 1986, piloted by IAI Chief Test Pilot Menachem Schmul. Handling was described as excellent, with a high degree of stability in crosswind landings, and the flight test programme proceeded apace. But even before it flew, the storm clouds were gathering. Lavi had been heavily financed by the USA, and a dispute arose as to the final unit cost, the Israeli figure being far less than American calculations showed. The end came when the US Congress withdrew financial support, by which time three Lavis were flying. It is doubtful whether the flight performance envelope had been completely explored, but it seems probable that Lavi would have been at least the equal of the F-16C in most departments, and possibly even superior in some. It had been calculated that Lavi could reef into a turn a full half second quicker than the F-16, simply because a conventional tailed fighter suffers a slight delay while the tailplane takes up a download, whereas with a canard fighter reaction is instantaneous. By the same token, pointability of canard fighters is quicker and more precise. Where Lavi might really have scored heavily was in supersonic manoeuvrability, basically due to the lower wave drag of a canard delta. But this was not to be.

115

Dassault Super Mirage 4000

In September 1976, just six months after the Mirage 2000C was ordered by l'Armee de l'Air, Dassault launched a new project. This was the Super Mirage 4000, a heavyweight multi-mission fighter. Basically it was a scaled up 2000 with twin engines, and much of the technology and aerodynamics developed for the smaller fighter was duplicated, thus minimising development costs; an important factor as this was initially a company funded private venture. There being no Armee de l'Air requirement, it was conceived primarily as an export fighter, with Saudi Arabia seen as the most likely launch customer. During the early years, it was widely believed, though never confirmed, that the Saudis made considerable development funding available.

The Super Mirage 4000 made its maiden flight from Istres on March 9, 1979, piloted by Dassault Chief Test Pilot Jean-Marie Saget, and reached Mach 1.2 on its first outing. It was obviously a much larger aeroplane than its sibling. Combat weight was 35,490lb, some 79 percent higher, while maximum takeoff weight was an astronomical 70,500lb; 94 percent up. It was powered by two SNECMA M53 afterburning turbofans as used in the smaller fighter, giving it a rather higher t/w ratio across the board, while the wing area of 783 square feet showed a 78 percent increase, giving an almost identical loading at combat weight. While maximum speeds at both high and low level were much the same as the Mirage 2000, gains were made across the rest of the performance spectrum. The operational ceiling was 5,000ft higher at 65,000ft. Time to Mach 2 at 50,000ft was just three minutes, a full minute less, while range with external tanks was more than doubled.

In external appearance the "large Mirage" was very similar to the smaller, the only differences being two engines instead of one, a more rounded radome, a true bubble canopy with no dorsal spine, a different system of engine bleed doors, and moving canard foreplanes mounted on the intake ducts in lieu of fixed strakes. The Super Mirage 4000 being a much heavier aircraft than the 2000, there was far more inertia to overcome when changing flight attitudes, and canards were found to be more effective than conventional control surfaces.

The wing was identical, with a 58deg leading edge sweep and full span slats, operated automatically in conjunction with two piece trailing edge flaperons to give variable camber. As in the Mirage 2000, quadruplex FBW and artificial stability combined to enhance manoeuvrability. A technological first for France was the use of an electron-beam welded titanium double frame to carry the canards, while a world first was the use of a composite fin structure as a fuel tank. Other advances were diffusion bonded and super-plastic formed titanium components, while composites were widely used, notably for the rudder, canards, wing control surfaces, and all fuselage doors. Internal fuel capacity was the secret of its greatly increased range, stated to be nine tonnes (19,840lb); roughly three times that of the Mirage 2000, with a fuel fraction of 0.39 compared to 0.27. The range could be increased still more by the addition of huge external fuel tanks holding a further 4,300lb each, and the use of flight refuelling, for which a retractable probe was fitted.

The proposed radar was a multi-mode pulse Doppler type with a 35in diameter antenna, which could have reasonably been expected to provide a detection range exceeding 100nm. Other proposed avionics kit followed that of the Mirage 2000 closely.

A total of twelve hardpoints allowed carriage of missiles and external fuel tanks. The probable AAM load would have been four Super 530Ds and four Magics, although the Super Mirage 4000 was also demonstrated with six Magics on the underwing pylons. Two 30mm DEFA 554 cannon with 125 rounds each, set in the wing roots, completed the air to air weaponry.

First seen in public at the Salon du Bourget in 1979, the Super Mirage 4000 showed remarkable agility for such a large aircraft, at both medium and low speeds. It also made a very spectacular low speed, high alpha flypast. While there could be no doubt of its capabilities, the sale to Saudi Arabia failed to materialise, almost certainly because they had bought the F-15 as an interceptor and were very interested in Tornado IDS (which they later also bought) for the interdiction mission. There can be little doubt that the 4000 would have been a worthy successor to the Mirage IVA in French service, but these aircraft still had plenty of life in them at this stage. With no sales forthcoming, the Super Mirage 4000 programme quietly lapsed.

When in 1986 Rafale neared its first flight, the Super Mirage 4000 was restored to flying status to test the effects of turbulence on canards. Then when in 1987 the Saudis encountered difficulties in acquiring a follow-on batch of F-15s, hopes were raised again, and the single prototype was dusted off and flown at Le Bourget that same year for the benefit of the Saudi military and government, culminating in a private demonstration before King Fahd at Nice. But nothing came of it, and a very potent fighter failed to enter service. Only the one prototype was built. Space had been provided for a second cockpit with no loss of internal fuel capacity, but lack of funding prevented the two holer from being manufactured.

Shenyang J-8 II Finback B

The People's Republic of China is a major aircraft producing nation, but has yet to make a fighter to match those of the West. For years the Chinese aircraft industry was shrouded in secrecy, apart from its ability to churn out rehashed Russian designs, and only in recent times have some of the veils been lifted. Rumours of swing wing fighters and deltas powered by licence-built twin Rolls-Royce Spey turbofans have abounded, but nothing firm has emerged. This section deals with their best shot to date, the J-8 II, NATO reporting name Finback B.

Way back in 1964, a Shenyang design team began work on a new high performance fighter. Experience had previously been gained in "reverse engineering" the Russian MiG-21, which entered Chinese service as the F-7, which retained the NATO reporting name of Fishbed. The simple solution of scaling up the J-7 and fitting it with two engines was adopted, giving it a marked resemblance to the Mikoyan Ye-152 Flipper, which had been passed over by the Soviet Union for the interceptor role in favour of Sukhoi's Su-15 Flagon.

Work on two J-8 prototypes began in 1967, and the first flight took place on 5 July 1969. Further development was then delayed until 1978 by the Cultural Revolution, although trials continued at a low rate, the two prototypes averaging one flight of 39 minutes duration per week each to the end of 1979, during which year small scale production of about 50 aircraft was ordered. Improvements resulted in the J-8 I, the second prototype of which took to the air on 24 April 1984, the first having been accidentally destroyed prior to its first flight. Like the J-7, the J-8 and J-8 I had MiG-21-style pitot intakes with translating shock-cones, which were too small to accommodate anything much more than a simple fire control radar.

Meanwhile, Chinese designers had carried out major surgery on another Russian design. The J-6 was a pitot-nosed MiG-19 lookalike which extensive redesign gave a pointed nose capable of holding avionics gear, and cheek intakes. Thus modified, it became the ground attack Q-5 Fantan. In order to accommodate a suitable multi-mode air to air radar, a similar rhinoplasty job was obviously wanted for the J-8. In fact Shenyang

117

went a bit further than this, and according to the book "China Today: Aviation Industry", 70 percent of it was redesigned, although nose section apart, the basic layout was retained. This, the J-8 II, reporting name Finback B, entered flight test in 1985, more or less at the same time as small scale production of the J-8 I Finback A commenced.

Not until June 1989 did the West get a good look at Finback B when it appeared at Le Bourget as a static exhibit, where it attracted only moderate attention, as it was overshadowed by the large Soviet contingent, of which Flanker, Frogfoot, Havoc, and Mriya with the Buran space shuttle mounted on top, were similarly all newcomers to the West.

First impressions of Finback B at close quarters were that it was long but not very bulky. Empty weight was similar to the Hornet, but dimensionally it was very different, nearly 15ft longer, but almost 6ft less in span, with 13.5 percent less wing area. Aspect ratio was also very different, 2.07 compared with 3.52 for the American fighter.

Two Wopen WP-13A afterburning turbojets rated at 9,608lb static thrust in military and 14,828lb at maximum power, gave a t/w ratio at normal takeoff weight of 0.94, rising at combat weight with 50 percent fuel to 1.10; a very respectable figure. Fuel fraction followed Western practice at 0.30. The sharply swept delta wing had a very thin section, a fixed leading edge with conical camber outboard, a fence at two thirds span, and was minimally cropped at the tips. The straight trailing edge had slotted ailerons outboard, with two section double slotted flaps inboard. The tail surfaces were swept at the same 60deg angle as the wing; with the horizontal surfaces located slightly lower than the plane of the wing, while the single vertical tail was mounted on a dorsal spine with a small intake for cooling air at its root.

Unlike many twin engined fighters, the engines were closely spaced and the intakes flared out dramatically from the sides of the fuselage, with horizontal flow fences internally. The intake lips were vertical, with MiG-23 type splitter plates, and bleed holes for boundary layer air on the fixed external ramp. Internal ramps are variable for speeds in excess of Mach 2.

By modern standards the cockpit was narrow and rather cramped, the available width restricted by the close spacing of the engines and the need to keep inlet curvature within reasonable limits. The radome was sized for the largest antenna diameter compatible with cockpit width. This allowed very little taper in nose planform, the result being an unusual flat sided front fuselage. Instrumentation was entirely conventional, and the radar display, set high on the right of the dash, was hooded against sunlight. Forward vision was restricted by thick metal framing to an optically flat windshield, heavy Hud framing and a massive canopy bow, while the view to the rear was not good, the canopy being faired into a dorsal spine which runs the length of the aircraft, ending in a drag chute housing. The radar was an unspecified Chinese continuous wave type, stated to provide guidance for PL-7 SARH missiles, but probably lacks look-down capability. Other avionics are also of indigenous design, but under the US Peace Pearl programme, Grumman was to supply 50 sets of Western avionics for Finback B, including a multi-mode radar based on the Westinghouse APG-66, but this was terminated in 1990 following the Tiananmen Square massacre.

Normal fighter armament of Finback B is stated to be two SARH and two IR homing missiles. The only Chinese radar homer at the time of writing is the PL-7A, but several IR homers have been developed. PL-2A is based on the AA-2 Atoll. A stern quadrant only weapon, its range is about 9nm, guidance time exceeds 21 seconds, and V_{max} is about Mach 2. PL-5B is slightly shorter but 20lb heavier, more manoeuvrable, able to pull 30g turns, and faster, with a stated V_{max} of Mach 4.5, although range remains the same. An all-aspect IR homer was shown at Le Bourget 91. This was the PL-9, which has a range of 8nm, and more than 35g manoeuvrability. Air to air armament is completed by a 23mm twin barrel cannon with 200 rounds located beneath the fuselage. As could be deduced from the rather dated configuration, subsonic manoeuvrability is not up to the standard of modern Western and Russian types, although in the supersonic regime, it is stated to be excellent. With its low aspect ratio one would expect it to be very snappy in the rolling plane, but its rather excessive length might make it sluggish in pitch. On the other hand, it has an excellent fineness ratio, and is aerodynamically very clean, which should give it sparkling acceleration. In 1991 improvements were stated to be in hand to improve subsonic manoeuvrability, and one of the obvious moves would be to introduce variable camber by using leading edge slats. There can be no doubt that FBW and relaxed stability would also benefit it considerably, while weight reduction could be achieved by the use of composites.

To date, only about 100 Finback As, in two separate batches, have entered service, and the situation regarding Finback B is unclear. In September 1991, the Peoples Republic commenced taking delivery of the Su-27 Flanker. There is no chance of Finback B ever matching the performance of this superb Russian fighter, and it seems probable that even if it enters production, it will be in small numbers only.

The Super-7 is a proposed Chinese variant of the MiG-21 but extensively modified to take an advanced turbofan engine. Western avionics were originally to be used, but this has since fallen through. Whether the Super-7 will ever become flyable hardware is questionable. (CATIC).

Grumman F-14D parked with the wings in the oversweep position. The engine compressor faces can clearly be seen, giving a large radar return from the head-on aspect. The television camera and IRST sensors are mounted beneath the nose. (Grumman).

CHAPTER TEN
Greater Capabilities

Modern fighters have a peacetime lifespan of 20 or even 30 years. During this time, both the threat that they are expected to counter, and the missions that they are expected to fly, can change radically. Of course, updating existing designs, usually by means of improved avionics, is an ongoing process which we have already seen at work, notably in Chapter 4, where the baseline fighter mission of the F-16 was quickly perceived to be inadequate and upgraded, firstly with better radar and avionics; secondly with improved armament, and finally with a more powerful engine to compensate for the growth in weight.

Where the updating process has been more or less continuous, it has been dealt with under the respective fighter heading, but in some cases radical changes have been made or proposed, often after long intervals. Some proposals were taken up; others were not; a few are scheduled for the future. These three categories are examined in this chapter.

Grumman F-14B, F-14D, and F-14/21 Super Tomcat

As related in Chapter 3, spiralling costs caused the F-14B to be cancelled, and the supposedly interim F-14A became the standard USN carrier fighter. The primary weakness of this aircraft was its over-sensitive TF30 turbofans. An F-14A driver had to nurse his engines which in any situation was undesirable. More power was required; t/w ratio was definitely on the low side, while attrition due to engine failure or malfunction was all too high. From the moment it entered service, the F-14A was a prime candidate for a re-engining job. Meanwhile as the years ticked by, the superb AWG-9 weapons system became dated. A planned avionics upgrade, which would have resulted in the F-14C, was also shelved for lack of funds.

Development of the F-14D was commenced in 1984. The Pratt & Whitney TF30-414A engines of the A model were replaced by the far more powerful F110-GE-400 turbofans while the avionics suite was upgraded with the Hughes APG-71 radar, digital systems, new jamming and communications links, and improved weaponry.

The first, and most urgent task, was to fit new engines. With the avionics coming along more slowly, the decision was taken to proceed with the engine modification alone as an interim measure. The trials aircraft first flew on 29 September 1986, and the subtype, at first designated F-14A+, entered service in November 1989. Alas for the wonders of modern technology. F-14A+ was not compatible with USN logistics computer programmes, and in May 1991 this was amended to F-14B.

The F110-GE-400 was a navalised version of the engine used in later models of the F-15 and F-16. Rated at 27,080lb static thrust in afterburner and 16,610lb at military power, it took the t/w ratio at combat weight from 0.83 to 1.07, conferring tremendous performance advantages in terms of sustained turn, acceleration, and rate of climb. As it was considerably shorter than the TF30, a plug 4.17ft long was inserted downstream of the engine proper, and the new nozzle, based on that of the F404, was shifted 0.92ft rearward to match the fuselage contours. Only minor structural changes were needed but the inlet ramp had to be rescheduled to accommodate the greater mass airflow.

Apart from performance gains, one of the greatest benefits to the Tomcat drivers was that they no longer had to consider the engine in every move they made. They could now slam the throttles from one end of the quadrant to the other without risking compressor stalls, and this allowed them to manoeuvre in a far more carefree manner than before. Furthermore they could launch from the carrier deck at quite high weights using military power only, which not only saved fuel, but assisted security during night operations in potentially hostile waters. The F-14A launching at night using afterburner could be seen for dozens of miles, and was generally considered a potential torpedo or missile magnet.

The fuel savings of a military power launch; the fact that in combat, afterburning would not need to be used so prodigally, plus the lower sfc, all combined to increase combat radius and range. Deck launched interception radius using a dash speed of Mach 1.5 increased from 134nm to 217nm, a massive 62 percent, while loiter time on station at 150nm radius went from 91min to 122min; over a third more. The final benefit came in reliability and lower maintenance requirements. Having got the propulsion system right at last, the way was clear to move on to the F-14D.

The heart of any modern fighter is its detection and sensor system. AWG-9 had been a world-beater in its day, but times had changed, and so had countermeasures techniques. Russian advances in this field had begun to make the elderly kit look a mite vulnerable. The APG-71 radar selected for the Super Tomcat was also a Hughes product, and was in many ways an improved version of its predecessor. High speed digital processing had increased its capability sixfold, and it incorporated many advances made in APG-70, which had been developed for the F-15E.

Monopulse angle tracking was used to locate a contact precisely within the 2.5deg wide radar beam. This contributed to the raid assessment mode by allowing individual targets to be detected from a close formation which previously would only have shown on the screen as a single contact. Track While Scan mode concentrates on a particular area of sky to the exclusion of all else, but digital scan control allowed an occasional sweep to be poached to search other areas at the same time. The increase in processing power provided non co-operative target recognition, with which a contact could be identified by the distinctive radar return from its compressor face. Both high and low prfs were used, while medium prf is a future possibility. Frequency agility combined with a guard channel which blanked off the sidelobes was used to enhance ECCM capability. Sidelobes are of course the most vulnerable areas for enemy ECM spoofing to enter the works.

The Northrop AXX-1 Television Camera Set(TCS) as used in the F-14A was retained, and supplemented by a General Electric Infra-Red Search and Track sensor. The former is used for long range identification, even in low light conditions, while the latter supplements the radar as a passive sensor which does not betray the fighter's presence. Both are mounted in separate pods under the nose. The F-14A had originally mounted an IR sensor, primarily to aid in raid assesment, as the angular discrimination of IR is far better than radar, but in practice it was found wanting and scrapped.

The new IRST operates in both the 3-5 micron(midwave) and 8-12 micron(long wave) bands, and uses computer algorithms to reject heat sources that are not targets. It has multiple target track capability, and the search volume can be varied. A passive sensor, it complements the radar, to which it can be slaved; alternatively it can be used to scan independently.

Other new avionics include a digital inertial navigation system, digital stores management, ALR-67 RWR, ALQ-165 ASPJ, and Jtids. Mission computers and data

Artist's impression of the proposed F-14 Super Tomcat 21. This was to have had revisions to the wings, and full attack capability, but there seems little chance of it ever being built. (Grumman).

buses considerably reduce the hard wiring of previous analogue systems. Software changes can provide growth, and programmable multi-function cockpit displays have replaced much of the original instrumentation, although the TID (Tactical Information Display) in the rear seat has been retained, supplemented by two MFDs. The TID range limit is 400nm. This is farther than the radar can see, but it allows the system to accept long range contacts from external sources via data link. In the front seat, a wide angle Hud would have been nice, but restrictions imposed by the windscreen frame made this impossible.

Just when it seemed that the Tomcat, rejuvenated with new engines and avionics, and with the Advanced Air to Air Missile scheduled to replace Phoenix, looked set to embark on a further two decades as the world's pre-eminent interceptor, the roof fell in. The disbandment of the Warsaw Pact and the breakup of the Soviet Union removed the primary threat. With this came demands for defence cuts, the so-called peace dividend.

F-14 production ended in July 1992 after 21 years. Only 37 new-build F-14Ds were produced, while a further 18 A models were remanufactured to D standard. New-build Bs amounted to 38, with a further 32 rebuilt from As.

In one way Tomcat is unique. It is the only dedicated fighter in modern times that in nearly two decades of squadron service had never had air to surface ordnance hung on it. But times have changed. The Pentagon's "review from the bottom up" in the summer of 1993 recommended the withdrawal from service of the antiquated A-6E Intruder all-weather attack aircraft and the termination of the proposed joint service A/F-X attack aircraft which might have replaced it. High on the list of priorities is the "Bombcat", the addition of an air to surface capability to the F-14. Trials have been in progress since 1991, and a bomb-laden Tomcat is virtually certain for the future. In many ways, this will mark the end of an era.

123

The USN has a requirement for a new fleet air defence fighter (NATF) at some point in the late 'nineties, which is expected to be based on the Lockheed F-22A (see Chapter 13). Whether this will happen must be open to doubt. With no serious threat on the horizon, the questions are raised whether it is (a) necessary, and (b) affordable.

Even before this, Grumman began to look for a viable alternative. Their answer, first revealed at Le Bourget in 1989, was the Tomcat 21. The premise was that the F-14 was a sound basis on which to build an affordable new fighter which retained the long distance multiple kill capability while being a true multi-role type.

One of the main operational constraints of the F-14 is carrier landing weight. A Tomcat taking the wire has an awful lot of kinetic energy to be absorbed somewhere. The dominant factor is not as might be thought, the weight of the aircraft, but the speed at which it comes aboard. For Tomcat 21, Grumman attacked this with high lift systems; increased chord leading edge slats and extending Fowler flaps. These had minimal impact on the basic wing design, while increasing available lift sufficiently to allow deck recovery with six Phoenix and two 'winders; something beyond present capabilities.

To extend mission range and endurance, more internal fuel can be carried in the wing glove, which will be redesigned accordingly; the glove vane deleted, and leading edge geometry tailored to give a close approximation of the airflow with the vane extended. As this has a destabilising effect, moving the centre of lift forward, it is presumed, although presently unconfirmed, that FBW would be used with relaxed stability. Other changes involve new engines, possibly the Pratt & Whitney F119, and state of the art avionics, with a possible doubling of radar range, and strike radar modes such as synthetic and inverse gain synthetic aperture, terrain following, ground moving target detection, FLIR, and all sorts of other goodies. In 1989 this looked good, but in 1994 there seems little chance of the Super Tomcat 21 ever being built.

McDonnell Douglas F-15E, F-15F and S, and S/MTD Eagle

Back in the late '70s, the USAF started to look for a tactical fighter to supplement, and later replace, the F-111 in the adverse weather interdiction role. With a breathtaking *volte face*, bearing in mind the Air Force's original insistence on a totally uncompromised air superiority mission, the F-15 Eagle became one of the contestants. Of course, had they simply wanted something to do the same job as the Aardvark, they could have bought Tornado IDS and had the capability instantly, but this would have been embarrassing.

In what at the time looked to be a bit of a smokescreen, but was in fact the first indication of changing tactical thinking, they asked for a dual role fighter for air superiority as well as the interdiction mission. By 1982 it was a two horse race, the other contestant being General Dynamics' F-16XL (see Chapter 9). The choice was made on 24 February 1984; the new USAF interdictor fighter was to be the F-15E.

A two holer, the Echo looked very similar to the earlier B and D models, but under the skin it was a very different bird. The main reason for this was that maximum takeoff weight had been increased to a colossal 81,000lb, while operational life was doubled to 16,000 flight hours. This involved an incredible amount of detailed structural strengthening, involving 60 percent of the airframe.

The most important structural changes involved the engine bays. A technique called Super Plastic Forming and Diffusion Bonding (SPF/DB) uses extremes of heat and pressure to mould titanium alloy into extremely complex curves and shapes, which previously had to be made up from many different components. The engine bay components formed in this manner became known as BLATS(Built-up Low cost

Two F-15Es of the 4th Fighter Wing. The F-15E is a true multirole aircraft with a two-man crew, and full night/adverse weather capability. Its capabilities were fully demonstrated in Desert Storm in 1991. (McDonnell Douglas).

Advanced Titanium Structures). The all-round savings were considerable: 240 fewer components, 6,400 fewer (this figure is not a typo) fasteners, 25 percent less weight, and 50 percent less cost. This resulted in a slightly larger engine bay which could house GE's F110 if need be. The other main internal change was the adoption of a triplex digital FBW system with mechanical backup. This was driven by the twin needs of automatic terrain following flight at ultra low levels, and extra pitch authority, made necessary by the fact that the cg of Echo is farther forward than in other models.

The original F-15E engine was Pratt & Whitney's F100-220, rated at 23,450lb static thrust. While this was actually a bit lower (380lb) than the -100 of earlier F-15s, it compensated with far greater reliability and maintainability, and was far less sensitive to disturbed airflow. But extra power was not to be sneezed at, and on 3 May 1990, testing of an F-15E powered by two -229s commenced. The F100-PW-229 is nominally rated at 29,000lb in full 'burner, giving a more than useful thrust increment, and is more cost effective than the -220. Both the -229 and GE's F110 are heavier than the originals, with the result that ballast has to be carried in the nose. Echos powered by F100-PW-229 engines commenced delivery in August 1991.

The most interesting thing about the F-15E is that the USAF decided that a two man crew was essential for the combined air superiority/interdiction mission. This was an open admission that the workload was too high for one man. As we saw in Chapter 3, there was no difficulty in providing space for the second seat, but the volume required to house the extra avionics kit caused a reduction to the size of the forward fuselage fuel tank. Internal fuel capacity of the Echo was down 332lb to 13,123lb. Not that this was any great problem, as like the C/D model, the F-15E carries FAST packs; by now known as CFTs (Conformal Fuel Tanks).

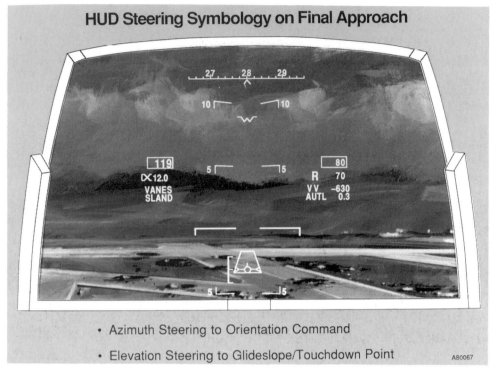

HUD Steering Symbology on Final Approach

27 . . 28 . . 29

10 ⌐   ⌐ 10

ᗐ

119
⋈ 12.0
VANES
SLAND

5 ⌐   ⌐ 5

80
R   70
V V   −630
AUTL 0.3

5 ⌐   ⌐ 5

- Azimuth Steering to Orientation Command
- Elevation Steering to Glideslope/Touchdown Point

A80067

The problems of landing on a damaged runway at night were addressed by this FLIR symbology used on the Agile Eagle demonstrator, which picks out an undamaged length of surface and cues the pilot onto it.
(McDonnell Douglas).

A new radar was needed, and Hughes developed APG-70 from the APG-63. More flexible and versatile than its predecessor, APG-70 differs mainly in air to ground modes, with synthetic aperture radar giving very accurate ground mapping, a degree of target identification, and a ground moving target indicator. Terrain following and terrain avoidance are other new modes. The radar is backed up with Lantirn, carried in two pods.

The accent on low level penetration meant increased risk of birdstrike, and a new and tougher polycarbonate wrap-around windshield was fitted to the Echo. As would be expected, cockpit displays were redesigned using MFDs, the pilot having three plus a wide angle holographic Hud, while the WSO is provided with four MFDs wall to wall across the panel. These display radar, EW or IR information; aircraft or weapons status, and a moving map. To operate the systems, the WSO uses two hand controllers.

Delivery of the F-15E to the USAF began in 1988, and IOC was attained the following year. Echo received its baptism of fire in the Gulf War in early 1991, where it performed well in the night interdiction role. Its air superiority capability though was hardly put to the test. The only air to air victory of that conflict scored by an F-15E came on February 14, when a hovering helicopter was knocked down by a laser guided bomb, which hardly counts.

The Eagle had proved to be the safest fighter in the USAF inventory, with an attrition rate of just 3.3 per 100,000 flight hours. While this compared well with the F-16's rate of 5.1, export sales had not been good, primarily due to the high initial cost. Then in 1990, McDonnell Douglas announced a variant purely for export. This was the F-15F which would keep costs down through a high degree of commonality with the F-15E.

The F-15F would be either a single or two holer according to customer choice, but would retain the lengthened canopy of the two seater. The baseline model would be powered by two F100-PW-220 turbofans, although the -229 or F110-GE-129 would be possible alternatives for approved clients. If the single seater was selected, provision for more fuel could be made in the rear cockpit area. The radar proposed was an export version of APG-70. As at 1994, the sole customer is Saudi Arabia, which in October 1992 ordered 72 aircraft with manufacturers designation F-15XP, later F-15S, which does not carry CFTs. Deliveries are scheduled to begin in mid 1995.

A uniquely modified F-15 flew for the first time in August 1988. This was the Short Takeoff Landing/Manoeuvre Technology Demonstrator(S/MTD) aircraft. During the

The F-15S/MTD demonstrator was modified with canard foreplanes and a digital quadruplex FBW system to test the ability to operate from damaged runways. Still later it was fitted with vectoring nozzles. (McDonnell Douglas).

'eighties there was increasing emphasis on the ability to operate from damaged runways, and the F-15S/MTD was modified from an F-15B to demonstrate the technologies needed to make this a practical proposition. Since thrust vectoring/reversing nozzles were part of the plan, the aim was expanded to include in-flight manoeuvring using these assets.

Runway limits were set at 1,500ft long by 50ft wide, with 4.5in bumps caused by Category E repairs. Conditions surrounding the test were no less stringent; a wet runway, at night, a 200ft cloud ceiling, a 30kt crosswind, visibility down to half a mile, and no external landing aids.

This is not easy. A suitable area of runway must be selected from many miles away, using only on-board systems. There is no margin for scatter; the touchdown point must be exact. The fighter then has to stop without being blown offcourse by crosswinds.

The solution to the first problem lay in the Autonomous Landing Guidance System (ALGS). This utilises the high resolution ground mapping mode of the APG-70 radar to select the landing area. Once selected, the touchdown spot and landing heading is designated, which provides steering and elevation guidance on the Hud. Once on short finals a perspective of the landing area can be superimposed on the Lantirn display. So successful has this been that ALGS is to be incorporated into all F-15Es, only a software change being needed.

Precision touchdown means a no-flare carrier-type approach. The main gear was redesigned to take this, and also to cope with a bumpy surface. Stopping is the next problem, and on a slippery surface, thrust reversal is the only real solution. For greater roll authority in the approach, canard foreplanes (actually tail surfaces from a Hornet) were fitted, with 18deg of dihedral. Finally, thrust vectoring/reversing nozzles were fitted, although the first series of flights was made without them.

The final problem, and an enormous one too, was was to tie all the extra bits into an integrated flight control system. Quadruplex FBW, based on that of the Hornet, was used to tie the canards and vectoring nozzles into a cohesive system that would not be overly demanding on the pilot.

In flight, the canards improve pitch and roll control while providing extra lift and yaw control at high alpha. They also give extra lift for short takeoff. The nozzles, which move vertically 20deg up or down at low speeds, give added control in pitch. At high speeds these are restricted to 5deg. In-flight thrust reversal is also under test; this could force an attacker to overshoot very rapidly without the need to throttle back, while resetting the nozzles would restore maximum thrust instantly.

Demonstrated performance improvements over the F-15A are: takeoff distance barely 1,000ft(38 percent shorter), landing roll 1,365ft(60 percent shorter). Thrust reversing at Mach 1.6 slowed the aircraft to Mach 0.8 in just 30 seconds; a deceleration rate of more than 18kt/sec. Pitch down rates from 30deg alpha were 110 percent faster than with conventional controls.

Refitted with standard nozzles, its next task was testing advanced avionics for the air superiority mission. Then on April 21 1993, in a convincing demonstration of what is now possible, NASA pilot C. Gordon Fullerton twice landed at Edwards using engine thrust alone for control; commanding flight path and bank angle via two thumbwheel controllers. In 1994 a flight test programme is scheduled for using axi-symmetric vectoring nozzles which will allow lateral as well was vertical thrust pointing. Whether all this will lead to a yet more improved F-15, or whether the technology will be used for a new generation fighter, remains to be seen.

General Dynamics YF-16CCV, AFTI F-16, Vista F-16, Agile Falcon, and F-16X

In close combat, one of the most important assets is pointability; the ability to quickly bring weapons to bear. This is normally limited by conventional flight modes, for example to aim at a receding target which is higher and off to one side, the fighter must bank to the desired angle while pulling the nose through obliquely to point at the target. If however the combat dynamics are such that it cannot pull its nose through the required angle in three dimensions fast enough, or at all, the firing opportunity is lost. Unconventional, or decoupled manoeuvre might compensate if the fighter could simultaneously use pitch and yaw to briefly line up on target without changing its flight path; in other words, to slew around long enough for a quick pot shot at a target of opportunity.

This was not a new concept; German ace Werner Voss used decoupled manoeuvres in his Fokker Dr.1 in September 1917 when, in an epic battle, he fought 11 British SE.5a's of No 56 and 60 Squadrons virtually singlehanded, writing three off and damaging all the rest before going down himself. On the other hand, this type of manoeuvring is a good way of departing controlled flight, and Voss' antics were not repeatable by the average squadron pilot. As fighter speeds and weights grew, so the difficulties increased.

The fact that something is difficult does not mean that it is impossible. High speed computerised flight control systems and FBW have moved the goalposts, making possible a CCV (control configured vehicle) able to explore unconventional flight modes.

The YF-16CCV first flew on 16 March 1976, piloted by GD's David Thigpen. Externally the only difference was that it had two all-moving ventral fins mounted on each side of the intake and canted out at a steep angle. Internally the fuel system was modified to allow the cg to be changed on demand, while the flight control system was altered to provide unconventional modes. A total of 87 flights was made by the end of July 1978, during which time the concept was demonstrated within the limits of the analogue FBW system.

In December 1978 trials recommenced with a triplex digital FBW system, which could fully exploit the new modes. At the same time, various attack systems were evaluated. An FSD F-16 was rebuilt for the task, differing from the YF-16CCV in having a large dorsal spine to carry extra equipment. This was the Advanced Fighter Technology Integrator (AFTI)/F-16, which commenced trials on 10 July 1982.

The AFTI/F-16 set out to explore various decoupled flight manoeuvres and attitudes. These were vertical translation, in which the fighter gained or lost height without pitching the nose up or down; direct lift to gain or lose height while maintaining constant alpha; lateral translation, in which the AFTI/F-16 moved sideways while holding its original heading; (called a skid before the jargoneers got at it); direct sideforce to allow unbanked turns; and pitch and yaw axis-pointing, in which the nose moves vertically, horizontally, or obliquely without altering the flight path.

It was found that in mock combat, many decoupled modes were physically disorienting to the pilot. Test pilots operating under controlled conditions could hack the course, but there were doubts about the ability of the average squadron jock to make use of them in air combat. Lateral g was also a problem, as it tended to flatten the pilot against one or other of the cockpit sides, reducing his effectiveness. But certain flight modes were found to have potential in the attack mission, allowing the aircraft to precisely adjust its aim by "sidestepping" or using direct lift.

The value of decoupled flight in air combat is doubtful, but it has been firmly established that it can give significant advantages in attacking surface targets. It is also

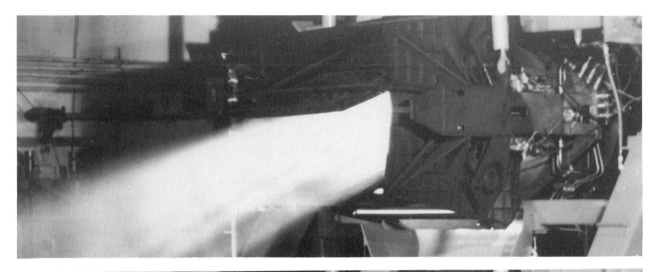

LEFT: *A Pratt & Whitney two dimensional vectoring nozzle seen on test using full augmentation. Vectored thrust increases agility and provides control power in the post-stall regime. (Pratt & Whitney).*

obvious, though nobody seems to have mentioned this, that it would be useful for anti-helicopter operations. Its first operational application may well be on the Mitsubishi FS-X, an attack/anti-shipping aircraft being developed for the Japanese Air Self Defense Force in conjunction with GD.

The Agile Falcon proposal was revealed in 1988. Basically this was intended to reduce the wing loading on what had become a much heavier airframe by incorporating a bigger wing, with span increased by 7.5ft to 40.3ft, area from 300ft^2 to 375ft^2, and aspect ratio from 3.2 to 4.33, with the leading edge sweep angle slightly reduced. This would have brought the wing loading back to the level of the F-16A, thus restoring turn capability. Interestingly, the aspect ratio would have been of the same order as Fulcrum and Flanker, while the extra fuel in the wing would have restored the fuel fraction to something like that of the original bird. Finally, the construction of the new wing would have mirrored that of FS-X, while development work for the Japanese aircraft wing would have amortized the costs involved. There were however no takers, and Agile Falcon quietly faded away.

Next came the Variable Stability In-Flight Simulator Test Aircraft (VISTA) F-16). This was a conversion of a standard F-16D two seater; the most obvious change being a large dorsal spine. This was a pure research vehicle intended to explore high speed control systems, and also the low speed handling characteristics of the proposed X-30 National Aero-Space Plane. The front cockpit was the simulator, for which it was equipped with a conventional central control column in addition to the normal F-16 sidestick, while the rear seat was occupied by the command pilot. Nearly four years in the making, it made just five flights in seven days in April 1992 before funding was withdrawn, and it was placed in flyable storage.

Not for long. Shortly after, it was dusted off and fitted with GE's F110-100 turbofan and a multi-axis vectoring nozzle. Tests to explore the effects of pitch/yaw thrust vectoring on high alpha manoeuvres, and to develop new close combat techniques, began in August of the same year, flown by company test pilot Joe Sweeny and Major Mike Gerzanics of the USAF. Early results were spectacular. In the first few weeks, the VISTA/F-16 reached a transient alpha of 110deg and a sustained alpha of 80 deg. Also demonstrated was a hammerhead manoeuvre, intended to force a pursuer to overshoot. this involved a hard pullup which in effect results in a backward somersault at the top, then pulling the nose through from the inverted position into a dive. Other manoeuvres still to be tried at the time of writing include high alpha gun tracking, and a so-called J-turn in which speed bleeds off from 300kt to zero in between five and ten seconds. At the time of writing, the test programme was due to complete by November 1993.

Meanwhile General Dynamics had, from April 1993, become Lockheed Fort Worth Division. In August 1993, the F-16X was offered as a contender for the next USAF multi-role fighter. This proposal obviously owes something to the F-16XL as it is tail-less and has the same fuselage stretch, but with a wing similar in many ways to that of the Lockheed F-22. While shortly after the proposal was made, the Pentagon called for the termination of the multi-role fighter project, the F-16X was aimed 15 years or more into the future, and a lot can happen in that time.

McDonnell Douglas F/A-18E/F Hornet; Hornet 2000

The F/A-18 multi-role carrier fighter was another project eminently suitable for comprehensive updating. First mooted during the summer of 1987 as the Super Hornet Plus, by October of that year it had become the Hornet 2000 study.

Hornet 2000 was actually a study of four development options, increasing capability and development costs in easy stages. Configuration I was externally identical to the F/A-18C, but with an improved cockpit layout, upgraded engines, state of the art electronics including the new APG-73 radar, and various survivability features. The operational benefits were better transonic/supersonic performance, and improved situational awareness aids for the pilot.

Configuration II added a stiffened wing, growth II engines, improved weapons systems and a bulged dorsal fuselage housing an extra 2,700lb of fuel. Configuration III built on this, adding a larger area wing; larger horizontal tail surfaces, and 3,700lb more internal fuel. Finally there came Configuration IV. This was a radically redesigned Hornet obviously intended to be a low cost contender in the EFA/Rafale class. Offered to various European nations, it featured a cranked delta wing with all-moving canards; a fuselage plug to give extra length, and completely revised twin fin and rudder assemblies. It was to have 3,200lb more internal fuel than the baseline model, and two more weapon stations.

At a later date, variations on Configuration III appeared, but failed to progress, although at one point the USN looked favourably on IIIC. While there can be little doubt that Configuration IV, the true Hornet 2000 proposal, would have provided a cut price alternative to EFA, this was politically unacceptable to potential client nations, as it would have meant dependence on the USA for the foreseeable future and the snuffing out of all indigenous fighter production capability.

This was not however the end of the road for the Hornet. The next generation USN attack aircraft, the stealthy A-12 Avenger scheduled to replace the A-6 Intruder, was cancelled early in 1991, leaving a gap to be filled by a nebulous A-X project, which also fell by the wayside two years later. To a degree the gap is being filled by dedicated Night Attack Hornets, F/A-18D two seaters with a systems operator in the back seat, which are operated by the USMC.

The obvious next step was the F/A-18E/F, details of which emerged in September 1991. The new Hornet will have F414-GE-400 engines, rated at 22,000lb thrust maximum, with a larger fan and a higher bypass ratio than the F404, based on the advanced core of the F412-400 developed for the A-12. This will involve larger, reshaped inlets. Other changes are 25 percent more wing are with increased thickness, and 25 percent larger LERX to improve high alpha capability. The "angle iron" strakes currently fitted on the LERX of existing Hornets are to be replaced by pop-up spoilers which double as speed brakes, allowing the existing dorsal article to be deleted. Other changes are new air to air sensors, the omission of mechanical backup to the flight control system, and two more weapons pylons. Fuel capacity is greater, and the fighter escort radius of action increased by 3.7 percent, while acceleration between Mach 0.8 and 1.2 is calculated as being 5.7 percent better.

A new radar, the Hughes APG-73, based on APG-65, was test flown in April 1992, and will equip production F/A-18C/Ds from June 1994. In the F/A-18E/F, it is to have an active phased array antenna that should double current detection range. In the cockpit, a large (195mm x 195mm) touch sensitive flat panel tactical situation display will be shoehorned in between the three MFDs, in what amounts to a "look level" position. Various stealth measures, aimed at reducing RCS to 1.19m 2 , roughly the same as that of the F-16, are to be incorporated. Seven flight and three ground test articles are under construction, with first flight scheduled for late 1995. The first 12 production aircraft are to be delivered to the USN late in 1998, with IOC in the following year.

CHAPTER ELEVEN

New Directions

Just occasionally a new technology gives birth to a new type of fighter, as vectored thrust did the Harrier, usually after a protracted and costly proof of concept phase. More often a new concept is found to give the predicted advantages, but like modern drugs, is also found to have side effects which negate the benefits. An example of this was the AFTI F-16 used to explore decoupled flight modes, most of which, after lengthy evaluation, were considered too disorienting for the ordinary squadron pilot to handle. There have also been total disasters, such as the ill-fated Rockwell XFV-12A vertical takeoff fighter which never flew. Other areas recently or currently under examination include wing technology; low observables, or stealth; and reducing the pilot's workload.

The Mission Adaptive Wing, AFTI/F-111

To state the obvious, wing efficiency is the most important factor in flight. It affects speed, acceleration, range, rate of climb, ceiling, agility, and turning capability. It is therefore worth going to a great deal of trouble to get it right. The main difficulty has traditionally been that a wing is a fixed shape and section, and these determine how well it will perform in different parts of the flight envelope. In fact, with a wing of completely fixed shape and section, there will be one fixed combination of speed and altitude where performance will be maximised, and elsewhere it will be less good. An essential part of fighter design has always been determining the fixed point for which the wing should be designed, to give the best compromise across the board. The introduction, some six decades ago, of high lift devices for low speed flight, simply allowed the design point to be raised in both speed and altitude, leaving the basic problem unsolved.

The emergence in the 1960s of a practical form of variable sweep allowed for the first time a degree of both flight regime and mission optimisation. The penalties were added weight and complexity, and a relatively small wing area, giving a high wing loading. Variable sweep, often wrongly called variable geometry, was followed by variable camber, in which a highly computerized flight control system optimised the shape of the wing section to meet the demands of the flight regime automatically.

The problem with variable camber is that it involves the use of a series of rigid surfaces; leading edge slats, fixed main section, trailing edge flaps etc. The joins between the moving and fixed sections are angular, and the movement opens up gaps which interfere with the smooth airflow, both of which reduce lift and create drag. 'Twas not always so; back in the early days of heavier than air flight, wing warping was commonly used as a method of control. But as aircraft performance improved, human muscle power became increasingly inadequate, and crude mechanical devices such as ailerons and flaps took over.

The wheel turned full circle after three quarters of a century, with the advent of the Mission Adaptive Wing(MAW). The aircraft selected for trials was a pre-production F-111 which had previously been used for other research projects. It was chosen because its variable sweep wing would allow investigation of MAW performance over a wide range of different sweep angles. It had also previously been fitted with a larger area wing of supercritical section.

LEFT: *Angular faceting is combined with RAM to minimise the radar cross-section of the Lockheed F-117A, plus a grille to shield the engine compressor face. The view from the cockpit appears to be very poor.* (Author).

BELOW: *The engine efflux is flattened to reduce IR signature by mixing the hot gases with the surrounding air as swiftly as possible.* (Eric Schulzinger and Denny Lombard).

Modification was undertaken by the Boeing Military Airplane Company. The variable camber leading and trailing edge wing sections were skinned with flexible fibreglass material, bending on the upper surfaces and close fitting sliding underneath. The camber changing mechanism was automatically controlled to match the flight regime, giving the effect of a one piece bending surface with no hard angles or drag-inducing discontinuities.

Leading edge camber was in a single piece, but that of the trailing edge was in three pieces, giving not only a high degree of variation, but with differential deflection of the outboard and mid sections providing control in the rolling plane as an alternative to the standard F-111 spoilers.

An extensive test programme was flown, commencing in late 1985. Takeoff and landing speeds were significantly reduced, as was cruise drag, giving greater range. Manoeuvre capability was enhanced, the buffet-free envelope increased, and direct lift control was investigated. It also seems obvious that stealth would benefit, although no MAW applications were visible on either ATF contender. While the powers that be have said neither yea or nay so far, it seems possible that the benefits are insufficient to repay the added cost and complexity of the MAW. It may equally be that the technology is not sufficiently mature, but there can be little doubt that MAW will be further explored in the future, if only to improve the range/payload performance on transports and airliners.

Forward Swept Wings, Grumman X-29A

Virtually all modern fighters have their wings swept aft to delay the onset of wave drag as supersonic speed is approached. The main drawback of an aft-swept wing is tip stalling, which occurs when the wing twists under lift loads, reducing the angle of incidence. This is known as wash-out. Lift is lost, causing problems with pitchup and loss of lateral control.

One method of eradicating tip stall while retaining the benefits of swept wings is to sweep the wing forward. This has further advantages. Compared to an aft-swept wing, lift induced drag is lower, lift coefficient is higher, and the sweep angle can be considerably reduced for the same effect. The centre of pressure is closer to the wing root, thus easing structural problems. Stall characteristics become more benign, and high alpha performance is also improved. With the airflow remaining attached to the tips, aileron effectiveness is assured. Finally the wing carry-through structure can be located aft of the centre of gravity, leaving this area free for more important things.

With a forward swept wing, manoeuvre causes wash-in, with the tip bending upwards, increasing the local incidence. When this happens the tip loading increases, which is potentially dangerous, as at high speeds and g, the loading continues to increase, bending the wing to the point where the structure fails (aero-elastic divergence) unless it is made far stiffer than a conventional aft swept wing. This could be done, but the weight penalty is prohibitive.

Like most things, the forward sweep concept was far from new. Its first real application was in the German Junkers Ju 287 four jet bomber, which first flew in August 1944. Both the USA and the USSR flirted with the idea after the war, but the advantages were dubious when measured against the problems. The breakthrough came with the introduction of composite materials which could be aero-elastically tailored by orienting the plies to give directional rigidity, at very light weight. Relaxed stability and FBW rounded out the FSW solution.

Studies began in the mid 'seventies, and in 1981 the Grumman Aircraft Corporation was awarded a contract to develop a FSW technology demonstrator. Calculations showed that for a given performance level, a FSW fighter would be considerably smaller, lighter, and more affordable (mustn't say cheaper), than a conventional aft swept type. While never officially mentioned, it was also obvious that a FSW fighter would provide enough aspect deception in a dogfight to terminally confuse opposing pilots used to dealing with more orthodox layouts.

The X-29A, as it was designated, used as many off the shelf components as practicable in order to keep costs down. The front end and nose gear was taken from an F-5A; main gears and engine accessories from an F-16, while the engine was a F404-GE-400. A supercritical wing section was used with a low thickness/chord ratio of 4.9 percent. Leading edge forward sweep was 30deg while aft sweep was used on small inboard sections to minimise root stall problems. From the wing root trailing edge, narrow strakes ran back to a point level with the engine nozzle. By providing extra area aft of the centre of gravity, these improved directional stability, while flaps on their extremities augmented the close coupled canard surfaces in providing extra pitch authority for recovery from high alpha.

Forward wing sweep has many aerodynamic benefits compared to aft sweep, but has only been made possible with the advent of aero-elastic tailoring of advanced composite materials. The Grumman X-29A is a technology demonstrator for FSW. (Grumman).

The leading edges were fixed, but two section full span flaperons, with the trailing section geared to operate in relation to the first, were used to provide discrete variable camber. This arrangement was stated by Grumman to be almost as efficient as Boeing's mission adaptive wing, while being far less complex and costly. If correct, this may explain the apparent lack of further development on the MAW project.

The first of two X-29As flew on 14 December 1984. Initial problems were found, and these had to be eradicated, but since then the flight test programme has moved steadily onwards. A high alpha test series was completed in February 1991, during which the X-29A demonstrated an alpha of 67deg, and pointing in pitch and all-axis manoeuvrability at up to 45deg alpha. While 67deg may seem small potatoes compared to the Cobra manoeuvre demonstrated by Flanker, it is doubtful whether the Russian fighter can even begin to match the all-axis manoeuvrability of the X-29A at 45deg alpha. And this is what is needed in combat, whereas the Cobra is just a spectacular circus trick.

A series of flight tests to take the X-29A up to 80deg alpha began in June 1991 and was concluded later that year, after which the two demonstrators were placed in storage at NASA's Dryden facility. With conventional aft-swept fighters now reaching very high alpha, it seems unlikely that the benefits of forward sweep will offer significant advantages over more traditional layouts.

Post Stall Manoeuvrability, MBB/Rockwell X-31A

Once close combat is joined, fighters traditionally engage using hard turns, in which speed bleeds off rapidly. While the current fashion is for sustained 9g turns, these can only be made in a small area of the envelope. For example, the Block 50 F-16C, powered by the F110-GE-129, rated at 28,982lb static thrust, can only sustain 9g between Mach 0.76 and Mach 0.98 at sea level, reducing to a single point at Mach 0.90 at about 6,000ft. And this is with only two Sidewinders, guns loaded, and 50 percent internal fuel. Any greater armament load than this and the 9g sustained envelope shrinks still further!

Of course, 9g instantaneous manoeuvre can be made over a much larger range of speeds and altitudes, but this reduces rapidly as speed bleeds off. In the stress of combat, with both victory and survival at stake, instantaneous manoeuvre will be used unhesitatingly where any advantage is to be gained, even if speed is lost in the process. Any combat extending beyond the first pass will therefore become slower and slower.

Aerodynamic considerations also enter into the equation. As a theoretical example, let us take a fighter with a minimum flying speed of 180kt. Move it up into the rarified air at 50,000ft and the minimum flying speed increases to 461kt. Lay on a moderate 4g turn, and minimum flying speed then becomes 922kt, or Mach 1.61, below which control will be lost.

To summarize, at lower altitudes where hard turning is possible, speed, and with it, manoeuvre capability, will be bled off rapidly, while at higher altitudes, lack of available lift will force the fighter to jockey slowly for position, making it predictable, and vulnerable to attack, bearing in mind that in the real world, multi-bogey engagements are the norm, and there can be no guarantee that other, previously unseen bandits, will not join the party from an unexpected quarter at any moment.

These limitations led to a requirement for the ability to manoeuvre in the post-stall flight regime, or to put it more simply, the ability to perform precise manoeuvres at altitude and speed combinations where conventional fighters lose control. This is called enhanced fighter manoeuvrability (EFM), or super-manoeuvrability.

Notwithstanding stories about Soviet fighters being able to launch missiles at attackers in their rear hemispheres, valid targets are only to be found in the front

quadrant, although helmet mounted sights do permit off-boresight missile launches to be
made. It therefore remains necessary for a fighter to point its nose in the general
direction of, if not directly at, the target, when launching AAMs. Missiles are not yet ten
feet tall, and to get the best results, a heart of the envelope shot gives them less work to
do. And while the gun remains a valid air to air weapon, precise nose pointing is a vital
fighter asset.

OPPOSITE: *The ability to manoeuvre with precision at speeds below the stall would confer tremendous advantages in close combat. The MBB/Rockwell X-31, an artist's impression of which is seen here, was designed to explore the possibilities.* (MBB).

A conventional fighter that has bled off most of its energy is unable to manoeuvre aggressively, while if it enters the post-stall regime it is unable to manoeuvre at all. When this happens, the best option is disengagement, but in a multi-bogey encounter this will be at best hazardous, and at worst impossible. Super-manoeuvrability will allow the nose to be snapped around precisely in the post stall condition, allowing the fighter to defend itself where a conventional machine would be helpless.

Back in 1977, Messerschmitt-Bolkow-Blohm (MBB), started work on the German TKF 90 requirement, a project since merged with EFA. Designed under the leadership of Dr. Wolfgang Herbst, TKF 90 was to remain manoeuvrable at very low airspeeds, while conceding nothing in conventional manoeuvre flight. It was to have combined a close-coupled canard delta layout with thrust vectoring nozzles located well aft of the centre of gravity to provide a long moment arm.

The US Defense Advanced Research Projects Agency(DARPA) soon took an interest, and in 1983 MBB was joined by Rockwell International, a company that had been involved in Highly Manoeuvrable Aircraft Technology (HiMAT), using an unmanned research aircraft. A preliminary design contract was awarded in September 1986, and the X-31A designation shortly after.

Studies predicted that post-stall manoeuvrability should double the number of first shots achieved and triple the exchange ratio, while enhanced agility should increase the exchange ratio by 160 percent while reducing non-combat losses by 15 percent. Enhanced deceleration, achieved by using very high alphas, should increase the number of first shots while improving survivability. Roll-coupled fuselage aiming was predicted to quadruple the exchange ratio in gunfights, while the ability to handle -4g would double the chance of evading a guns attack.

Two X-31As were built, the first of which flew on 11 October 1990 piloted by Rockwell's Ken Dyson, the second on January 19, 1991, with MBB's Dietrich Seeckt at the controls. The X-31A is a cranked canard delta, with 56.6deg sweep inboard and 45deg sweep outboard. The planform is a compromise between low drag at supersonic speeds, maximum lift at corner velocity, minimum lift/ drag at the design manoeuvre points, with a fine balance being struck between relaxed stability at low alpha and pitch down recovery moments at high alpha. The wing is cambered, although the canard surfaces are not. Neither are the canards close coupled as in Eurofighter 2000 or Rafale. Lightly loaded, and set well forward, they are primarily pitch recovery controls.

The X-31A uses many off the shelf parts, but unlike the X-29 was unable to use large sections of an existing fighter. The fuselage is deep and slab sided with a chin intake, and rather surprisingly, a single fin was selected. The engine is the F404-GE-400, chosen for its known tolerance of disturbed airflow at high alpha, plus its reliability. It was at first intended to use vectoring nozzles, but calculations showed that three paddles at the hot end would suffice. These, which were originally developed for the F-14 spin demonstrator, are far simpler and lighter, and can divert about 17 percent of the available thrust either vertically or laterally.

What the X-31A is designed to do is to perform a rapid pull-up to high alpha akin to Flanker's Cobra, but reaching 9g rather than 3g, with a far greater speed loss. Then with its nose still high, it will reef into a very tight turn of perhaps 1,000ft radius as its nose falls through. This will be done with enough precision to allow guns tracking. This manoeuvre is far beyond anything the Su-27 can do, as any attempt by the big Russian fighter to emulate it would shortly be followed by wing drop, loss of control, and probably an expensive noise.

The first two phases of flight testing were successfully completed in 1991 and 1992 respectively. Then on April 29, 1993, the number two demonstrator, piloted by German Project Pilot Karl Lang, starting at an altitude of 19,400ft and an entry speed of 200kt, pitched up nearly vertically, decelerating hard by using the entire airframe as a speed brake. With speed well below the normal stall and alpha at 70deg, he used thrust vectoring to roll rapidly back to reverse through 180deg before commencing a nose-down acceleration. This has been dubbed the "Herbst manoeuvre" after its originator, the late Dr. Wolfgang Herbst. This was the last and most difficult of the four high alpha agility milestones that the aircraft was called upon to demonstrate, the others including Split-S's, pull-ups, wind-up turns, and bank to bank rolls.

The next stage includes simulated combat, but at the time of writing, no results have been released. It will be interesting to see whether the computer predictions are borne out. The future of super-manoeuvrability depends very much on advances in medium range combat. Should this succeed in dominating the air to air arena, super-manoeuvrability will have little application. But should advances in stealth and counter-measures largely negate medium range combat, EFM will become increasingly important.

Stealth and the Lockheed F-117A

Another technology which has recently come to the fore is low observability, or stealth. As the villains in the Invisible Man films discovered, it is impossible to fight someone you can't see. While technology is far from reaching this ultimate stage, the reduction of radar cross sections and infra red emissions to very low levels complicates the task of the defenders out of all proportion.

The stealth concept is far from new, and the first recorded instance occurred in Austria in 1912, when transparent materials were used in an attempt to minimise visual signature. Some 65 years further on, things had changed. Visual detection had been far outranged and supplanted by radar and to a lesser degree, infra-red. It was these that now needed to be defeated.

By 1970 a certain amount of low observables technology had already been applied to service aircraft, notably the Lockheed A-12 and SR-71. Then in 1973, DARPA asked half a dozen companies to submit design studies for low observables aircraft under project *Have Blue*. The winner was Lockheed, who the following year were awarded a contract for three proof of concept prototypes.

Radar detection depends on radar impulses returning to the receiver, rather like the way a ball thrown against a wall bounces back to the thrower. If the ball is thrown at an angle to the wall, it bounces away from the thrower. Conventional aircraft tend to have a lot of areas where the radar impulse will be returned in the direction of the receiver, not necessarily from the curved surfaces, but from angles formed by them, or from angles in the internal structure. One of the worst offenders is the engine compressor face, which rotating at high speed, acts virtually as a flat plate.

Lockheed's main intent was to minimise radar signature by deflecting the impulses off at an angle, thus dispersing them away from the receiver. At the time, computer limitations prevented accurate simulation of radar returns from curved surfaces, and they elected to use a series of flat plates. The other main anti-radar measure was the liberal use of Radar Absorbent Material(RAM). It was then determined that detection was normally made by emitters located within a 30deg angle of the plane of the aircraft, either above or below. The angles between the flat plates should therefore exceed this figure in order to deflect the emissions rather than return them.

The *Have Blue* prototypes, often referred to as XSTs, were most peculiar looking aeroplanes. A wing leading edge sweep of 72.5deg commenced at the nose pitot boom and carried out to the tips in an unbroken line. The underside was completely flat, while the upper surfaces were composed of flat plates meeting at unlikely angles. Even the wing and tail sections were angular, with no smooth curves. In a competition to produce an aeroplane which could generate the most in-flight vortices, it would have won hands down. The transparencies were also made up of flat plates in heavy framing, with a V-shaped windshield. Twin vertical tails mounted on booms were canted steeply inward. It was powered by two General Electric J85 turbojets, the intakes for which were set in a grotesquely wide body, and covered with grilles calculated to minimise radar returns from the compressor face. The rear end was equally weird. Flattened jet nozzles gave a wide efflux, ensuring rapid mixing with the ambient air to reduce the IR signature.

Testing commenced from the secure facility at Groom Lake some time in 1977, with Lockheed test pilot Bill Park making the first flight. Evaluation was rapid, and it was soon decided to go ahead with an operational aircraft based on *Have Blue*.

The first task was to determine what missions it should fly. It was never suitable for air superiority or interceptor roles. Non-afterburning engines and what must have been the draggiest airframe designed in the past 50 years saw to that. On-board radar, being an emitter, would have compromised its stealthy qualities, while forward view from the cockpit was terrible, and rear view non-existent. Finally, even quite mild (2g) manoeuvres would compromise stealth by presenting facets at angles other than those designed to deflect radar emissions away. Apart from any other considerations, the fact that the stealth aircraft would be a turkey if caught within visual range by enemy fighters, and vulnerable to optically laid ground weapons, restricted it to night operations. Given these factors, the operational version could only realistically be used for night precision attack and defence suppression.

Design work began on the full scale development aircraft in December 1978, and it first flew from Groom Lake, piloted by Hal Farley, in June 1981. For added security, the radio call sign of 117 was allotted, and it was the widespread use of this that finally led to the designation F-117A, rather than any of the fanciful theories later advanced. The press had a lovely time. They knew something top secret was around, gave it the obvious (and erroneous) designation of F-19, and even published three-views of it which had foundation only in their overheated imaginations. Not until November 1988 was the existence of the F-117A revealed, and even then the heavily retouched photo released gave a totally wrong impression of its outline.

The F-117A differed quite a bit from the proof of concept bird. For a start, it was a lot larger, and two F404-GE-F1D2 unaugmented turbofans were used to handle the extra size and weight. The wing leading edge sweep was reduced to a more reasonable 67.5deg to improve payload/range performance. The centre framing of the original V-shaped windshield obstructed the view through the Hud, and the nose was redesigned to allow a flat plate transparency. A small triangular section was grafted on the front to maintain the integrity of the leading edge straight line from nose to wingtip. The inward canted fins were replaced by a steeply swept butterfly tail set on a central spine, the main reason for this being that the inward canted tails had directed the jet efflux downwards, increasing the chance of IR detection from below. Weapons load was carried internally, forward looking and downward looking infra-red sensors were fitted, plus a laser designator. An air to air refuelling receptacle was installed behind the cockpit, with a rear facing lamp in the cockpit peak to illuminate it at night. Every effort was made to allow it to carry out its mission without the use of emitters; a super-accurate INS is reported, coupled with the Global Positioning System. The F-117A entered service in 1982, and IOC was achieved in October 1983. The last of 59 examples was delivered in July 1990.

Despite its F prefix, the F-117A is solely an attack aircraft, and as such has no real place in this book. However, it justifies inclusion because of the operational implications of low observable technology for future fighters.

The combat debut of the F-117A took place in Panama, as part of Operation Just Cause, but its real test came in the Gulf War in 1991. There it carried out precision attacks on targets in the heavily defended Baghdad area apparently without being detected. Its nav/attack kit gives a very accurate time on target, which enabled a small and obviously widely spaced force of F-117As flying singly, to put down their bombs within a matter of seconds of each other. The importance of this is made clear when one realises that bombs going down are an immediate signal for anti-aircraft barrage fire to start coming up.

What are the difficulties of stealth operations? Firstly they must be carried out with a total absence of emissions, and in radio silence. Friendly fighters must be kept well out of the way for two reasons. Firstly, even at night a chance visual contact, and with it the possibility of mistaken identity, cannot be entirely discounted. Secondly, the risk of mid-air collision between friendlies is higher than normal, the F-117A having no radar to warn it of impending disaster although it does have RWR, while the conventional radar-equipped fighter is unable to detect it. One of the unofficial Gulf War stories has an F-15 driver being startled to see an F-117A whizzing past, while his radar screen remained clear.

Other potential problem areas are air refuelling in radio silence where more than one bird is scheduled to a tanker, and the creation of safe corridors through the defences for the F-117A to ingress and egress. Nor can the F-117A be used in daylight, except in the almost total absence of opposition, while any attempt to operate in formation to comply with the cardinal principle of concentration of force, would be doomed to failure. Finally, confined to medium altitude attacks at night, its sensors and precision weaponry still has no answer to adverse weather, and on many occasions during the Gulf War, the Black Jets were unable to identify their targets, and were forced to bring their loads home.

What are the weaknesses of the F-117A? Firstly, it is vulnerable to a sudden advance in radar technology, which could conceivably make it obsolete overnight. Secondly, if it should be detected visually by an enemy fighter, it stands little chance of escape. At Le Bourget 1991, an F-117A driver assured me that it handles just like a T-38. If true, this speaks volumes for the quadruplex digital FBW system, which was based on that of the F-16, but the thought of all those vortices swirling around the angles makes me dubious. And the high drag caused cannot do anything for acceleration and climb rate. But even if it does handle well, all those flat plates tilting about as the Black Jet manoeuvres would be likely to make it visible on radar, even if only for short periods. The fact is, in the combat zone, it is not supposed to manoeuvre. Finally, its sharply swept wings and low aspect ratio make it dependent on long runways and fixed bases, and these are vulnerable in turn.

To summarize, low observables are very much a thing of the future, but they must be combined with the traditional fighter virtues of speed and agility. But the angular F-117A is very much previous generation stealth technology, as the rather later B-2, and the now cancelled A-12 configurations show. The two Advanced Tactical Fighter contenders, which are dealt with in the next chapter, show a carefully honed compromise between low observables and traditional fighter performance and agility. The F-117A appears to be very much a "one off" design which made use of the technology available at the time of its conception. Since then, computers have attained the capability of predicting radar reflective characteristics of curved surfaces.

Pilots Associate, Voice Control, and Big Picture

As aircraft have become ever more complicated, so flying and fighting them has become increasingly demanding. Workload is very high, and it is not unknown for a pilot to "max out" under pressure, while intensive training is needed to get the best out of the systems. An increasing amount of effort has been put into finding ways of reducing the pilot's workload to more manageable proportions. Improved Huds, CRT cockpit displays, and HOTAS have all been part of this process, but all of these need operating, and make extra demands on eyes, brain, and manual dexterity.

Pilot's Associate is a programme developed for the ATF. This is intended to fill much of the function of a backseater in a two-place aircraft; monitoring systems and advising the pilot on such matters as situation assessment and changes, aircraft systems status, on-going mission planning etc. It is highly dependent on artificial intelligence, with software programmes based on human thought processes. One of its functions, already tested on an F-15, will be to reconfigure a damaged aircraft to fly as near normally as possible by changing the ways in which control surfaces interact with each other.

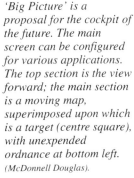

'Big Picture' is a proposal for the cockpit of the future. The main screen can be configured for various applications. The top section is the view forward; the main section is a moving map, superimposed upon which is a target (centre square), with unexpended ordnance at bottom left. (McDonnell Douglas).

In a confused tactical situation, PA will assess the threat and offer an optimum solution which can be acted upon or rejected by the pilot. It will not be a battle-winning system in its own right, but merely an adviser, offering a choice of standard solutions to complex but standard or near-standard problems. PA may also take over ECM functions at need, freeing some of the pilot's concentration for more urgent matters.

It has been said that in modern air combat, the difference between the ace and the turkey is that the ace monitors only the data which he needs to know, while the turkey tries to monitor everything in sight and mentally overloads as a result. The main function of PA is to present priorities in a critical situation by presenting information rather than data, thereby increasing pilot efficiency.

Presentation of information is one of the great problems of PA. Voice control and warning is a favoured method, and it is conceivable that PA might blare "break left you dumb shmuck!" in the manner of the ultimate back seat driver.

Voice control has certain problems to be overcome, and work in this field is continuing. The first is speech recognition. As many pilots fly the same machine, it has to be able to interpret accents correctly, from the Yeager-type hillbilly drawl to the British exchange officer's "I say chaps!" It also has to be able to decipher the strangled grunts of a pilot under high g loads. Nor are the problems all one way. Many pilots find spoken instruction (one particular system is known as "Bitchin' Betty") irritating, while others, concentrating on a critical phase in combat, have been known to mentally blot out warning calls, totally failing to hear them. But this notwithstanding, voice warning and control is part of the fighter future.

Well into the future is Big Picture, under development by McDonnell Douglas. The areas devoted to display in current fighters are tiny. At one point it was proposed to put the Joint Tactical Information Display System (JTIDS) in the cockpit of every F-15, but in practice it was found that trying to cram the tactical situation for 300 miles around onto a five inch square screen produced a good simulation of a disturbed ants nest, and the idea was dropped. Big Picture is an attempt to remedy this, but making the entire dash area one large screen on which a variety of presentations can be shown. These would include the overall tactical situation, or the terrain ahead, showing the engagement envelopes of known missile and AAA batteries while predicting the safest path between them, or attack profiles. Other information needed can be superimposed in small patches set on the periphery of the critical information. The display will of course be in colour, to make interpretation easier. Changes can be made by voice control, or simply by touching the sensitive screen.

Big Picture is the technology of the far future, and while it offers tremendous advantages, it also sets tremendous challenges. It has even been suggested that it could be thought controlled, but this might have hilarious consquences if the pilot's mind wandered briefly.

Many of the things described in this chapter may feature on the future generation of fighters. It does however seem that the long predicted era of the fully automated, unmanned fighter, has moved at least a little nearer.

TOP: *The Super Mirage 4000 was basically a scaled-up, twin-engined 2000, with canard foreplanes. Very capable, it was also very costly. (AMD-BA/Aviaplans).*

BOTTOM: *The F-20 Tigershark at high speed over the Nevada Desert. A potent little aeroplane, it failed to attract enough customers. (Northrop).*

CHAPTER TWELVE
The European Canard Deltas

When it first appeared in January 1974, the F-16 set new standards in fighter manoeuvrability. As with the fad for Mach 2 a couple of decades earlier, it became fashionable to stress all later fighters for 9g and make them actually sustain this loading over a portion of the flight envelope, be it never so small. But while equalling the agility of the F-16 appeared not too difficult, surpassing it by a margin large enough to warrant putting a totally new fighter into production was something else again. The reason was not too hard to find. 9g was pushing the limit of what the pilot was able to take and still be effective. In effect, this meant that turn performance had reached a plateau, beyond which it was very hard to advance without straying into the unexplored territory of post-stall manoeuvres.

There were however certain areas in which improvements could be made. Payload/range was an obvious choice; acceleration and rate of climb were others, by using higher specific excess power. In the agility stakes, a larger sustained 9g envelope, faster instantaneous rates of turn, faster pitch rates, and greater high alpha capability (the F-16 is a little short in this department), would all contribute towards a better fighter. Naturally there was further scope in terms of avionics and weaponry, but the baseline aircraft to be outdone in the black box field was the F/A-18 rather than the F-16.

Unlike the 1950's, when a whole rash of different shapes filled the sky, by 1980 the science of aerodynamics had reached the stage where similar requirements gave birth to similar configurations. In Western Europe the canard delta, which reduced trim drag and enhanced supersonic manoeuvrability, reigned supreme. This trend did not however extend to the USA, for the simple reason that replacement fighters were needed in Europe on a shorter timescale. The USA, still building Tomcats, Eagles, Falcons and Hornets in improved versions, could afford to take a longer view, and go for a replacement fighter which was much further advanced.

Four canard delta fighters were spawned in this period; the Israeli IAI Lavi, which was not really European anyway, and as related in The Nearly Birds, foundered on cost at an early stage; the Swedish JAS 39 Gripen; the British /German/ Italian/Spanish European Fighter Aircraft (EFA); and the French AMD/BA Rafale.

Saab JAS 39 Gripen

Intended to replace the elderly Draken and rather limited Viggen in Swedish service, Gripen was conceived in 1980 as a single seat multi-role lightweight fighter, and a consortium of Swedish companies called IG JAS, covering airframe, systems, propulsion, and avionics, was set up to develop it. An initial contract for five prototypes and 30 production aircraft was signed in June 1982, with an option for 110 further aircraft.

Having produced the multi-role Viggen, Sweden was familiar with the canard delta layout, and unsurprisingly this was chosen for the new fighter. But whereas Viggen canards were fixed, with control surfaces on the trailing edge, those of the Gripen were all-moving and close coupled. The Viggen layout had been adopted to provide STOL capability, and also to allow a flat angle on takeoff and landing. Combined with negative stability and FBW, those of the Gripen enhance manoeuvrability by improving lift/ drag ratio, and also give a better ride at low level, flattening out the bumps by responding automatically to wind gusts.

A further advantage of the close coupled canard delta configuration is that its greater aerodynamic efficiency allowed the smaller Gripen to carry much the same payload as the rather large machine it was to replace, while providing a higher level of manoeuvrability. The design empty weight of the Gripen was set at about 11,000lb or so, half that of the Viggen, and barely two thirds that of the F-16A.

Small size, low weight, and a single engined layout made the choice of powerplant crucial. The contenders were P & W's PW 120; GE's F404; and Turbo Union's RB 199. The first was too heavy, the last not ideally suited to the fighter mission. The F404 was selected for further development by GE and Volvo Flygmotor to become the RM12 turbofan. Tolerance to birdstrike was brought in line with exacting Swedish standards, mass flow was increased and turbine entry temperature raised to provid 18,100lb of static thrust at maximum power and 12,140lb at military rating; 12 and 15 percent improvements respectively over the original F404. It was further anticipated that maximum power could be raised to 20,000lb, and finally to 22,000lb after further development.

Gripen was rolled out in April 1987, and it was immediately obvious that everything possible had been done to reduce size and weight. A chin intake would probably have been the optimum aerodynamic solution, but this position would have deepened the forward fuselage considerably, and given the Swedish practice of operating from public highways, would have increased the FOD risk. Cheek inlets were used, accepting the airflow distortion during sideslip caused by this location. With no Mach 2 requirement to meet, these were fixed geometry. Large all-moving canards with slight dihedral were mounted on the sides of the inlets, rather higher than the plane of the mid-set wings.

A wrap-around windshield was combined with a single piece canopy hinged on the left side, which was faired into the line of the fuselage in the manner of the Mirage 2000. The fairing immediately astern of the transparency housed the environmental control system and heat exchangers; making a virtue of necessity, these last exhausted here, with the fairing bulged on either side of a dorsal spine to allow the efflux to escape. The spine itself housed control and cable runs.

The wing had a few degrees of anhedral, and was of cropped delta configuration which allowed carriage of AAMs on wingtip rails. The leading edge was straight, with a fixed inboard section and very small root extensions, while two piece slats occupied the remainder, a dogtooth discontinuity forcing the break at about two thirds span. The trailing edge was swept slightly forward, with two piece differentially moving flaperons on each side. Meeting the fuselage with a small fillet, it ended sufficiently far forward to allow speed brakes to be mounted on the fuselage sides astern of it. A certain amount of wing/body blending was evident, which although adopted for aerodynamic reasons, would have the effect of reducing radar cross-section.

The vertical tail was swept at a steep angle on the leading edge, with single piece rudder, and a large housing for ECM gear near the top. Carbon fibre spars and skinning over honeycomb made up much of the fin structure. Carbon fibre was widely used throughout, accounting for about 30 percent of the structure.

Surprisingly for a fighter intended to operate from road surfaces no more than 800m long by 17m wide, Gripen had no reverse thrust, no braking parachute, and no tail hook.

Like Viggen, it was designed to make a hard, no-flare touchdown, but then, unlike Viggen, be pulled up by braking alone. To aid this, a sturdy, aft-retracting twin-wheel nosegear was stressed for heavy braking, with the canard surfaces deflected steeply down to provide extra aerodynamic braking.

Radar is the Ericsson PS-05A multi-mode pulse Doppler set, developed in conjunction with Ferranti specifically for Gripen. Little more than half the size of Viggen's PS-46/A, it has double the power output. Operating in X band, PS-05/A uses low, medium and high PRFs, with Frequency Modulation for high resolution and long range detection. The actual range has not been revealed, but is probably of the order of 50nm against a standard fighter sized target. Air to air modes include long range search and track, multi-target track while scan, short range wide angle search and track, and automated missile and gun fire control.

The cockpit is essentially of the 'eighties, with the by now almost obligatory three multi-function displays, HOTAS, and a wide angle diffraction-optics Hud. The control column is central, and the lightweight ejection seat developed by Martin Baker from their Mk 10 has the usual 22deg rake angle. Nor does the pilot sit up very high, the cockpit sills being only just below shoulder level.

Standard air to air weaponry consists of two RB 72 Skyflash SARH missiles and four RB 24 Sidewinder heat homers, although Amraam is projected for the future subject to agreement by the US DoD. A single 27mm Mauser BK27 cannon is located low on the left fuselage. Air to surface ordnance is the same as carried by Viggen, including up to two RBS 15F anti-ship missiles.

Nearly two years passed between rollout and first flight, which took place in December 1988 with test pilot Stig Holmstrom at the controls. Much of the intervening period had been spent in validating the software for the triplex digital FBW system. No mechanical reversion had been provided, the backup being a triplex analogue system. To digress for a moment, one of the buzzwords of the late 'eighties was "it's only a software change", thereby implying something easy, quick, and cheap. The complexity of software programmes has since ensured that it is none of these things, and this expression is no longer heard.

Returning to Gripen, it was therefore not good news to find that handling was a bit twitchy. It became even worse when in February 1989, the prototype piled up on landing and was written off, apparently as a result of deficiencies in the control laws which at low speed put test pilot Lars Radestrom out of phase with the aircraft motion. He survived with minor injuries.

It was May 1990 before the software was corrected and the second and subsequent prototypes were cleared to resume the flight test programme. Other problems concerned the engines. Compressor resonance, slow build-up of thrust, and insufficient durability in the afterburner lining, all demanded solutions. In an attempt to make up lost ground, an intensive flying programme was instituted, which delayed Gripen's international debut until Farnborough '92. Seen on the ground, its tiny dimensions were emphasised by the proximity of the hardware around it. Its flying display was rather muted, with no more than 7g and little use of afterburner. As Lars Radestrom commented, the intensive flight test programme had left insufficient time to work up a really polished display. It also prevented it from making an appearance at Le Bourget '93.

Gripen was originally to have entered Flygvapnet service in 1990, with F.10 Wing at Angelholm the first unit scheduled to receive the type. This has now slipped badly, and matters were made worse on 8 August 1993 when what was described as a software anomaly forced Lars Radestrom to abandon a production aircraft over Stockholm, fortunately with no casualties on the ground.

Many attempts have been made to produce a true multi-role bird. These have all foundered due to the conflicting aerodynamic and avionic requirements of the different missions. Whether the Swedes have done any better remains to be seen, but the size and weight constraints have certainly stacked the odds against them.

Eurofighter EF 2000

When one considers how many promising fighters have sunk without trace as a result of the inability of two services, typically air force and navy, to agree on requirements, it seems downright amazing that any international programme involving three or four nations can even get started, let alone succeed. Even when they do, when one considers what a small nation like Sweden can achieve virtually unaided, one wonders why major industrial nations bother.

Once upon a time, Britain, France, West Germany (as it then was), and Italy decided that they needed an Agile Combat Aircraft (ACA) to enter service in the 1990s. Total requirements were estimated as 800 aircraft, enough to gain the benefits of a large production run, even though this would have to be split four ways. Initial agreement was surprisingly swift. The new fighter was to be a single seater canard delta, with two engines. While air to air performance was primary, it was to be given a significant ground attack capability. The prospective partners agreed that the target weight should be around 10 tonnes; all except France that is, who with an eye on the export market, wanted to keep it down to 8.5 tonnes. Avions Marcel Dassault also wanted project leadership, arguing that their greater experience with tail-less deltas made them the natural choice. The result was inevitable; France went her own way with the Avion de Combat Experimentale(ACX); later Rafale, while the remaining partners, joined by Spain in 1985, stayed with what had become the European Fighter Aircraft(EFA).

The first prototype EF 2000 takes to the air for the first time on 27 March 1994 at Manching, flown by DASA Chief Test Pilot Peter Weger. (BAe).

EAP was a technology demonstrator for EF 2000. Although it had a similar canard delta layout, it differed in many respects, notably the cranked leading edge, the much taller vertical tail, and the box-like intake. (BAe).

A technology demonstrator, clumsily called Experimental Aircraft Programme(EAP), made its first flight from Warton in August 1988, flown by BAe test pilot Dave Eagles. It was then rushed through the initial phase of flight testing in order to make its public debut at Farnborough that September.

EAP was a stumpy, solid aircraft, its truncated appearance accentuating its size. The wing was a cranked delta, swept at 57deg inboard, reducing to 45deg outboard. Sized for high turn rate and short landing, construction was almost entirely of composite materials, aeroelastically tailored to take up an optimum shape under high g loadings. The cropped tips were left plain, with low drag missile rails under rather than on them. Wing cambering, via split leading edge slats and trailing edge flaperons, was automatically controlled by the quadruplex FBW system as a function of airspeed and alpha to maximise lift/drag ratio in manoeuvring flight and minimise the shock wave in supersonic straight line flight.

Swept canard surfaces with a marked amount of anhedral were set actually in line with the canopy, unlike Gripen and Rafale, which had them located well back. This provided a long moment arm for optimum high alpha control, although it rather obscured the view sideways and downwards. This was not thought to matter too much, as studies showed that the majority of targets appear either above the fighter, where they are easily seen, or below and astern, where they are masked by the wing. Very few appear in a position where they would be masked by the foreplanes. When manoeuvring, the foreplanes offer even less area to obstruct the view, whereas a rearward location restricts aft visibility in turning flight. The forward position was therefore considered advantageous overall.

A wrap-around windshield followed by a two piece canopy long enough to accommodate a second crew position without alteration gave an excellent view from the cockpit. It was then faired into a dorsal spine from which rose a massive fin, based on that of Tornado and extending almost halfway along the fuselage. The spine housing just aft of the canopy doubled as a speed brake.

EAP was powered by two Turbo Union RB 199 turbofans as used in Tornado, pending the development of the definitive powerplant. A fixed chin intake featured a hinged lower lip which could be drooped at low speeds or high alpha to improve inlet airflow.

The cockpit was state of the art, with three colour MFDs to present information; HOTAS, and an ejection seat raked at rather more than the usual 22deg angle. This was still not as radical as that of the F-16, for reasons stated earlier.

EAP gave a welcome if restrained performance at Farnborough 86. Barely a month into the flight test programme, it was limited at that time to 5g and 20deg alpha, which made it look rather subdued against Rafale, also making its international debut. The French fighter, having flown a month earlier, had had a greater portion of its flight envelope cleared beforehand.

EAP explored the flight regime in easy stages. It handled well, and was very precise in control, even at low speeds. On many trials it carried dummy weaponry; two Asraam and four Skyflash missiles. Cleared to 7g (out of the design loading of +9/-3g) in time for Le Bourget 87, it was able to give a far more convincing performance than hitherto.

Meanwhile development of the definitive EFA prototype had been proceeding apace. Early artist's impressions showed considerable differences between EFA and EAP. The cranked leading edge had been straightened, giving a cropped delta planform of 53deg sweep. Trials showed that the maximum coefficient of lift (CLmax) with a cranked delta changed non-linearly, going from totally unstable just before CLmax to totally stable just afterwards. The change did not reflect a remedy so much as an improvement.

The elongated EAP canopy was replaced by a more orthodox bubble, and the dorsal spine had been tapered into a flat upper fuselage from which an all-moving vertical tail projected, looking as disproportionately small as EAP's tail had appeared oversized. An ECM housing was situated near the top, while a bullet fairing appeared low on the trailing edge. The plain wingtips had been supplanted by cigar shaped ECM housings, and four Skyflash missiles were now carried semi-conformally along the corners of the lower fuselage. Finally, the canards had been moved forward to a position level with the windshield.

At Le Bourget 87, a full scale mockup was exhibited which showed further changes. The most noticeable of these was the "smiling" intake, which now assumed an upward curve. This gave lower drag and better stealth characteristics. A press briefing released at the time stated that stealth technology had been applied extensively throughout the design, although nobody at the Eurofighter Chalet was prepared to enlarge on this. Just down the road, Dassault were being equally coy on stealth; it appears that both projects were aiming at a head-on RCS roughly one quarter to one fifth that of a conventional fighter. It has since emerged that curved intake ducts are used to mask the engine compressor faces, stealth tiles shield reflective internal components, while radar-absorbent material will coat some other areas, such as leading edges.

Another obvious change was the vertical tail. Gone was the all-moving slab surface, which had been changed to a larger (though not as large as EAP) fixed fin and moving rudder. This was said to give better handling characteristics in the extreme corners of the flight envelope. The bullet fairing was now at the base of the fin and a small air scoop had appeared low on the leading edge. The fin-mounted pod disappeared shortly after when the avionics consortium announced that the self-protection kit would almost all be contained in the wing pods.

Later still came the adoption of a circular section radar nose, replacing the former ogive; and a general slimming of the fuselage, made possible by improved installation of internal equipment. These gave a slight drag reduction. The number of AAMs increased from six to eight, and finally to ten, with three under each wing. Up to six AIM-120 Amraam could be carried, plus four 'winders or Asraam. The air to air armament was completed with a 27mm Mauser cannon. In all there were 13 hardpoints, seven of which could carry air to surface ordnance.

The project crept along at a snail's pace until 1992, when German intransigence, arising from a lack of funds, and fuelled by the disappearance of the Soviet threat, looked like torpedoing the whole shebang. It survived, thanks to strenuous efforts by Britain and Italy, to emerge with a handful of compromises and a new name. It was now Eurofighter 2000.

The first two Eurofighter 2000 prototypes are powered by two RB 199 Mk 104Es, but the definitive engine is the Eurojet EJ200, based on the experimental Rolls-Royce XG40. The decision to use a totally new powerplant was taken primarily because there was no modern engine in the right thrust class. Uprating an existing engine is unsatisfactory; it is not only limited by the original design, but has reduced growth potential. This ruled out GE's F404, which was by then approaching twenty years old.

EJ 200 is a two spool engine rated at 20,000lb max. and 12,000lb military power, with considerable growth potential. Bypass ratio is a nominal 0.4, overall pressure ratio is 25, while thrust/weight ratio is a massive 10. The latest advances in metallurgy and cooling are incorporated, including wide chord compressor blades for increased efficiency and FOD resistance. Simple and modular, it is optimised for the fighter mission.

The primary airborne sensor is the European Collaborative Radar(ECR) 90, a third generation X-band pulse-Doppler set developed by a Ferranti-led consortium. Unhappy early experiences with Tornado's Foxhunter caused many people to worry that ECR 90 was a new and totally unproven set, possibly full of bugs. In fact it is largely based on Ferranti's Blue Vixen, yet still contains much up to the minute technology. A mechanically scanned planar array antenna driven by electric motors was selected as best able to provide the scan rates and angular changes demanded by the air to air role.

Few performance details are available, but it is known that ECR 90 has a total of 31 air/air, air/surface, and navigational modes, many of which already meet the specification. It is also claimed that ECR 90 has superior automated functions, target detection, covert features, and ECCM. It includes adaptive scanning and fine range resolution, and has a low transmitter duty ratio, which increases the probability of detection of targets with a small radar cross-section. Rumour control gives it the ability to carry out at least ten simultaneous attacks.

ECR 90 is supplemented by IRST developed by a Thorn-EMI-led consortium, and a helmet mounted sight and night aids will be an integral part of the weapons system. Defensive Aids SubSystems (DASS) is however an area where savings have been made, and both Germany and Spain are going to be several pfennigs short of a mark. Initially DASS included active radar jamming, with phased array antennae; electronic support kit, and a missile launch and approach warning system, in addition to the usual chaff and flares, plus a laser warning receiver. In addition, Towed Radar Decoys, unappetisingly referred to as Turds, will be mounted. These last, first used operationally by RAF

Nimrods in the Gulf War, are streamed 100m astern of the parent aircraft to attract the attentions of hostile missiles.

Carbon fibre composites are extensively used by Eurofighter 2000, and cover 70 percent of the surface area. In addition to structural members, titanium is also used for the canards, which are superplastically formed, and the outboard flaperons, as well as around the hot end. Aluminium lithium is widely used, on the leading edge slats, the leading and trailing edges of the tail; and the wing/fuselage and wing/fin junctions. This material is also used for small strakes, similar to the Mirage 2000, located beneath the cockpit sills and above the level of the wings.

Political infighting apart, long delays have been caused by the unusually protracted validation period of the flight control system software. Taxying trials began in the early summer of 1993, but first flight, from Manching, was delayed until 27 March 1994. The second prototype followed from Warton on 6 April. The earliest that Eurofighter 2000 can enter service is now 2000, more than four years late. Perhaps this time could be usefully spent in thinking up a decent name, such as Spitfire 2.

Dassault Rafale

Designed originally for the air superiority mission with a secondary attack capability, Rafale has a similar configuration to EFA, although it is rather smaller and lighter. It also has a further function. It is the one aircraft which can keep France in the forefront of aerospace technology, and therefore for reasons of national prestige it could not be allowed to fail.

The Avion de Combat Experimentale (ACX) first appeared in the guise of a technology demonstrator, later named Rafale A. Powered by two F404-GE-400 augmented turbofans, Rafale A was dimensionally larger and heavier than the definitive article, but otherwise almost indistinguishable from it. Piloted by Chief Test Pilot Guy Mitaux-Maurouard, it first flew in July 1986 in striking red, white and blue livery, which contrasted sharply with the black and gold worn by a model at Le Bourget '85, and which had caused it to be dubbed "The John Player Special" by irreverent Brits.

Although of similar canard delta configuration, it differed from EFA in many ways. The most striking of these was the engine inlet design, which represented an original way of combining the excellent pressure recovery characteristics of the side inlets of the Mirage 2000, with the high alpha efficiency of a chin intake. This was done by constricting the fuselage below the cockpit to give a segmental shaped inlet beneath a large streamlined bulge. Like EFA, there was no requirement to exceed Mach 2; the inlets were therefore fixed, with no moving ramps.

The sharply swept all-moving canards were located on the bulged section of fuselage above the inlets, well astern of the cockpit, and rather higher than the mid-set wing. The wing itself was sharply swept, with a small root extension inboard, and cropped at the tips to allow missile rails. Three section slats and three section elevons occupied leading and trailing edges respectively in Rafale A; in later aircraft these were reduced to two. The trailing edge was swept forward a tad, with a shelf-type fillet where it met the fuselage.

The fuselage ran smoothly back from the sharply pointed radome to the hot end, broken only by a long and sleek cockpit transparency. This tapered gently into a dorsal spine which ran the length of the fuselage, terminating in a bullet fairing which housed the drag 'chute. On the spine was mounted a sharply swept fin and rudder with an air scoop at its base, similar to that of the Mirage 2000, and featuring the same horizontal VOR aerials. Twin speed brakes were located on either side of the forward base of the fin.

The F404 engines were an interim measure until such time as the operational Rafale engine was available. The M53 as used for the Mirage 2000 was optimised for very high speed, high altitude performance, and was not ideally suited to an agile fighter at lower levels. The engine chosen was the new SNECMA M88-2, a twin spool augmented turbofan, rated at 16,875lb maximum and 11,250lb military thrust. These figures are rather lower than those of EJ200, but Rafale being a smaller aircraft, two M88-2s will provide a comparable t/w ratio to that of Eurofighter. Further development has produced 19,558lb for the M88-3 which powers production aircraft, while 23,000lb maximum and 15,000lb military thrust may become available at some future date.

With few exceptions the cockpit layout differs little from Eurofighter 2000, with colour MFDs, although one is the "head-level" tactical situation display as described for the Mirage 2000, located immediately below the wide field collimated holographic Hud. The ejection seat is raked back at a 29deg angle to increase pilot g tolerance, and a sidestick controller is fitted to the right hand console. The now almost obligatory quadruplex FBW flight control system gives carefree handling, and it is quite possible this may end up as fly-by-light. Crouzet voice control, with a vocabulary of 37 words, oddly enough in English, will probably be installed in the production article.

Radar is the RBE(radar à balayage electronique 2) multi-mode pulse Doppler set, developed by Thomson CSF and Electronique Serge Dassault. The first European radar to use an active array antenna, RBE 2 uses passive electronic scanning to form and direct multiple radar beams, allowing different modes, i.e. air search and terrain avoidance, to be used simultaneously. During its development, the air to ground mission came to take equal importance with air to air, and this is reflected in the radar more than any other feature. Detection range is stated to be 50nm even against low level targets, with a high degree of resolution, and high, medium or low PRFs are automatically selected as required. Up to six targets can be engaged simultaneously. RBE 2 computer power is stated to exceed one billion operations per second, and as with ECR 90, gallium arsenide modules provide ultra fast data processing. IRST and a helmet mounted sight are integrated into the weapons system.

Designed to take off and land in 400m, Rafale has a beefy main gear to absorb the shock of a no-flare landing. Both Armee de l'Air and Aeronavale variants are fitted with tail hooks. Like Eurofighter 2000, Rafale uses a high proportion of advanced composites, some of them second generation, in its construction. Aluminium lithium is used at the wing/body blend, while the leading edge slats are of titanium alloy.

Rafale C has 14 hardpoints, five of which are wet, and can carry up to eight tonnes of stores externally. Air to air armament is a maximum of eight MICA AAMs, with an alternative load of six MICA, with two Magics on the wingtip rails. Other weapons carried will be the AS 30L and Apache AGMs, the nuclear ASMP and ASLP, and the supersonic ANS anti-ship missile. A 30mm cannon, the new, fast firing GIAT M791B, is carried low in the left fuselage side.

The first flight undertaken with the M88-2 engine took place in February 1990. Four development aircraft were ordered; C 01, M 01 and M 02 single seaters, and B 01 as a two seater. The M prefix stands for Marine, the carrier based variant.

Rafale M, the carrier fighter, varies little from the land based Rafale C. A rather heavier main gear and arrester hook, plus local structural strengthening, and nose gear designed for extra energy absorption, are the main differences, while Rafale M has one less hardpoint. Initial deck trials, consisting of bolters, were carried out on *Clemenceau* in 1987 by former Aeronavale pilot Yves Kerherve. He found that while alpha on landing was, at 16 or 17deg, a bit steep, there were no real problems; low speed handling in the unstable airflow over the round-down was satisfactory, while rapid throttle response ensured safe touch and goes.

In flight, Rafale is reported to have reached a stabilized alpha of plus 32 and minus 6deg, and has sustained a speed of Mach 1.4 without afterburning. This was probably attained by using augmentation to attain a high Mach number, then cutting the 'burners and letting the speed drop back and stabilize at full military power. Mach 2 was reached in March 1987, and 750kt has been demonstrated at low level, against a requirement for 800kt. Manoeuvrability is good, and Rafale has been flown down to speeds of 80kt. At Farnborough '88, Dassault's Henri Suisse asked me to time Rafale through a 360deg turn. It took just 15 seconds, an impressive sustained turn rate of 24deg/sec. Design loading is +9/-3.6g.

As at late 1991, Rafale's situation had considerably altered. Firstly the Armee de l'Air version was relabelled Rafale D (D = discret, or stealth). Secondly, Gulf War operations by A de l'A Jaguars highlighted the excessive workload of attack pilots. As the ground attack aspect had taken on ever increasing importance, it was decided that most A de l'A Rafales were to be two seaters, in order to share the load, leaving Aeronavale as main operator of the single seat variant. Delivery is now scheduled for 1997.

Cockpit of Rafale, showing the wide-angle Hud with a 'look-level' display just below it; three colour multi-function displays, and a sidestick controller.
(Photo AMD-BA/Aviaplans).

CHAPTER THIRTEEN

The 21st Century Fighter

While the Europeans were taking the next step forward from the capability levels of the F-16 and F/A-18, the USA began to chart new and unexplored territory. The air is essentially an arena of offensive action, in which the greatest effectiveness is gained by carrying the fight to the enemy. A defensive posture may sometimes be necessary, but it means ceding the initiative; being forced to respond to threats as they arise, and allowing an enemy the freedom to exploit any perceived weaknesses. Much depends on the area of operations. Those over friendly territory are backed by SAM and AAA defences, and have all the advantages of ground radar and control, plus friendly ECM. Operations over neutral territory, such as the North Sea would have been had the Cold War erupted, give the advantage to the side best equipped for autonomous action. But operations over hostile territory mean that multi-layered defences; air, ground, and electronic, must be neutralised and penetrated.

The first indication of what might be possible came in the Beka'a action of 1982, described earlier, which ended in a turkey shoot. In a matter of days, the Israelis gained absolute air superiority, albeit over a limited area. But in the "worst case" scenario of all-out conventional war in Central Europe, operating over a much larger area against a determined, well trained, well equipped and numerically superior opponent, there was little or no chance of reducing the defenders to a similar degree of impotence. The alternative was to acquire the ability to operate successfully in hostile airspace. But how?

Modern air warfare had become almost completely dependent on radar; for early warning, for GCI, and for air combat. Without radar, air defence systems were almost completely helpless. If resources to sufficiently disrupt the opposition were lacking, some other means must be found. The Americans attacked the problem on two fronts; stealth and speed.

While it was obviously impossible to build a totally radar-invisible aircraft, significant reductions of its RCS would give several advantages. It would become more difficult to detect by enemy ground or airborne radars, and even if detectable, the range would shorten considerably. These factors would combine to make it far more difficult to track. In BVR combat it would allow first shots to be taken at bandits in the front hemisphere with relative impunity. It would also close down the range at which an active radar guided missile could commence its terminal homing phase, while greatly increasing the probability of it breaking lock if it did. The engagement envelopes of radar-laid SAMs and guns would be reduced by a significant amount, often to the point where they had insufficient time after detection to track, predict, and launch, before the low RCS aircraft vanished from their screens.

Low heat signature was another important factor. While IRST cannot give range, its angular discrimination is rather better than that of radar. A possible future threat is a series of co-ordinated ground IRST stations, able to provide accurate tracking of heat sources, providing range and altitude data by means of triangulation. Finally there was the obvious threat of heat homing missiles to be countered.

155

The second American thrust was speed. During the first half-century of air combat, speed reigned supreme, even at the expense of manoeuvrability. Speed conferred surprise and this, more often than not, gave victory. Only with the combat debut of the Mach 2 wonderplanes in the late '60s did the importance of speed appear to lapse, and even then it was illusory. Up to and including the Korean War, there had been little difference between fast cruise and maximum speed, and maximum speed had traditionally been taken as the most important parameter. In the supersonic era, this misconception continued, primarily due to the need for speed to intercept fast and high flying jet bombers.

It was a long while before it became obvious that fast cruise, sustainable for long periods, was a truer measure of air combat advantage. Back in World War 2, this had been recognised by the Soviet Union. Russian fighter pilots in the combat zone flew always at full throttle; not at emergency power, which would have blown up their engines in short order, but at maximum sustainable speed. This reduced the time between sighting and engaging an opponent, while increasing the time between being sighted and being engaged. In the first case, achieving surprise was easier; in the second avoiding being surprised was easier, with the advantage to the Russians in both cases.

In the jet and missile era, two factors were ultimately convincing in the V_{max} versus V_{cruise} debate. The first was that Mach 2 was never used in combat. Acceleration was a lengthy process; it took forever to get there, and when you did, the fuel warning light came on and it was time to go home. Not that you could do much at Mach 2, other than fly in a straight line. The second factor was the way that missile launch envelopes shrank in the presence of a rapidly receding target. A speed of Mach 1.4 plus is one of the most reliable ways of clearing six oclock, firstly because missile launch range from astern reduces tremendously as a function of target speed; secondly because the interception geometry and timing for an attack becomes incredibly precise, and only an extremely fortuitously placed interceptor would be able to attempt it. Against a beam attack, such high speeds create angle off very quickly, possibly exceeding the seeker look angle, and certainly shrinking the launch envelope drastically, to say nothing of the missile fuzing problems involved. A fighter with low radar and IR signatures, cruising at supersonic speed, makes effective interception very risky from head-on, and nearly impossible from other angles.

Studies for a new fighter were launched in 1981, and by 1984, the USAF had decided pretty much what it wanted. The foundations of the Advanced Tactical Fighter (ATF) were laid. STOL capability was both obvious and unglamorous, with a runway length minimum of 2,000ft. Stealth was regarded as essential, and whereas the European manufacturers were aiming at a reduction to perhaps 25 percent in head-on RCS as compared to a conventional fighter, against fighter radar wavelengths only, the target for ATF was set at 1/100th that of the F-15 against all wavelengths used by fighter, ground and AWACS radars. This was a much harder task, and was far more reliant on the deflection of radar emissions than their absorbtion. Not only was stealth a matter of low RCS and IR signature; emissions such as radar and jamming transmitters had to be very tightly controlled. On the other hand, stealth could not be allowed to compromise fighting capability to any great extent, particularly in the field of traditional fighter manoeuvring. There could be no guarantee that combat would never occur at subsonic speeds and visual ranges, in which stealth could play only a marginal part, and so the ATF had to be able to hold its own in this regime as well.

Maximum speed was set at Mach 2.5, but more importantly, ATF had to be able to supercruise in military power at more than Mach 1.4, while having an operational radius on internal fuel significantly greater than that of current fighters; a figure of 700nm being quoted. Manoeuvre capability of 6g at Mach 1.8 was called for. A further feature was high operational altitude. ATF had to be able to fly and fight at up to 70,000ft. This would eliminate most of the hostile SAM threats and severely reduce the effectiveness of the remainder, while placing a high premium on look-down, shoot-down capability. Turnround time was to be less than half that of the F-15, while maintenance man hours per flight hour were barely one third. The final requirement was a clean takeoff weight of 50,000lb. These were target figures; not specifications which had to be met at all costs.

A request for proposals issued in 1985 drew seven responses. Of these, submissions by Lockheed and Northrop were selected for further development, and in 1986, an order was placed for two prototypes from each company to be flown and evaluated. Lockheed teamed with Boeing and General Dynamics to produce the YF-22, and Northrop with McDonnell Douglas for the YF-23. First flight was set for 1989. Engines need more lead time, as they must be well advanced even before the prototype airframe flies, and both General Electric and Pratt & Whitney were commissioned in 1982 to develop new engines, the XF120 and XF119 respectively. Two aircraft of each type were to be built, one of each powered by the YF120, the other by the YF119, as the pre-production engines were designated, for evaluation of the airframe/engine combination.

The canted surfaces seen here on the Lockheed YF-22A obviously owe much to the faceting of the F-117A, but the technology has moved on, allowing more aerodynamic shaping to be incorporated. Particularly noticeable are the diamond cross-section of the nose, and the canopy shaping. (Lockheed).

Both ATF engines were nominally rated at 35,000lb static thrust with full augmentation, and something in the region of 28,000lb at full military power, in order to meet supercruise requirements. Pratt & Whitney favoured a conventional layout based on their tried and proven F100, but with new blade designs and the latest advances in combuster and cooling technology and materials. It has fewer and more durable parts than engines currently in service. It is reasonable to assume that the YF119 has a rather higher pressure ratio than the F100-PW-129, attained with fewer compressor stages, and runs appreciably hotter, at up to 1,700deg Celsius.

General Electric, on the other hand, went for a more exotic solution. The turbofan has largely supplanted the turbojet in both military and civil service because of it's far better fuel economy. The larger the bypass ratio, the better the specific fuel consumption(sfc). But a really economical engine, such as one has on an airliner, is totally unsuitable for the fighter mission. In fact, at extremes of altitude and speed, the turbojet actually performs better than a turbofan.

Fighter engines have low bypass ratios, and are thus a compromise between an economical but staid HBR turbofan and a thirsty but lively turbojet. GE decided to have the best of both worlds, by using a variable cycle engine. In this, bypass air was drawn off in two places; downstream of the fan, and just ahead of the core. The airflow through these could be regulated so that the bypass air could be virtually closed off at need, turning the engine into a near-turbojet. Like almost all else in aviation, this was not new. Only recently revealed, in 1991, was the fact that Pratt & Whitney used a similar scheme in their J58, used to power the SR-71 to Mach 3. It is also possible that GE may have used a similar system in their J93, used for the B-70 Valkyrie, which also had sustained Mach 3 capability. Apart from the variable cycle, which obviously had repercussions on both weight and cost, GE used much the same technical advances as P&W in producing the YF120, which had 40 percent fewer parts than the F110-GE-229 fighter engine.

One thing both engines had in common were vectoring nozzles for short takeoff, enhanced manoeuvre, especially up high where the thin air offers little for aerodynamic controls to bite on; and to give recovery power from high alpha. Originally, thrust reversers were to be fitted, but these were eliminated at an early stage on weight and cost grounds. Lack of stealth may have been a further consideration, but in any event a 50 percent penalty in landing distance was deemed an acceptable tradeoff.

Weaponry was to consist of eight missiles; a mix of Amraam and Sidewinders carried in internal bays. On launch the weapons bay doors would open momentarily and a missile be extended into the slipstream before its rocket motor fired. Again this idea was not new; it had been used on Convair's 1950's vintage F-102 and F-106 interceptors. The main difference was that ATF would have to launch missiles at high g loadings as well as supersonic speeds.

An internal gun was also a necessity. Two options were available. The first was the Advanced Technology Gun(ATG) which was in the trials stage. Simpler than the M61 Vulcan, with only half as many parts, this was to fire case-telescoped ammunition developed by Ford Aerospace, which could be stored and handled in a smaller volume than traditional shells. ATG offered a very high muzzle velocity of 1,500m/sec, giving greater accuracy, longer range, and enhanced hitting power.

The alternative was an advanced version of the proven six barrel M61, with barrels lengthened by nearly 19 inches, which increased muzzle velocity from 1,050m/sec to 1,100m/sec by allowing the propellant to be more fully burnt before the projectile left the barrel. Component changes and new materials were used to hold the gun weight down to that of the original weapon. New 20mm ammunition with a ballistically better projectile shape would give greater range and accuracy. The standard 20mm projectile had been sadly lacking in this respect.

While ATG offered significant advantages over the rehashed M61, problems dogged the new weapon. The advanced M61 thus became the safe choice. It should be remembered that as missiles have become more able, guns have been pushed further down the pecking order. While they are still an important last ditch, instantly available weapon, which when fired are not vulnerable to countermeasures other than hard

manoeuvring, their value is greatly diminished in the primary scenario for which ATF was conceived. The advantages of higher muzzle velocity of the ATG were therefore not quite as great as might be supposed, and the selection of the advanced M61 was only a minor handicap.

Far more important was the avionics suite, and in fact this was more costly than the airframe. Active array technology was proposed for the radar, despite affordability doubts, and an INtegrated Electronic Warfare System (INEWS) and an Integrated Communication/Navigation/Identification System (ICNIA). Data transmission was by fibre optics, while Very High Speed Integrated Circuits (VHSIC) were used to handle the formidable processing power needed by the new fighter, which had an integrated computer core to tie everything together. This had the advantage of ensuring that different systems, for instance radar and active ECM emitters, do not interact with each other, a problem sometimes encountered in the Gulf War. Low observable antennas were shared between systems. Reliability requirements were high, and Pave Pillar fault tolerant architecture, capable of automatically reconfiguring itself in the event of a module failure, was used. This meant that systems failures could be avoided altogether in many cases, while in others, affected systems would degrade gradually rather go completely off-line. A glass cockpit with integrated colour displays able to show data from more than one system at a time, Pilots Associate as described previously, and voice control, were all incorporated. Surprisingly, the USAF decided late in 1990 that IRST was not sufficiently advanced to be included. Laser warning sensors were deemed non cost-effective, as only one laser threat existed in the world at that time.

A cloak of secrecy descended on the project, and the years following the initial contract award were filled with lots of speculation but little hard fact. From time to time, artists impressions were published, showing all manner of hypothetical configurations, many of them sharply pointed canard deltas. An element of disinformation appeared to have crept in, because when in 1990 the two ATF contenders were finally revealed, they bore no resemblance to anything previously seen.

Northrop/McDonnell Douglas YF-23A

The first ATF contender to appear in public was the YF-23A, which was rolled out on 22 June 1991. It looked nothing like any previous fighter; in a nutshell it was futuristic. So radical was it that there was barely a single feature that could not be singled out for special comment.

The wing shape was a total surprise. Instead of the highly swept delta that virtually everyone had expected, it was trapezoidal in planform, with leading edges swept back at about 40deg, and trailing edges swept forward at a similar angle. The tips were cropped plain, with no missile rails or EW fairings.

This planform had certain advantages. It gave a simply enormous area for its span, with consequent low wing loading and low aspect ratio. The tremendously long chord inboard gave depth where it was most needed, which simplified structural problems and allowed wing/body blending over more than half the fuselage length. The sweep angles adopted were a response to stealth requirements, reflecting radar emissions in directions well clear of the line of flight. On the other hand, one would normally expect tip stalling to be a potential problem on such a wing shape, unless some form of aero-elastic tailoring had been used to counter it.

Single piece flaps occupied most of the leading edge outboard of the intakes, with no attempt to make use of the continuous flexible surfaces pioneered by the MAW F-111, which would have been more stealthy. Two piece flaperons occupied the trailing edge, the inner of which had much greater chord than the outer. Flaperon effectiveness must however suffer from the steeply swept hinge line, and additional roll control must be provided by differential tail movement.

The body of the YF-23A, one hesitates to call it a fuselage, had a layout in common with, although no similarity to, the Tomcat, in that it consisted of a forebody housing the cockpit, and two widely spaced engines nacelles aft, joined by a flattish pancake afterbody into which the forebody tapered.

The nose was quite small, with no huge drooped radome as in the F-15 or Su-27, and the cockpit was set well forward. Its cross-section was a unique blend of straight lines with smoothed off corners, calculated to deflect radar impulses away from the emitter. A sharp chine rather like that of the SR-71 ran around the nose, level with the wing leading edge. Sharply angular in plan view, this probably acts as a vortex generator in place of root extensions. It may also reduce vortex shedding during high alpha manoeuvres, improving yaw control. The underside of the forebody was flat, with a single wheel nose gear hinged beneath the cockpit and retracting forward, and with two tandem internal missile bays just aft of it.

The cockpit canopy consisted of two pieces; a wrap around polycarbonate windshield with metal framing, and a single piece transparency, which was not only shorter than might have been expected, but had strange double curvatures to sides and rear, varying from convex to concave. High sills were obviously shaped for stealth, helping keep radar emissions out of the cockpit and avoiding radar reflecting angles. Rearward vision was not in the same league as the previous fighter generation, but with supercruise this is less important. Or is it? Don't say I said it, but remember the Phantom?

The engine inlets were rhomboidal in section, and were widely spaced beneath the wings. Stagnant boundary layer air was removed through panels in the inlet roof and ejected through doors on the upper wing surface, thus removing the need for radar reflecting splitter plates. Curved ducts lined with RAM led inwards and upwards to the compressor face, effectively shielding it from prying radars.

Single wheel main gears were housed in the underwing duct sections, while the engines were located above the wing section, causing two large flat-topped bulges. As these rose, so the forebody tapered away to nothing, probably to conform to area ruling. The tailpipes were flattened in section, exhausting into channels leading back to the familiar sawtooth trailing edge of the afterbody as pioneered on the B-2; also a Northrop design. The channels shielded the hot efflux from the low rear aspect, but also appeared to eliminate, or at best reduce the use of thrust vectoring, which was not fitted.

The afterbody looked as if someone had sat on it. The flattened rear fuselage, broken only by the engine humps, was finished off by butterfly tail surfaces, described by Northrop as ruddervators. These were set at an extremely flat angle, about 40deg from the horizontal. Both leading and trailing edges of the tail surfaces matched those of the wing, as did the angles of the sawtooth rear fuselage.

The abiding impression of the YF-23A was that it was a dream machine, optimised for high speed and stealth, possibly at the expense of subsonic manoeuvrability. This was denied by Northrop, who claimed that it's large wing area and low wing loading gave excellent manoeuvre capability at the bottom end of the performance envelope.

The first ATF prototype to fly, the YF119 powered YF-23A, made its maiden flight on 27 August 1990, piloted by Northrop's Chief ATF Test Pilot Paul Metz. On the first flight it was found that drag calculations had been a bit pessimistic. On the climb-out, lower than predicted power settings were used, and the F-15 and F-16 flying chase had to use 'burner to keep up, even though the YF-23A's gear was down and it was only using military power. The second YF-23A, powered by GE's YF120, joined it in the evaluation programme in October.

Lockheed/Boeing/ General Dynamics YF-22A

Compared with its Northrop rival, the YF-22A looked far more chunky and workmanlike. This disappointed many people, who rather expected it to look like a refined F-117A. In fact, it looked more like an extrapolation of the F-15 with few unusual features thrown in. The wing planform was more or less orthodox, a cropped delta with about 48deg of sweep on the leading edge, and moderate forward sweep on the trailing edge. Single piece flaps on the leading edge were unusual in that they ran right out to the wingtip, and had a strange V-shaped junction inboard where they met the fixed portion of leading edge, possibly for vortex generation. Two-piece flaperons occupied the trailing edge; the inboard section having a much broader chord than the outer.

The forward fuselage was V-shaped below the midpoint with the underside sharply rounded, and domed above it, with a small chine at the junction of the two. Like the YF-23A, the radar nose was short and sharply pointed by current standards. The single piece canopy, (reflections in some pictures give the impression of a metal bow) had a rather abrupt hump, almost triangular in section and curving steeply down at the back, before fairing into the fuselage. This was in direct contrast to the modern trend of bulging the canopy outwards to improve downward view.

The engines of the YF-22A were located below the wing and set fairly close together to reduce inertia in the rolling plane. Plain intakes, RAM-lined and serpentine, combined to screen the compressor face. Splitter plates were used to divert the boundary layer flow from the forebody, dumping it into the low pressure area on top of the wing. From head-on, the intakes appeared as parallelograms, leaning outwards at the same angle as the lower section of the forward fuselage. The inlet lips were raked at about 60deg both in plan view and in elevation, and commenced well forward of the wing roots, dispensing with any form of compression wedge to straighten high alpha airflow.

The main fuselage was quite deep and rather wide, and flat on top and bottom, providing extra lifting surface, while the sides followed the slant angle of the forebody. The single wheel nose gear was situated beneath the cockpit, while the main gears retracted into the fuselage sides beneath the wing roots. A single weapons bay was located ventrally, with one more in each of the sloping sides astern of the inlet ducts.

At the back end, apparently oversized twin vertical tails of low aspect ratio, with the by now familiar aft sweep on the leading edge and forward sweep on the trailing edge, sprouted from the dorsal surface of the fuselage. They were canted outward at a fairly sharp angle, in what certainly did not appear to be a particularly stealthy manner. The moving rudder was, like the leading edge flaps, unusual in that it ran right to the top of the fin.

The vertical tails were supplemented by traditional all-moving tailerons, set only slightly lower than the plane of the wings, and mounted on shelves outside the lines of the engine nacelles. The engines themselves had vectoring nozzles; the tailerons overhung these by a considerable amount. Some effort towards low observability had been made at the rear end of the YF-22A, but the use of fully vectoring nozzles made this difficult. In all, the back end of the Lockheed aircraft lacked the finished appearance of the rear of the Northrop article.

Flown by Lockheed Chief Test Pilot Dave Ferguson, the YF-22A left the ground for the first time on 29 September 1990, powered by two General Electric YF120s, with the YF119-powered second prototype following in October.

* * * *

During the remainder of 1990, the flight envelope was gradually explored by the two contenders. The two YF-22As flew 74 sorties totalling more than 91 hours in the space of 91 days, which is pretty good for a totally new type with two new engines. During this period, Mach 1.8 was exceeded, and supercruise at Mach 1.58 was achieved using the GE engines, although it is understood that to attain this, the aircraft was accelerated to a high Mach number using augmentation before reverting to military power and allowing the speed to stabilize. It having been established that shock waves impinging on the horizontal tail caused it to lose authority at speeds in excess of Mach 1.4, thrust vectoring was used to achieve high turn rates at speeds above this mark. Missiles were launched, one Amraam and one Sidewinder, and an alpha of 62deg was reached at an equivalent airspeed of about 60kt, with plenty of control authority left. Lockheed claim that the YF-22A has no alpha limits.

The two YF-23As flew a total of 50 sorties totalling 65.2 hours during the evaluation period. The Northrop fighter was widely believed to be rather faster than the YF-22A, and while the F119 powered aircraft achieved a supercruise of Mach 1.43, the GE powered article reached a speed that was immediately put under wraps, perhaps because it significantly exceeded the Mach 1.58 reached by the YF-22A.

165

Other points demonstrated by the YF-23A were a speed of Mach 1.8 and an altitude of 50,000ft; a stabilized alpha of 25deg at low speed with precise control; "very high" pitch, roll and turn performance in the supercruise regime. It also had what Paul Metz called "the best gun tracking to 4g I've seen".

Crunch time came in April 1991. Apparently all four airframe/ engine combinations met the specification, but the decision was made on the basis of lowest risk. The USAF Advanced Tactical Fighter was to be the Lockheed F-22A, powered by the Pratt & Whitney F119. The final question, which will probably not be answered for many years to come is, lowest risk in which field? It was stated at the time that the YF-22A/YF119 combination was the most mature, but could it rather have been a question of the lowest risk for the decision makers? To an outside observer, the options seem to have been a high degree of stealth/supercruise versus a bit less stealth/supercruise plus a bit more traditional fighter agility. The last time the USAF went out on a limb was with the A-10A, an aircraft now heading for premature retirement because its concept is no longer considered viable.

So where does this leave us? The YF-23As have been stored. They contain too much classified technology to be retired to a museum during the next couple of decades. An engineering and manufacturing development contract was awarded to Lockheed/Boeing in August 1991 to complete design work, make production tooling, and manufacture 13 aircraft, two of which are to be static test vehicles. This was later reduced to seven single seater F-22As and two twin seat F-22Bs.

Even during the flight evaluation phase, the design was being further refined, details of which were released in March 1992 when the configuration was finally frozen. Wingspan was increased by 18in to 44.50ft, although alterations to the planform left the area unchanged. Leading edge sweep was reduced to 42deg, and the trailing edge clipped outboard. Wing root thickness was reduced, and twist and camber modified. At the same time, the two piece trailing edge flaperons were considerably revised in shape. The horizontal stabilizers were also reshaped, the leading edge angle matching that of the wing and given a broader chord, and the inboard section of trailing edges aligned with the booms. These changes are stated to reduce RCS, improve manoeuvrability across the board, and reduce drag.

Weight saving has also featured. The inlets have been cut back 18in, which also improves stability; while the huge fins have been reduced in size, 14in in height and 20 square feet in area per side.

Overall length is reduced by 25in; the nose is blunter, and the cockpit has been nudged forward a tad. The canopy has a revised, sleeker shape, and the landing gear revised, with the nosewheel now retracting aft rather than forward.

Meanwhile flight testing continued. Then on April 25 of that year, disaster struck. Flying from Edwards AFB, the YF-22A was scheduled to explore supersonic flight characteristics when the air to ground telemetry link failed, causing the flight to be aborted. Having just refuelled, the aircraft was well above its maximum landing weight, and test pilot Tom Morgenfeld began a series of low altitude passes along the runway to burn off the excess fuel prior to landing. On the second pass, an uncommanded pitch-up occurred when the gear was raised and the 'burners engaged. As Morgenfeld corrected, the thrust vectoring system increased the forward stick authority by a factor of three, which resulted in a sharp pitch-down. From then on, pilot and computers were out of synchronization, and seven seconds of oscillations in pitch ended when the aircraft bellied in, skidded almost a mile along the runway, and caught fire. Fortunately

Morgenfeld was only slightly injured, but the incident, due to a software anomaly, brought the programme to an only slightly premature halt, as it was 90 percent complete at that time. The other prototype had already been grounded to use as an engineering mockup.

Construction of the EMD aircraft was scheduled to have begun late in 1993, with first flight in June 1996, and service entry in 2002 or thereabouts. But behind the scenes, other factors were at work. The evaporation of the Soviet threat had called the very existence of the F-22A into question. This had been followed by the Gulf War, which had caused the powers that be to take a long hard look at the air superiority mission.

With no opposing superpower, future wars could reasonably be expected to take the form of limited clashes against technically and possibly numerically inferior opponents. Air superiority over Iraq had not been attained by the time-honoured method of air combat. A total of less than 40 air to air victories against an oponent possessing over 400 combat aircraft demonstrated that quite conclusively. Air superiority had been attained by other means. Precision attacks against detection, communication and control centres; airfield strikes, and electronic warfare, had combined to render the Iraqi Air Force impotent. Yet within this victory, there was another, far more significant. The ability of the F-117As to make precision attacks on vital targets deep in the most the most densely defended areas of Iraq, without any semblance of traditional fighter protection, demonstrated air superiority of another sort. Penetration became the new buzzword.

Far from the uncompromised air combat role, the F-22 is now to be equipped to carry air to surface munitions. Two Joint Direct Attack Munitions (JDAMs) are now to be carried internally, at the expense of air to air ordnance, and for deep strike missions, two Northrop AGM-137 stand-off attack missiles will be carried under the wings.

What does look very dubious is the future of the proposed new carrier fighter to replace Tomcat. This was to be based on the ATF winner, and Lockheed have proposed a less stealthy variant of the F-22, a rather larger and longer legged fighter, using variable sweep wings to improve carrier compatibility. Whether it will ever materialise we can only guess.

And what of the distant future? Advanced STOVL, stealth, automated systems, smart skins which act as aerials, Big Picture cockpits, artificial intelligence, laser weaponry, are all possible players in the arena of the future. Air combat, once the supreme arbiter of air superiority, looks to have been ousted by stealthy penetration and precision stand-off attack, unless a quantum leap in detection technology restores the balance.

The contest to achieve air superiority has always devolved around threat and response; theory and practice; scientist and fighting man; drawing board and cockpit. Given man's propensity for settling his differences by muscular means, it will be so for the foreseeable future.

Aircraft Data

BRITISH AEROSPACE SEA HARRIER FRS.2
Dimensions: Span 25.25ft(7.70m); Length 47.58ft(14.50m); Height 12.16ft(3.71m); Wing Area 201 sq.ft(18.69m²); Aspect Ratio 3.17.
Weights: Empty 13,000lb(5,900kg); Normal TO 19,650lb(8,915kg); Max. TO 26,200lb (11,880kg); Int. Fuel 5,050lb(2,290kg); Fuel Fraction 0.26.
Power: one Rolls-Royce Pegasus 106 vectored thrust turbofan rated at 21,500lb(95.5kN).
Loadings, Normal TO Wt: Wing 98lb/sq.ft (477kg/m²); Thrust 1.09.
Performance: Max. Dive Speed Mach 1.25 at altitude; Service Ceiling 51,200ft (15,600m); Combat Radius 400nm(741km); S/L Climb Rate 50,000ft/min(254m/sec).
Armament: four AIM-120 Amraam BVR or four AIM-9L or R550 Magic IR missiles; or two 30mm Aden cannon pods with 100 rounds per gun (replacing two Amraams).

DASSAULT MIRAGE 2000C
Dimensions: Span 29.50ft(8.99m); Length 46.50ft(14.17m); Height 17.06ft(5.20m); Wing Area 441 sq.ft(40.98m²); Aspect Ratio 1.97.
Weights: Empty 16,835lb (7,636kg); Normal TO 25,928lb (11,761kg); Max TO 37,480lb (17,000kg); Int. Fuel 7,055lb (3,200kg); Fuel Fraction 0.27.
Power: One SNECMA M53-P2 afterburning turbofan rated at 14,400lb(64kN) mil and 21,400lb(95.0kN) max.
Loadings, Normal TO Wt: Wing 59lb/sq.ft (287kg/m²); Thrust 0.83.
Performance: Maximum Speed Mach 2.35 at altitude; Service Ceiling 60,000ft (18,300m); Combat Radius c300nm(556km); S/L Climb Rate 49,212ft/min(250m/sec).
Armament: Two Matra Super 530D SARH missiles and two R550 Magic 2 IR missiles, or four MICA; plus two 30mm DEFA 554 cannon with 125 rpg.

DASSAULT SUPER MIRAGE 4000
Some data estimated.
Dimensions: Span 39.14ft(11.93m); Length 61.42ft(18.72m); Height 19.69ft(6.00m); Wing Area 783sq.ft(72.70m²); Aspect Ratio 1.96.
Weights: Empty c30,313lb(13,750kg); Normal TO with full int. fuel and two missiles 50,706lb(23,000kg); Max. TO 70,547lb (32,000kg); Int. Fuel 19,841lb(9,000kg); Fuel Fraction 0.39.
Power: two SNECMA M53-P2 afterburning turbofans rated at 14,400lb(64kN) mil. and 21,400lb(95kN) max.
Loadings at Normal TO Wt: Wing 65lb/sq.ft(316kg/m²); Thrust 0.84
Performance: Max. Speed Mach 2.2 at altitude; Service Ceiling 65,620ft(20,000m); Operational Radius c648nm(1,200km); S/L Climb Rate <60,000ft/min(305m/sec).
Armament: up to ten AAMs; Super 530D and Magic 2s; two 30mm DEFA 554 cannon with 125rpg.

DASSAULT RAFALE D
Dimensions: Span 35.17ft(10.72m); Length 49.15ft(14.98m); Height 15.52ft(5.34m); Wing Area 474 sq.ft(44m²); Aspect Ratio 2.61.
Weights: Empty 18,739lb(8,500kg); Normal TO 28,219lb(12,800kg); Max. TO 40,124lb (18,200kg); Int. Fuel 8,818lb(4,000kg); Fuel Fraction 0.31.
Power: two SNECMA M88-2 afterburning turbofans rated at 11,250lb(50kN) mil. and 16,875lb(75kN) max.
Loadings, Normal TO Wt: Wing 60lb/sq.ft (291kg/m²); Thrust 1.20.
Performance: Max. Speed Mach 2 at altitude; Service Ceiling 60,000ft(18,287m), Combat Radius c350nm(650km); S/L Climb Rate c55,000ft/min(279m/sec).
Armament: eight MICA AAMs, mix of active radar and IR homing; one 30mm GIAT M791B cannon.

EUROFIGHTER EF 2000
Dimensions: Span 34.46ft(10.50m); Length 47.58ft(14.50m); Height c16.41ft(5.00m); Wing Area 538 sq.ft(50m²); Aspect Ratio 2.21.
Weights: Empty 21,495lb (9,750kg); Normal TO c32,750lb(14,855kg); Max TO 37,480lb(17,000kg); Int. Fuel 8,818lb (4,000kg); Fuel Fraction 0.27.

Power: two Eurojet EJ 200 afterburning turbofans rated at c12,000lb(53.3kN) mil and 20,000lb(89kN) max.
Loadings, Normal TO Wt: Wing 61lb/sq.ft(297kg/m²); Thrust 1.22.
Performance: Max. Speed Mach 1.8+ at altitude; Service Ceiling 60,000ft (18,287m)plus; Combat Radius 300nm(556km); S/L Climb Rate 60,000ft/m(305m/sec) plus.
Armament: typically four AIM-120 Amraam and four AIM-130 Asraam or AIM-9 IR missiles, and one 27mm Mauser cannon. Up to 10 AAMs may be carried.

GENERAL DYNAMICS F-16F
Dimensions: Span 34.25ft(10.44m); Length 54.16ft(16.51m); Height 17.58ft(5.36m); Wing Area 646sq.ft(60m²); Aspect Ratio 1.82.
Weights: Empty c19,000lb(8,618kg); Normal TO c32,000lb(14,515kg). Max. TO c48,000lb(21,773kg). Int. Fuel c12,700lb(5,760kg); Fuel Fraction 0.40.
Power: as F-16A for single seater, GE F101 DFE for two seater.
Loadings at Normal TO Wt: Wing 50lb/sq.ft(242kg/m²); Thrust 0.74
Performance: Max. Speed Mach 2 at altitude; Service Ceiling 50,000ft(15,239m) plus; Combat Radius c730nm(1,340km).
Armament: two Sidewinders; 20mm M61 cannon with 500 rounds.

GRUMMAN F-14A TOMCAT.
Dimensions: Span 64.13ft(19.55m) max; 38.20ft(11.65m) min; Length 62.88ft (19.17m); Height 16ft(4.88m); Wing Area 656 sq.ft (52.50m²); Aspect Ratio 7.28 to 2.58.
Weights: Empty 39,921lb(18,110kg); Normal TO 58,571lb(26,570kg); Max. TO 74,349lb(33,724kg); Int. Fuel 16,200lb (7,350kg); Fuel Fraction 0.28.
Power: two P&W TF30-414A afterburning turbofans rated at 12,350lb(54.9kN) mil. and 20,900lb(93kN) max.
Loadings, Normal TO Wt: Wing 104lb/sq.ft(506kg/m²); Thrust 0.71.
Performance: Max. Speed Mach 2.31 at altitude; Service Ceiling 56,000ft (17,068m); Combat Radius 750nm(1,390km); S/L Climb Rate 30,000ft/min(152m/sec).
Armament: six AIM-54 Phoenix, four or six AIM-7 with four or two AIM-9, or eight Amraam. One 20mm M61A cannon with 675 rounds.

GRUMMAN F-14D TOMCAT
Dimensions: Span 64.13ft(19.55m) max; 38.20ft(11.65m) min; Length 61.92ft(18.87m); Height 16ft(4.88m); Wing Area 565sq.ft (52.50m²); Aspect Ratio 7.28 to 2.58.
Weights: Empty 41,780lb(18,951kg); Normal TO 61,200lb(27,760kg); Max. TO 74,349lb(33,724kg); Int. Fuel 16,200lb(7,350kg); Fuel Fraction 0.26.
Power: two F110-GE-400 afterburning turbofans rated at 16,610lb (73.82kN) mil. and 27,080lb(120.36kN) max.
Loadings at Normal TO Wt: Wing 108lb/sq.ft(529kg/m²); Thrust 0.88.
Performance: Max. Speed Mach 1.88; Service Ceiling 53,000ft (16,154m) plus; Combat Radius c850nm(1,575km); S/L Climb Rate c48,000ft/min(244m/sec).
Armament: as F-14A.

ISRAEL AIRCRAFT INDUSTRIES LAVI
Dimensions: Span 28.61ft(8.72m); Length 47.21ft(14.39m); Height 15.68ft(4.78m); Wing Area 414sq.ft(30.50m²); Aspect Ratio 2.10.
Weights: Empty 17,000lb(7,771kg); Normal TO c25,000lb(11,340kg); Max. TO 37,500lb(17,000kg); Int. Fuel 6,000lb(2,722kg); Fuel Fraction 0.24.
Power: one Pratt & Whitney PW 1120 afterburning turbofan rated at 13,550lb(60.2kN) mil. and 20,620lb(91.6kN) max.
Loadings at Normal TO Wt: Wing 60lb/sq.ft(372kg/m²); Thrust 0.82
Performance: Max. Speed Mach 1.85 at altitude, Mach 1.05 at sea level; Service Ceiling 50,000ft(15,239m) plus; Mission Radius 1,000nm(1,853km); S/L Climb Rate 50,000ft/min(254m/sec) plus.
Armament: four Shafrir or Python AAMs; one 30mm DEFA cannon.

LOCKHEED F-16A FIGHTING FALCON
Dimensions: Span 31ft(9.45m); Length 49.25ft(15.01m); Height 16.58ft(5.05m); Wing Area 300sq.ft(27.88m²); Aspect Ratio 3.20.
Weights: Empty 16,292lb(7,390kg); Normal TO 23,810lb(10,800kg); Max. TO 37,500lb(17,010kg); Int. Fuel 6,846lb(3,105kg); Fuel Fraction 0.29.
Power: one P & W F100-100 augmented turbofan rated at 14,670lb (65.2kN)mil. and 23,830lb(105.9kN) max.

Loadings at Normal TO Wt: Wing 79lb/sq.ft(387kg/m²); Thrust 0.94

Performance: Max. Speed Mach 2 at altitude, Mach 1.2 at low level; Service Ceiling 50,000ft(15,239m)plus; Combat Radius 430nm(797km); S/L Climb Rate 50,000ft/min(254m/sec).

Armament: two or four AIM-9L Sidewinders, Magics, Pythons or Shafrirs; one 20mm M61 Vulcan cannon with 500 rounds.

LOCKHEED F-16C FIGHTING FALCON

Dimensions: Span 31ft(9.45m); Length 49.25ft(15.01m); Height 16.58ft(5.05m); Wing Area 300 sq.ft(27.88m²); Aspect Ratio 3.20. Weights: Empty 17,960lb(8,150kg); Normal TO 26,536lb(12,040kg); Max TO 42,300lb (19,187kg); Int. Fuel 6,972lb(3,162kg); Fuel Fraction 0.26.

Power: one P&W F100-220 afterburning turbofan rated at 14,370lb (63.9kN) mil. and 23,450lb(104.2kN) max.

Loadings, Normal TO Wt: Wing 88lb/sq.ft (432kg/m²); Thrust 0.94.

Performance: Max. Speed Mach 2 at altitude; Service Ceiling 50,000ft (15,239m); Combat Radius < 500nm(927km); S/L Climb Rate 50,000ft/min(254m/sec).

Armament: up to six AIM-9 or Magic IR missiles, some variants AIM-7 or Amraam; one 20mm M61A cannon with 515 rounds.

LOCKHEED F-117A

All data except external dimensions and maximum takeoff weight estimated.

Dimensions: Span 43.33ft(13.20m); Length 65.92ft(20.08m); Height 12.42ft(3.78m); Wing Area 880 sq.ft(81.75m²); Aspect Ratio 2.13.

Weights: Max. TO 52,500lb(23,814kg).

Power: two General Electric F404-F1D2 unaugmented turbofans rated at 10,800lb(48kN).

Loadings, Max TO Wt; Wing 60lb/sq.ft(291kg/m²); Thrust 0.41.

Performance: Max. Speed Mach 0.95; Combat Radius 650nm(1,205km).

Armament: "full range of tactical fighter ordnance", but no air to air weaponry.

LOCKHEED YF-22A

Some data provisional.

Dimensions: Span 44.50ft(13.56m); Length 62.14ft(18.94m); Height 16.54ft(5.04m); Wing Area 840 sq.ft(78.04m²); Aspect Ratio 2.36.

Weights: Empty 34,000lb(15,422kg); Normal TO 62,000lb(28,123kg); Max. TO not applicable; Int. Fuel 25,000lb (11,340kg); Fuel Fraction 0.40.

Power: two P&W F119 afterburning turbofans rated at c28,000lb (124.4kN) mil. and 35,000lb(155.6kN) max, with thrust vectoring nozzles.

Loadings, Normal TO Wt: Wing 74lb/sq.ft(360kg/m²); Thrust 1.13.

Performance: Maximum Speed Mach 1.8 plus; sustained cruising speed on military power cMach 1.5; Combat radius c700nm(1,297km).

Armament: four Amraam BVR and four AIM-9 IR missiles internally, one 20mm cannon.

McDONNELL DOUGLAS F-15A EAGLE

Dimensions: Span 42.81ft(13.05m); Length 63.75ft(19.43m); Height 18.46ft(5.63m); Wing Area 608sq.ft(56.50m²); Aspect Ratio 3.01.

Weights: Empty 28,000lb(12,701kg); Normal TO 41,500lb(18,824kg); Int. Fuel 11,635lb(5,280kg); Fuel Fraction 0.28.

Power: two F100-PW-100 augmented turbofans rated at 14,670lb (65.2kN) mil. and 23,830lb(105.9kN) max.

Loadings at Normal TO Wt: Wing 68lb/sq.ft(333kg/m²); Thrust 1.15

Performance: Max. Speed Mach 2.5 plus at altitude; Mach 1.2 at low level; Service Ceiling 65,000ft(19,811m); Combat Radius c380nm(704km); S/L Climb Rate 50,000ft/min(254m/sec).

Armament: four AIM-7 Sparrows and four AIM-9 Sidewinders; one 20mm M61 Vulcan cannon with 675 rounds.

McDONNELL DOUGLAS F-15C EAGLE

Dimensions: Span 42.81ft(13.05m); Length 63.75ft(19.43m); Height 18.46ft(5.63m); Wing Area 608 sq.ft(56.50m²); Aspect Ratio 3.01.

Weights: Empty 29,180lb(13,240kg); Normal TO 44,500lb(20,185kg); Max. TO 68,000lb(30,845kg); Int. Fuel 13,455lb (6,103kg); Fuel Fraction 0.30.

Power: two P&W F100-220 afterburning turbofans rated at 14,370lb (63.9kN) mil. and 23,450lb(104.2kN) max.

Loadings, Normal TO Wt: Wing 73lb/sq.ft (357kg/m²); Thrust 1.05.

Performance: Max. Speed Mach 2.5+ at altitude; Service Ceiling 65,000ft (19,811m); Combat Radius c500nm(927km); S/L Climb Rate 50,000ft/min(254m/sec).

Armament: four AIM-7 SARH and four AIM-9 IR missiles; later eight Amraam; and one 20mm M61A cannon with 675 rounds.

McDONNELL DOUGLAS F-15E EAGLE.
Dimensions: Span 42.81ft(13.05m); Length 63.75ft(19.43m); Height 18.46ft(5.63m); Wing Area 608sq.ft(56.50m²); Aspect Ratio 3.01.
Weights: Empty 32,000lb(14,515kg); Normal TO c72,000lb(32,659kg) Max. TO 81,000lb(36,742kg); Int. Fuel 22,904lb(10,389kg); fuel Fraction 0.32.
Power: two F100-PW-220 augmented turbofans rated at 14,370lb (63.9kN) mil. and 23,450lb(104.2kN) max.
Loadings at Normal TO Wt: Wing 118lb/sq.ft(578kg/m²); Thrust 0.65.
Performance: Max. Speed Mach 2.5 at altitude; Service Ceiling 65,000ft(19,811m); Combat Radius 685nm(1,269km); S/L Climb Rate n/a.
Armament: air to air as F-15C.

McDONNELL DOUGLAS F/A-18A HORNET
Dimensions: Span 37.50ft(11.43m); Length 56ft(17.07m); Height 15.29ft(4.66m); Wing Area 400sq.ft(37.17m²); Aspect Ratio 3.52.
Weights: Empty 21,830lb(9,900kg); Normal TO 35,800lb(16,240kg); Max. TO 51,900lb(23,540kg); Int. Fuel 10,860lb(4,925kg); Fuel Fraction 0.30.
Power: two General Electric F404-400 afterburning turbofans rated at 10,600lb(47.2kN) mil. and 16,000lb(71.2kN) max.
Loadings, Normal TO Wt: Wing 90lb/sq.ft(437kg/m²); thrust 0.89.
Performance: Max. Speed Mach 1.7 at altitude; Mach 1.01 at sea level; Service Ceiling 50,000ft(15,239m); Combat Radius 434nm (804km); S/L Climb Rate 50,000ft/min(254m/sec).
Armament: two AIM-7M Sparrows(Amraam later), two or four AIM-7P Sidewinders; one 20mm M61 Vulcan cannon with 570 rounds.

McDONNELL DOUGLAS F/A-18E HORNET
All data approximate.
Dimensions: Span 44.70ft(13.62m); Length 60.10ft(18.32m); Height 15.80ft(4.82m); Wing Area 500sq.ft(46.45m²); Aspect Ratio 4.00
Weights: Empty 30,000lb(13,608kg); Normal TO 46,000lb(20,865kg); Max. TO 63,500lb(28,803kg); Int. Fuel 13,900lb(6,305kg); Fuel Fraction 0.30.
Power: two General Electric F414-400 afterburning turbofans rated at 22,000lb(97.78kN) max.
Loadings at Normal TO Wt: Wing 92lb/sq.ft(449kg/m²); Thrust 0.96
Performance: all as F/A-18A, but combat radius increased to 591nm(1,095km).
Armament: as F/A-18A but Amraam in lieu of AIM-7.

MIKOYAN MIG-29 FULCRUM A
Dimensions: Span 37.25ft(11.36m); Length 56.82ft(17.32m); Height 15.52ft(4.73m); Wing Area 379 sq.ft(35.21m²); Aspect Ratio 3.66.
Weights: Empty 18,025lb(8,175kg); Normal TO 33,065lb(15,000kg); Max. TO 39,683lb (18,000kg); Internal Fuel 7,495lb (3,400kg); Fuel Fraction 0.23.
Power: two Isotov RD-33 afterburning turbofans rated at 11,240lb (50kN) mil. and 18,300lb(81.4kN) max.
Loadings, Normal TO Wt: Wing 87lb/sq.ft (426kg/m²); Thrust 1.11.
Performance: Max. Speed Mach <2.3 at altitude; Service Ceiling 55,777ft (17,000m); Combat Radius c300nm(556km); S/L Climb Rate 65,000ft/min(330m/sec).
Armament: six AA-10 Alamo medium range or AA-11 Archer close range missiles; eight Amraamski on later models; one 30mm GS-301 cannon with 150 rounds.

MIKOYAN MIG-31 FOXHOUND
Some data estimated.
Dimensions: Span 44.18ft(13.46m); Length 74.44ft(22.69m); Height 20.18ft(6.15m); Wing Area c657sq.ft(61m²); Aspect Ratio 2.97.
Weights: Empty c46,297lb(22,000kg); Max. TO with full internal fuel load 90,389lb(41,000kg); Max TO with ext. fuel 101,853lb (46,200kg); Int. Fuel 36,045lb(16,350kg); Fuel Fraction 0.40.
Power: two Perm D30F-6 afterburning turbofans rated at 20,944lb (93.1kN) mil; 34,171lb(151.9kN) max. and 41,843lb(186kN) for "frontal takeoff".
Loadings, Max.TO Wt without ext. fuel: Wing 138lb/sq.ft (672kg/m²); Thrust 0.76.

Performance: Max. Speed Mach 2.83 at altitude; Mach 1.22 at low level; Service Ceiling 67,588ft(20,600m); Combat Radius 755nm (1,400km); Supersonic Interception Radius(Mach 2.35) 389nm (720km) S/L Climb Rate c41,000ft/min (208m/sec).

Armament: four long range AA-9 Amos SARH missiles, plus four AA-8 Aphid or AA-11 Archer, and one 30mm GS-301 cannon.

NORTHROP F-18L HORNET

Dimensions: all as F/A-18A except height 14.50ft(4.42m).

Weights: Empty c19,600lb(8,900kg); Normal TO 33,090lb(15,010kg); Max. TO 52,000lb(23,588kg); Int. Fuel 10,380lb(4,708kg); Fuel Fraction 0.31.

Power: as F/A-18A.

Loadings at Normal TO Wt: Wing 83lb/sq.ft(404kg/m²); Thrust 0.97

Performance: Max. Speed Mach 2 at altitude; Service Ceiling 55,000ft(16,763m); Combat Radius <500nm(927km); S/L Climb Rate 56,000ft/min(284m/sec). Armament: six AIM-7 Sparrows or six AIM-9 Sidewinders or mix; one 20mm M61 Vulcan cannon with 570 rounds.

NORTHROP F-20 TIGERSHARK

Dimensions: Span 26.19ft(7.98m); Length 53.92ft(16.44m); Height 13.73ft(4.19m); Wing Area 186sq.ft(17.28m²); Aspect Ratio 3.69.

Weights: Empty 13,376lb(6,070kg); Normal TO 18,540lb(8,510kg); Int. Fuel 4,364lb(1,980kg); Fuel Fraction 0.24.

Power: one General Electric F404-100 augmented turbofan rated at 12,000lb(53.3kN) mil. and 18,000lb(80.0kN) max.

Loadings at Normal TO Wt: Wing 100lb/sq,ft(487kg/m²) Thrust 0.97

Performance: Max. Speed Mach 2 at altitude; Mach 1.2 at low level; Service Ceiling 55,000ft(16,763m); Combat Radius 385nm (713km); S/L Climb Rate 53,800ft/min(273m/sec).

Armament: two AIM-7F Sparrows and two AIM-9L Sidewinders; two 20mm M39 revolver cannon with 225rpg.

NORTHROP YF-23A

Some data is provisional.

Dimensions: Span 43.60ft(13.29m); Length 67.40ft(20.54m); Height 13.75ft(4.19m); Wing Area 950 sq.ft(88.26m²); Aspect Ratio 2.00.

Weights: Empty 37,000lb(16,783kg); Normal TO 64,000lb(29,030kg); Max TO not applicable; Int. Fuel 24,000lb (10,886kg); Fuel Fraction 0.375.

Power: two P&W YF119 or GE YF120 after-burning turbofans rated at c28,000lb (124.4kN) mil, 35,000lb (155.6kN) max.

Loadings, Normal TO Wt: Wing 67lb/sq.ft (329kg/m²); Thrust 1.09.

Performance: Supercruise (sustained cruising speed on military power), Mach 1.4 to 1.5. Combat radius c700nm(1,297km).

Armament: four Amraam BVR and four AIM-9 IR missiles internally; one 20mm cannon.

PANAVIA TORNADO F.3

Dimensions: Span 45.58ft(13.89m) at min. sweep; 28.21ft(8.60m) max. sweep; Length 59.25ft(18.06m); Height 18.31ft(5.53m); Wing Area 323 sq.ft(30.01m²); Aspect Ratio 6.43 to 2.46.

Weights: Empty 31,500lb(14,290kg); Normal TO 50,200lb(22,770kg); Max. TO 61,700lb(27,986kg); Int. Fuel 12,500lb (5,670kg); Fuel Fraction 0.25.

Power: two Turbo Union RB.199 Mk 104 afterburning turbofans rated at 9,656lb (42.9kN) mil. and 16,920lb(75.2kN) max.

Loadings, Normal TO Wt: Wing 155lb/sq.ft(759kg/m²); Thrust 0.67.

Performance: Max. Speed Mach 2.27 at altitude; Service Ceiling 50,000ft (15,250m) plus; Combat Radius 1,000nm (1,835km) plus; S/L Climb Rate 40,000ft/ min(203m/sec) plus.Armament: four Skyflash SARH missiles (later Amraam), four AIM-9 IR missiles, and one 27mm IWKA Mauser cannon.

SAAB JAS 39 GRIPEN

Some data estimated.

Dimensions: Span 27.56ft(8.40m); Length 46.25ft(14.10m); Height 14.76ft(4.50m); Wing Area c275 sq.ft(25.54m²); Aspect Ratio 2.76.

Weights: Empty c11,000lb(4,990kg); Normal TO 17,635lb(8,000kg); Max.TO 21,000lb(9,526kg); Int. Fuel 5,000lb(2,268kg); Fuel Fraction 0.28.

Power: one GE-Volvo RM 12 afterburning turbofan rated at 12,140lb(54kN) mil. and 18,000lb(80kN) max.

Loadings, Normal TO Wt: Wing 64lb/sq.ft (313kg/m²); Thrust 1.02.

Performance: Max. Speed Mach 1.8 at altitude; Service Ceiling 50,000ft (15,239m); Combat Radius 200nm(371km); S/L Climb Rate 50,000ft/min(254m/sec).

Armament: two Skyflash SARH and four AIM-9 IR missiles, and one 27mm Mauser BK cannon.

SHENYANG J.8 II FINBACK B
Dimensions: Span 30.66ft(9.34m) Length 70.84ft(21.59m); Height 17.75ft(5.41m): Wing Area 454 sq.ft(42.2m²); Aspect Ratio 2.07.

Weights: Empty 21,649lb (9,820kg); Normal TO 31,526lb (14,300kg); Max TO 39,242lb (17,800kg); Int. Fuel 9,269lb 4,204kg); Fuel Fraction 0.29.

Power: Two Wopen WP-13A II after-burning turbojets rated at 9,608lb(42.7kN) mil and 14,828lb(65.9kN) max.

Loadings, Normal TO Wt: Wing 69lb/sq.ft(339kg/m²); Thrust: 0.94.

Performance: Max. Speed Mach 2.2 at altitude; Service Ceiling 65,620ft (20,000m); Combat Radius 432nm(800km). S/L Climb Rate 39,370ft/min(200m/sec).

Armament: 2xPL-7A SARH missiles; 2xPL-2B, -5 or -9 IR missiles; 23mm twin barrel Type 23-3 cannon with 200 rounds.

SUKHOI Su-27 FLANKER B
Some data estimated.

Dimensions: Span 48.23ft(14.70m); Length 71.97ft(21.94m); Height 19.46ft(5.93m); Wing Area 695 sq.ft(64.57m²); Aspect Ratio 3.35.

Weights: Empty 35,000lb(15,876kg); Normal TO 50,706lb(23,000kg); Max. TO 72,752lb(33,000kg); Int. Fuel 22,000lb(9,979kg) in overload; Fuel Fraction in overload 0.37.

Power: two Lyulka AL-31F afterburning turbofans rated at 19,000lb(84.4kN) mil. and 27,558lb(122.5kN) max.

Loadings, Normal TO Wt: Wing 73lb/sq.ft (356kg/m²); Thrust 1.09.

Performance: Max. Speed Mach 2.35 at altitude; Service Ceiling 59,058ft (18,000m); Combat Radius 810nm(1,500km); S/L Climb Rate 60,000ft/min(305m/sec).

Armament: Ten missiles total, mix of AA-8 Aphid, AA-10 Alamo, AA-11 Archer, or AA-12 Amraamski; one 30mm GS-301 cannon with 240 rounds.

SUKHOI Su-35 SUPER FLANKER
Available brochure figures only.

Dimensions: Span 49.22ft(15.00m); Length 72.18ft(22.00m); Height 19.69ft(6.00m).

Weights: slightly heavier than Flanker B.

Power: two Lyulka AL-31SM afterburning turbofans giving approx. five percent more power than the AL-31F of Flanker B.

Performance: Max. Speed at altitude Mach 2.4; at sea level Mach 1.14; Service Ceiling 59,058ft(18,000m); Operating Range on int. fuel 2,159nm(4,000km) plus; with flight refuelling 3,508nm (6,500km) plus.

Armament: 14 AAMs, same mix as Flanker B plus one 30mm GS-301 cannon with 240 rounds.

YAKOVLEV YAK-141 FREESTYLE
Some data estimated.

Dimensions: Span 33.14ft(10.10m); Length 60.04ft(18.30m); Height 16.41ft(5.00m); Wing Area c334sq.ft(31m²); Aspect Ratio 3.29.

Weights: Empty c25,353lb(11,500kg); VTO c35,274lb(16,000kg); Max. STO 42,990lb(19,500kg); Int. Fuel c8,598lb(3,900kg); Fuel Fraction 0.26.

Power: one vectored thrust Soyuz R-79V-300 afterburning turbofan rated at 34,170lb(151.86kN) max; two Rybinsk RD-41 lift engines.

Loadings at Max. STO Wt: Wing 129lb/sq.ft(629kg/m²); Thrust 0.79

Performance: Max. Speed Mach 1.8 at altitude; Service Ceiling 49,215ft(15,000m) plus; Combat Radius in the air to air role with a centreline tank 485nm(900km); S/L Climb Rate 49,000ft/min (249m/sec) plus.

Armament: four AA-10 Alamo, AA-11 Archer or AA-12 Amraamski AAMs; one 30mm GS-301 cannon with 120 rounds.

Index